Silver Throat of the Moon

*For Stanley, Timothy
and Jeremy Langer*

Silver Throat of the Moon: Writing in Exile

Edited by Jennifer Langer

**Five Leaves
Publications**
in association with
Long Journey Home

www.fiveleaves.co.uk

Silver Throat of the Moon:
Writing in Exile
Edited by Jennifer Langer

Published in 2005 by
Five Leaves Publications,
PO Box 81, Nottingham NG5 4ER
in association with Long Journey Home
info@fiveleaves.co.uk   www.fiveleaves.co.uk

Five Leaves gratefully acknowledges financial assistance
from Arts Council England

ARTS COUNCIL
ENGLAND

Design by 4 Sheet Design and Print
Printed in Great Britain

ISBN: 0907123651

Cover illustration by Yasser Ganem

Acknowledgements

Jennifer Langer and Five Leaves gratefully acknowledge the following authors and publishers for permission to reprint work in this volume.

Ahmed Omar Askar, *Sharks and Soldiers*, 1992, distributed by Haan Associates

B.W. Andrzejewski with Sheila Andrzejewski, *Anthology of Somali Poetry*, 1993, Indiana University Press

Erewhon, 1994, Stichting Ex-Yu PEN, Amsterdam

Reesom Haile, *We Have Our Voice*, 2000, Red Sea Press

Miroslav Jancic, *The Flying Bosnian*, 1996, Hearing Eye

Esmail Kho'i, *Outlandia: Songs of Exile*, 1999, Nik Publishers, Vancouver

Esmail Kho'i, *Voice of Exile, 2002*, Omega Printing LLC

Hadi Khorsandi, *The Ayatollah and I: New Iranian Satire*, 1987, Readers International

Igor Klikovac and Ken Smith, *Stone Soup*, No 1, 1995

Kurdish Solidarity and Yashar Ismail, *Anthology of Contemporary Kurdish Poetry*, 1994

Abdirahman Mirreh, *A Gob Tree Beside the Hargeisa Wadi*, 1995, Tuba Press

Abdirahman Mirreh, *Songs of a Nomad Son*, 1990, Tuba Press

Kamal Mirawdeli, *Passage to Dawn*, 2002, self-published

Simon Mol, *Africa... My Africa*, 2002, Verbinum, Warsaw

Mabiala Molu, *Aujourd'hui Le Soleil*, Universal Connection, Paris

Nazanin Rakhshandeh, *Runway of Words*, 2003, Iranian Arts Projects

Storm, Out of Yugoslavia, 1994, Storm

Shadab Vajdi, *To the Thirst of the Southern Mountain Slopes*, self-published

Saadi Youssef, *Without an Alphabet, Without a Face*, 2003, Graywoolf Press Haifa Zangana, *Through the Vast Halls of Memory*, 1991, Hourglass

Contents

Introduction

Part 1

Exile

Part 2

Introduction

The Silver Throat of the Moon is by writers in exile who were forced to flee from their countries in recent times, from Afghanistan, Algeria, Angola, Bangladesh, Bosnia, Cameroon, China, Colombia, Democratic Republic of Congo, Croatia, Eritrea, Iran, Iraq, Kosova, Kurdistan, Peru, Somalia, South Africa, Turkey, Yemen and Zimbabwe. While for some writers exile is a new phenomenon, others have been in exile for a considerable period, sometimes constituting reluctant global travellers moving from country to country. Interestingly, the poet Saadi Youssef prefers to describe himself as a resident of the world, not an exile, feeling at home wherever he is. The vast majority of the contributors reside in the UK but some live in the USA, Sweden, Norway, Canada and Poland.

This follows *The Bend in the Road* published in 1998. At that time, refugee and exiled writers had a low profile so that considerable effort was required to locate them and the literature they had created, whereas with the establishment of the organisation Exiled Writers Ink, I have met large numbers of writers. This anthology contains some of the original work. However, since 1998 there have sadly been human rights abuses in a range of new countries and other voices have emerged, so that a considerable number of new writers are represented. However, I felt it was essential to include some of the earlier work by writers from countries where the conflict has now ended, although the countries concerned may now face different scenarios and may have had to metamorphose because of the original trouble. The literature by these writers, records a time which must not be forgotten and fresh work by some of the original writers is evidence of the emotional journeys taken since the early days of arrival in exile. Post September 11th, a new consciousness has emerged about values, culture, post and neo-colonialism, world orders and the clash of civilisations which is reflected in the literature categorised under "New World Order".

Prior to the publication of *The Bend in the Road*, I recall that there was minimal interest in and awareness about the cultural aspects that the new refugees and exiles brought with them compared to Afro-Carribean and Asian culture, which was quite segregated from mainstream culture. The anthology stimulated considerable interest in the literature of the new exiled writers and led to the formation of Exiled Writers Ink! This was not planned but grew organically. There is now more activity around the literature of exile both by mainstream literature organisations and by refugee groups, with small anthologies published in the parts of the UK to which asylum seekers have been dispersed.

Naturally, most writers articulate their thoughts and ideas in their mother tongue. There is a great demand by the writers for translation into English, which is a challenging area to be developed. Not surprisingly, writers remain marginalised if they do not write in English as publishers are generally unwilling to deploy resources for translation or risk publishing the work of a non-mainstream writer. However, some publishers have been adventurous enough to give a voice to exiled writers and the Independent Foreign Fiction Prize is an acknowledgement of the importance of literature in translation, with Lebanese writer Hanan Al Sheykh's novel *Only in London* being shortlisted in 2002.

Some of the contributors were distinguished writers in their countries. Other exiled writers began the creative process in the UK, often stimulated by the experience of being a refugee, living in exile and the desire to communicate something of their identity to audiences and readers outside their own communities. Many of the writers have found the angst of exile to be a powerful contributory factor, which inspires them to write — as Ted Hughes, the poet, stated "Every work of art stems from a wound in the soul of the artist." Some of the writers use writing as a catharsis with the page as the receiver of emotions and thoughts, which cannot be articulated elsewhere so that through the pen and the page the thought processes unravel and become defined.

This book provides an opportunity to understand not only the pain of the refugee experience, manifested in alienation, marginalisation and identity crises, but also into the complexity and diversity of literary styles and cultures and the experiences and concerns of writers from different regions. There are very different literary traditions and forms, which may be unfamiliar to those imbued with a Eurocentric literary perspective. Whilst categorising the work according to themes that enable the reader to compare experience and genre, I am aware of the limitations of this method.

Much of the literature by exiled writers represents the intersection of the personal and the political. This is certainly a complex interface with politics inextricably linked with the literary work by writers who fled from their countries because of persecution, war, imprisonment, lack of freedom of speech or censorship. It may be many years before refugees externalise the events of persecution or conflict. To deal with trauma takes a considerable period. Experiences are probably mediated because of the passing of time and so the reconstruction of events and feelings takes place through memory. Only now are Afghan exiles openly articulating the experience of being victimised under the Taliban.

The writer's role was often quite different to his/her role in Britain in mobilising ideological opposition and expressing the anger of the people in stories and poems. Given that in most of the countries covered, the writer is a revered, well-known figure in the community and the power of the pen is respected, often their words are the only means of opposition and therefore, extremely dangerous for the writer. Salman Rushdie stated that it was the duty of the writer to say the unsayable, speak the unspeakable and to ask difficult questions while Taslima Nasreen, the Bangladeshi writer in exile, has stated that it was the writer's responsibility to tell the truth. In Iran, poetry was known as the "symbolic language of political dissidence". Many women writers in particular are writing to expose the iniquities of their patriarchal societies and their connections with state policy. This is *politicised* literature, which tries to change the status quo. It would certainly be banned or censored in many of the writers' countries. The courage of the writers is admirable with some at risk for speaking out, even in exile. An unsuccessful plot to assassinate Hadi Khorsandi, the satirist, was uncovered by Scotland Yard and various writers have received death threats and as a result, police protection.

Censorship is one of the serious threats to the freedom of the writer. In many cases, for a writer to remain in his or her country, there is a compulsion to operate a system of self-censorship or to veil one's ideas in allegory and imagery. Many writers in exile continue to have difficulty in writing openly partly because of this but also because of fear of retribution in exile. Mahmud Kianush, the Iranian poet in exile in London, tells how he visited the poet, Ahmad Shamloo, who told him "In these days I cannot write poems. My style, my language, my symbols, all had taken form in the time of repression and censorship. Now that I am free to say what I want, I have no poetical language for it."

The late Miroslav Jancic, at a poetry reading in 1996, stated that there were two definitions of homeland: "Language is my homeland" and "My country is where I feel." Esmail Kho'i has stated that a refugee is a split person — a typical example of a person in between, physically here but mentally there, unwilling to be in the host society but unable to go back.

Writers in exile face specific problems, some of which are articulated in the extract from the article: 'Refugee Blues' by Predrag Finci, formerly Professor of Aesthetics at Sarajevo University. Finci expresses the psycho-linguistic traumas and the disempowerment of the refugee writer.

A refugee is not welcome anywhere. A person without a homeland is redundant everywhere. A newcomer is not exactly denied his rights, but is never an equal, for he can never be 'the equal' with his hosts. He is an alien, a potential cause of mayhem and disorder and an extra burden in times of economic crisis. And there is no return. Or at least not for the time being.

Once we had a country and we thought it fair,
Look in the atlas and you'll find it there;
We cannot go there now, my dear, we cannot go there now.
FROM *REFUGEE BLUES* BY W.H. AUDEN.

The first great shock is language. The language keeps reminding us that we are in a completely foreign country. Wittgenstein's words that the boundaries of our language are the boundaries of our world acquire a clear existential meaning. As much as the lack of knowledge of the language torments the poorly educated, it troubles so much more those for whom a language is a medium of self-expression. What can a writer do whose mother-tongue is not English? "Poetry is what is lost in translation," claimed Verlaine. A translated text is never my text. A language is my homeland, says a writer. From now on, his language will be the one he lives in, and the other one, revived in his dreams. A new language — a completely new culture. Many of them remain forever rooted in a world that no longer exists, spiritually absent in a world where they found themselves. Their past is destroyed, the present wretched, and the future?

A refugee is a person with no direction, disorientated in every way possible. It is all the same if he says the homeland is where the heart is or where he feels safe. It is of little consequence whether he was driven away from home or just fled. In the hell of militant nationalism, one could stay no longer; it is not a matter of whether one is a Serb, a Muslim, or a Croat any more... the question is whether one can be at all.

Clearly, the writer's role changes in an alien society and may alter perspective.

It is worth considering to what extent writing in liberty causes the writer to adapt their theme, style or language. In his or her country feelings were expressed about conflict, conflict between individuals and authority, tradition and modernity, men and women. Widespread corruption or oppression and torture may have been exposed whereas in the West to which most writers have fled, these conflicts are more low key or nonexistent. The writer may lose his or her position of importance through working out of context and the reading or listening public may diminish substantially.

The second part of the book consists of papers by exiled writers, given at various conferences. These outline many of the practical and emotional problems faced by writers in exile.

With heartfelt gratitude to all the contributors and may the voices of exiled writers resound loudly in their diasporas.

Jennifer Langer

1. Finci Predrag, 'Refugee Blues', *Third Text* (30): Spring 1995, p.47-52

Part 1

INCARCERATION AND BEYOND

The Doves
Reza Baraheni
(Iran)

outside doves perch everywhere
it is clear from
their cooings of love and delight
it is clear from
the whirr of their wings
wings which seem to fan me in my prisoner's sleep
it is clear outside
doves perch everywhere

the night is like day on the other side of the bars
on this side the day is like night

Doctor Azudi, The Professional

Reza Baraheni
(Iran)

Azudi is just like
Genghis Khan when he walks
he walks on a pile of fresh corpses

the Khan did not clean his teeth either
the Khan also belched the Khan
did not take off his boots either Azudi
has shattered the mouths of twenty poets today

Azudi wears a tie something
Genghis Khan never did
only this splendid detail reveals the prodigious march of
history

White Rock
Ghazi Rabihavi
(Iran)

The photographer jumped down over the gallows and his three cameras jumped around with him. We were worried something might happen to them. The gallows were still lying on the floor of the pick-up truck. He dusted off his trousers and said:

"Are you kids from around here?"

We looked at each other and one of us said:

"Are you going to take pictures of us or the dead man?"

The photographer blinked nervously and asked:

"Is he dead?" and ran, complete with the solid looking black cameras, to the patrol car. It had arrived with these three *pasdars* carrying G-3 guns about an hour earlier. And one of us had said:

"I bet those guns aren't loaded."

Two of the officers threw their guns onto the back seat of the car and walked over to the pick-up. And one of us had said then:

"I bet those guns are loaded."

They began to help take out the gallows posts from the truck and to set them up on either side of the white rock where they had already dug two shallow holes to support them. Before they had found the rock, one of the *pasdars* — the revolutionary guards — had asked us:

"Hey, you. Can any of you get us a stool?" and one of us had said:

"He's going to be hanged, isn't he. Because you have to hang him."

But the other guy said:

"Don't bother with a stool: this white rock will do."

A few local men were coming our way from different parts of the town. It was a good Friday morning for a hanging, only it would have been even better if it hadn't started to snow, or if we'd had gloves. They said if it snowed they wouldn't hang him. It wasn't snowing when they brought the dead man. When they brought him he was alive.

He came out of the ambulance and sniffed the air. He had pulled up the zipper of his grey and green jumper — or someone had done it up for him because his hands were strapped behind his back. The first snowflakes settled on his hair. A group of locals ran towards him. The photographer was checking out his cameras. The headlights of the ambulance had been left on. The snowflakes were light and soft. They melted even before they touched the lights. One of us said:

"Pity. I wasn't even born when they executed the Shah's guard." One of us answered:

"My brother was born then; my dad sat him up on his shoulders so he could see the guy being executed. Bang! Bang!"

The truck driver said:

"I'd love to stay and watch. It'd mean a blessing for me. But I've got to deliver this food for the troops." The fat *pasdar* scratched his beard with the gun barrel and said:

"Good luck." The truck driver ran to the pick-up cursing the snow.

The prisoner was pacing up and down in the snow without any idea that he was moving closer and closer to the gallows. Sometimes he just stood there, with his long, thin legs, turning his head this way and that, sniffing the air. He wrinkled his nose and waggled his eyebrows, trying to shift the blindfold to find out where he was. But the blindfold was too tight. One of us said:

"Shout out his name so he knows where he is." Another said:

"When I used to know his name he was a different person."

A couple of people were still working on trying to get the gallows firm in the ground. Only men and children could come to watch. One of the guys, who had been given a leg up on the cupped hands of another, jumped down and said:

"Where's the other one?" The prisoner turned his head and said:

"Yeah. Where is he?" We didn't know the other guy; he wasn't from our town. We only saw him once — no, it was twice — on the same night. It was the beginning of autumn. The sun was just setting when we saw him entering the gates. He had a long turtle-neck sweater pulled down over his trousers. His clothes were black; like his hair. The officer on the gate was eating meat and rice. The stranger was carrying a bouquet of pink roses, and he was trying to hide a black plastic bag underneath it. He didn't like us watching him. But we did anyway and worked out that there were two bottles in the bag. He had the address of the prisoner but didn't know which way to go. So we showed him. At first, we thought he was a rather tall boxer. He ran his fingers through his hair and lifted his head. Then he looked down at us from under his eyelids. His eyebrows were shaved across his nose where they should have run together and he smiled at us. The sun trembling through the plane tree splashed his face with light and shade. He smiled and turned in the direction we had pointed. The security guy was washing his plate under the tap and asked us:

"Who was that?" and we told him. He looked over to the prisoner's house.

People were moving closer to the gallows, gathering in front of it. The photographer was sitting in the ambulance having a smoke. The prisoner, walking towards the gallows, was still unaware of where he was. One of the guards took his arm and pulled him over to the rock. The photographer grabbed his cameras and jumped out of the ambulance. He was wearing one of those safari vests with a lot of pockets. He got out a wire contraption from one of them and hooked them onto the shoulder tabs. Then he got out some white cloth and stretched it over the frame he had made. Now the snow wouldn't bother him. He ran across to the gallows with the umbrella that had sprouted from his shoulder.

None of the spectators were related to the prisoner; we didn't know if he had any relations. He was a loner; he built the wooden bodies for stringed instruments and twice a week went out of town. People said he had a wife and children somewhere that he had abandoned. The grocer had said to him:

"Give it another chance. You're only 45. It's just the right time to get married." The prisoner had smiled and said:

"Just the right time."

The guy holding onto the prisoner's arm was still looking at the hanging rope. Then he told the prisoner:

"Stand on top of this stone, will you, pal. Just to test everything's OK."

The prisoner's feet searched for the stone. Found it. If we could have seen his eyes, we could have told if he was frightened or not. That midnight, in the autumn, when the guards attacked his house and arrested both of them, he pressed his face against the rear window of the car, his eyes searching everywhere for his lover. Then, his voice trembling, he yelled from behind the glass:

"Leave him alone!" The car drove off; a crushed pink rose was still sticking to the back tyre.

The prisoner asked:

"Is it time?" The *pasdar* said:

"No. The *Hadji* — the Mullah — hasn't arrived yet. We can't start without him." He said:

"Then what?" The officer said:

"Take your shoes off. This is only a trial run." The prisoner took his bare feet out of the loose-fitting canvas shoes and stood on them. His long, thin toes were red with cold. They had up-ended the white rock and were holding it in position; the slightest kick would topple it, leaving his feet dangling in space.

"Now climb up." He put one foot on the rock. It shifted, swayed, nearly fell over. The guard jumped forward and

14

set it straight again.

"What's with you? Are you in a hurry?" he said. Then he got up and one by one, carefully placed the prisoner's feet on the stone. The prisoner stood on the stone and was raised up above the crowd. His shoes were left below, on the ground, and everything around him was white: the sky, the snow. The rest of the officers and the driver were standing under a big umbrella like you have on a beach, next to the patrol car. It was a long way from the gallows. The photographer said:

"What are you doing? *Hadji* isn't here yet." The guard said:

"No, he isn't" The photographer said:

"Then come over here and have some saffron dates." The guard said:

"Only if you let me stand under your umbrella," and burst out laughing. The photographer looked up at his umbrella and said:

"It's for the cameras," and walked towards the patrol car. The spectators were not saying anything. They were just standing there, silent, looking at the prisoner. Hanging onto one side of the gallows, the guard pulled himself up next to him. If he hadn't been wearing boots, there would have been enough room for another pair of feet. The stone wobbled again, but didn't fall over. The guard grabbed the hanging rope and struggled to get it round the prisoner's neck. The prisoner was trying to help, but couldn't see what the other guy was doing. Then he jumped down and the rock stayed firm. He said:

"Now you see how steady it is?"

In the distance a car was approaching. One of the *psadars* called out: "Hurry up!" He looked at the patrol car and then at the prisoner and said: "Try to get used to it, then, when the time comes, you won't panic." The only movement in the landscape was the distant car. We could only just see it, but because of the whiteness of the snow, we could make out what make it was: either a Mercedes or a Hillman. The *Hadji* must have been lounging in the back

15

seat. The guard said:

"Make sure it doesn't work loose. I'll be right back." The prisoner said:

"What?" But the guard had already moved off to the patrol car. The boot of the approaching car sagged low to the ground from the weight on the back seat. It drew nearer to where we were, but it was still a good way off. The guards were still eating their dates near the patrol car.

Women were not allowed to watch because this was not their business: it had nothing to do with them. The prisoner tried to shift the rock with his feet. It refused to move. One of the spectators jumped forward but quickly froze to the spot. All of us were waiting for the approaching car. The *psadars* and the photographer were throwing the date stones into the snow. The snowflakes were melting as they hit the ground. The prisoner again tried to shift the rock. It moved, but didn't fall. The silent spectators stood stock still as if they were frozen to the spot and it wasn't snowing. Our hands were red with cold. Red as the wine the guards found in the prisoner's house the night of his arrest. One of the bottles was empty; the other still half full. The guards also took the two long-stemmed crystal glasses. By now we could see the car. It was a Hillman. One of the officers threw the date box away. The rest quickly ate up what was left in their hands. One of the *psadars* went to meet the car and the rest followed. The photographer glanced at the gallows. He started to move closer, but changed his mind and walked over to the ambulance instead. The prisoner was kicking at the rock with his feet. It tottered, fell down and left his bare feet hanging in the air. His long, thin toes were searching for the stone. But by then it was too late. Then the movement stopped and his feet hung motionless. The car finally arrived dazzling us with its headlights. We went to warm our hands at the headlights of the ambulance because that was what the photographer was doing.

Through the Vast Halls of Memory 1
Haifa Zangana
(Iraq)

Pointing to the last cell at the end of the corridor, the guard said in a loud voice:

"There is barely any room left for more prisoners. You must stay with Um Wahid, Um Jassim and Um Ali."

Slowly I followed the big woman's steps. She was in her forties. Her hair was jet-black and her body a huge mass of fat that vibrated with every step; buttock up, the rest of her body down, left, right. I did not know what to do with my right hand. I kept trying to adjust the strap of my handbag, but then realised I was not even carrying one. I put my hands in the pockets of my navy blue skirt, took them out, put them back in. Slowly I followed the guard's steps. She was wearing a grey uniform. The walls were concrete, the floor concrete, the ceiling concrete. Were the women too made of the same substance?

The front of each cell was made of iron bars with a door on the right-hand side. There were two rows of cells with iron bars facing each other. The corridor was a metre wide. To maintain some privacy, the women had used old, grey blankets as curtains, knotted to the bars in the most bizarre ways.

Many eyes stared at me, the eyes of women with their bodies wrapped in black clothes. The whole place was in black and grey, like an old photo from a family album. The women's faces were a funny colour, not pale in the usual way, the pallor of illness and fatigue. In their faces, I beheld the dryness and cracking of earth that has suffered drought for many years. The concrete floor did not nourish seeds, the light bulbs surrounded by wire did not give light.

The guard stopped at the last cell and told the three prisoners:

17

"This is the new prisoner. She's a political." She pronounced that slowly and firmly as if introducing a new breed of animal and then she slowly left.

I did not know what to do, so I stood where I was, hoping one of them would make the first move. The cell was a cube with a small barred window looking onto another concrete wall a few metres away. In the right-hand corner, there was a cubicle big enough to accommodate one person sitting or standing. In it was a tap and a flask. It was the toilet, the bathroom, the place where the three women could wash their cutlery, clothes and their bodies. The two walls of the cubicle were so low, they barely covered the lower part of the body. The entrance was decorated with an old cotton night-dress.

For years, the women had continued cutting up old blankets and clothes for use as curtains, hanging them up in the afternoon when the prison warden left, and taking them down in the morning before she arrived for inspection. With endless determination, they persisted in the same ritual, as if proving to themselves and the others that, in enjoying some privacy, they could still defy the system.

It was evening. One of the women, the smallest one, with long plaits, was wearing a black, long-sleeved dress over striped pyjamas. She carried her mattress on her head and walked out of the cell, staggering under the heavy load. The second woman did the same. She was very old, wrinkled, with gums that made unusual sounds. Her wrinkled face was covered in tattoos. The blue tattoos began at her eyebrows and continued to her navel, as she later proudly showed us. Was she in her eighties? She carried her mattress on her head and left. The third woman stood next to me:

"Do you have a mattress? Have you any clothes apart from what you're wearing?" She peered at my face, particularly my chin covered in sores. Then she put her mattress on her head and indicated to me to follow her.

"My name is Um Wahid. The little woman is Um

18

Jassim. She's sentenced to fifteen years. Old Um Ali will be released in two years. The warden lets us sleep in the yard because it's impossible to sleep inside because of this heat."

I sat down on the mattress Um Wahid had lent me. Um Wahid was the longest serving prisoner in the women's prison. She had been sentenced to life along with her brother. They had murdered her husband together. Shortly after their wedding, he had treated her badly, beating her up and forcing her to entertain his friends. One morning, while her husband was at work, she had packed her bags and left, returning to her family in the south. Her mother had sent her back straightaway, saying.

"Your home now is with your husband. We don't want you anymore."

Her uncle accompanied her to Baghdad. Um Wahid told her young brother that her husband was forcing her to be a prostitute. Together they agreed the only solution was to kill him. So they killed him. At the time she was nineteen and her brother seventeen. Over the years, Um Wahid had accumulated many aluminium plates, pans, spoons, pillows, clothes and blankets. Being there for such a long time, she was the official recipient of the prisoners' leftovers, the things they did not want to take with them on release, reminders of prison.

My bed was next to Um Jassim's in the concrete yard surrounded by a high barbed wire fence. My continual coughing drove someone to complain. I heard one of them say:

"Maybe she's suffering from TB."

At that moment, and for no good reason (maybe it was the sympathy shown by Um Wahid, the other women's silence, or the complaints some of them made), the mask I had worn for some weeks now began to crack. The mask had protected me from seeing, smelling, touching, but not from hearing. Hearing the voices of the tortured, trying to recognise their identities, hearing the torturers' footfall in the corridors of the Qasir, listening to the sound of keys

19

turning in locks, trying to identify the last click before the torturer would appear before me. I touched my dishevelled hair, matted with dirt and dried blood. I smelt the odour of my body, touched my hair, my face and cried. I cried quietly, a painful, continuous moaning that lasted all night, during which I mourned my disappointments, my fear and the longing I had to see my friends and comrades. Can the soul be separated from its shell and leave it behind to wander the open fields?

I gaze into the darkness. I see a green mountain, heavy with bushes and cypress trees. At its foot are vineyards, overlooking a village. The tinkling of water can be heard inside the houses. I see a group of children picking up camomile leaves, putting them in cotton bags, competing with each other to fill them up. I see them eating figs on their way home, and throwing walnuts at each other. I see myself laughing happily.

The Silence of the Living

Nafissa Boudalia
(Algeria)
Translated from French

The silence of the living
Is deafening
The dead are there
They question me again
The assassins are there
Now, Howl louder
They shout again
You are a spy... you are a spy
Bring hither
The pincers
Bring here
The syringe
It's easy to confess
You are a spy... you are a spy
We found this feather
It's all so clear now
The nib in the end
The spacing of the ink
The shapes of the faces
And the expression of the eyelids

You are a spy... you are a spy
We found this frame
It's all in the canvas
You believe in the spirit
Where you dip your brushes
Ethereal in different sizes
Your blues are threatening
Your reds are too deep

You are a spy... you are a spy

I Hate Wednesdays

Sokol Syla
(Kosova)

Tanks noisy, gun-fire and gunpowder smell,
Assassinations, executions,
Mournful voice of mothers
And even —
Innocent screams everywhere:
June 24 '98 — a very gloomy summer,
My first arrest in Gjakova town;
It is Wednesday....!

Through my cell's improvised window
I've become a former observer of yellow leaves,
On the only tree in the prison yard —
Where just a bird is resting on a twig.
I covet its freedom,
And am glad it is not a human slave,
Otherwise,
I'm still in a state of anxious anticipation,
Waiting for the three minute visit of my dearest,
When suddenly:
"There is no meeting for you today" — a guard shouts,
I forget what day it is,
Ah...! What a pity... I realise (Oct 99) —
It's Wednesday today....!

"Get ready p...plea...se" another strange voice requests,
"No more than 25kgs" says the other,
"It's your deportation today!" says the third,
"Thank you!" I want to say,
Because of a longing for my children,
But how can I make this mistake, I had to...!
And why an Ipswich cell I don't know,
I've become a prisoner again!

But this time of my new-found friends,
Where it's impossible to see anything through a window,
No tree, no bird!
Does the "Phoenix" need to engulf itself in flames again?
That would break the rule,
Does it need more inspiration through suffering?
I must finish this poem and complete my diary;
That's what I tell myself,
However I do not forget
This is the other autumn day —
Nov 2002,
Wednesday... again!

Helped by true friends,
I start to breathe freely again
And go on my way,
Not knowing how long I can resist,
Counting the weekdays,
Afraid of the third,
I cross it out off my calendar, but
Still it follows me,
Even faster,
And comes again,
That evil day,
Like a ghost, vampire or monster,
Oh, may God take if away from me!
Let it be six days only —
I really hate Wednesdays.

My Teeth Are Talking to Me

Nasrin Parvaz

(Iran)

Pary's story

I am ashamed of myself. I hate myself because I did a terrible thing.

They wanted to beat me and they showed me the feet of one of the prisoners covered with blood. Before, I had heard the noises of flogging and the voice calling for God, Mohammed and Ali before each lash, and there was a weak moaning. I had no idea what would be the outcome of all that I was hearing. But when I finally saw the prisoner's feet I was scared and I agreed to betray my friend. I just hoped she wouldn't come back to work. After all, she had witnessed my arrest and she might suspect danger. But, when I took them to the factory where I had been working, there she was, and I pointed her out to them.

How horrible I am. I've always been bad. Everybody said I was bad. My father and brother used to tell me I was just like that whore, my mother. I never knew whether she was a prostitute or if they just called her that because she left us. I never knew why she left us. Maybe she could not bear my father's attitude. I was still a child that day I escaped from home and I went to my uncle's house and asked if I could stay with them forever. They agreed and I grew up with my cousins, who helped me to study and I married one of them later. Until then I believed in God and I used to pray; after all, my father was religious, but my cousin didn't pray.

When people stood up against the Shah and the whole atmosphere changed, my cousins became left-wing revolutionaries. At that time I was working in a factory and my marriage to one of my cousins let me see the world from another point of view. There were always meetings in our house and after some time I joined them. I remember one evening after work, I fell asleep during one of these meetings and my cousins sat in such a way that the others didn't realise that I was asleep — until the meeting was over and my cousins had to move to make the tea. When they stood up I fell and woke up and everybody realised that I had been asleep. What nice days I had, there was no fear at all of anything. Nor the fear of God that was my companion all my childhood, and no fear of authority. We were like birds, free of all the burdens that I always felt on my shoulders before. For a couple of years I enjoyed my life; everything about it is a dream now. The partner that I had, his kisses, the way he touched me, the way he looked at me, the way he talked to me, I miss all of that. I even began to like myself, and feel happy being alive.

That situation didn't last long. Nor did those meetings. One day the security guards surrounded our house. They took my husband and I to Evin prison and I could not face the torture. After that I felt so guilty that I decided to proclaim Marxism so that they would execute me and I would be freed of my guilt feelings. But instead they gave me a life-sentence and everyday life in prison means that torture is always just behind the door. If I do something that they don't like, they beat me up even in front of other prisoners. The fear of torture accompanies my everyday life. Once though, I did manage to cope with it, and that was during one of the most excruciating periods of the entire prison regime. I had to sit down all day long in a *chador*, blindfolded, in a small space with the loudspeaker telling us all the time about the goodies of the god and mullahs' regime. I wasn't to move or make any noise. If I did I would be beaten very hard by the *Haji*. This torture was known as Grave and I was one of only about fifteen out of more than one hundred who came out of it after nine months without breaking down and "confessing". For a while I was proud of that and it helped me to keep the fear away a bit.

After Grave it was important for me to find a group I could be with. Everybody here belongs to a group and each group behaves differently. In prison nobody can be by themselves or unattached. I decided to be among a group of mostly Grave survivors. They were inactive, passive you could say, because they knew all too well what the price was of doing something. However it wasn't easy to be accepted by them. I had to prove that I was worthy of their relationship. So I tried to do everything that their leader did — saying "hello" to those she said "hello" to, ignoring those she ignored, talking only to those she talked to. However she spent most of her time on her own, walking by herself, gazing at the wall, thinking, or reading books. By changing my attitude towards the other prisoners and ignoring them, I lost my friends. To be alone is what I like to do too. I had to get used to it when I was in Grave and ever since that time it's still my habit to sit facing the wall for hours on end, not making a noise and keeping perfectly still. It's what we had to do in Grave, if we didn't want to be tortured, and I like doing it even now, it makes me feel safe from torture.

Sometimes I just like to watch her, to see what my leader is doing. After I started copying all her activities, she began to see me and smile at me sometimes and even to talk to me after my visits. That's when I felt they accepted me, because after she talked to me, the others did too. It was important for me to keep this relationship, so I continued acting like her. Even when she felt everybody in our prison was a counter-revolutionary and asked the jailer to take her to the penitents'[1] ward, I waited to see if they would move her and was ready to ask if I could go too. She sensed something was going to happen in our ward soon and she didn't want to be around when it did. It is true that sometimes even if you stay neutral, you can end up being punished. What can we do if we don't want to pay a price for someone else's action? Anyway the jailer didn't agree to her demands and we both stayed in that ward together. But after that time she set herself apart from

26

everybody else, making her life quite separate. She refused to take her meals in the rota order, insisting on taking her food straight from the communal dish, rather than waiting for it to be handed to her when her turn came, and so I did the same. I didn't mean to imply by my action that the other prisoners were untouchable[2], after all I wasn't religious, but I just wanted to follow my leader, because she was the smartest and the best and I would die for her. However some of the prisoners didn't like our way of not complying with the ward regulations, would not leave our food in the main pan and would divide it to the rooms that we were in physically. So those times we didn't eat.

I could bear everyday life in prison forever if they didn't beat me, but now everything has changed. Every few days they call ten of us out, to be beaten three times a day at prayer times, until the prisoner denounces her belief or dies. The guards, male and female, are beating prisoners and calling for God and Mohammed with each lash to give them strength. I know they will come for me soon and then what can I do? Some girls under torture agreed to their conditions. They come back broken, with tears in their eyes, ten years older than a month ago. They want to die; sometimes you can hear their crying. They don't talk; they just wait for their release. What release? With heads hanging down and lips that will never laugh. Laugh? Will they ever be able to forget what has happened to them? Will they be able to forgive themselves for their weakness? I haven't forgiven myself and I won't let them make me feel weaker. How do I know if I go under torture again, I'll manage to bear it?

Once you agree to be humiliated by doing what they want, you are defeated and it will change your whole spirit. Like the penitents, you act like a defeated person, frightened, aimless, hopeless, full of hate. Then to cure yourself, you try to go further and further from what you were and do more for them. Like a diseased person you will carry this personality until death, the very death you tried to escape from. Death is the end I'm choosing now so

27

that my spirit can survive; it will come to us sooner or later anyway. Only death can take me away from this crowded earth. Even silence is now noisy for me.

By the time they call out my name, I'll be dead and they won't be able to do anything to me. If they broke me for a second time, how could I go on living? I'm already ashamed of myself for the first time it happened. Oh yes they will let me go after they have broken me, after they have. I'll be allowed to see my husband more frequently and he will tell me that I did the right thing in agreeing to their conditions. It's what he did, and that's why he can come and see me whenever he wants. He tells me to stop acting as a communist and talks to me about tactics. He says that in prison we have to act differently from our aims. But isn't that just what the jailers want? "Act in the way they want; give your information, and pray to a god that they created to fool us. Don't laugh, because there is nothing to laugh about. You can think in your own way inside your head." Which way? The way you act or the way that you believe and are not brave enough to show?

When my husband comes to see me, he brings a lot of beautiful dresses and he says that I should do what he did. But the way he talks now is different from his words before prison. I liked him then because of how he used to speak, and if I believe him now how can I love him? He was a decent person then and I don't know what prison has done to him. I said that I loved him, but what is love? I don't know anything about love any more. I have forgotten how to love someone. It is now many years since I touched anybody. Prisoners cannot even hold each other's hands. If we do they call us lesbians and even punish us for that. I miss being hugged — by anyone. I wish I could be hugged so tightly I could feel it in my bones. Perhaps I must wait for the earth to give me this final embrace.

Sometimes I put on the clothes that he sends me, but I cannot wear them for more than ten minutes. Then I change back again, into my old dark dresses. When I wear those beautiful clothes everybody looks at me because they are beautiful, soft and colourful, and their attention makes me angry. They must know that my husband has sent them to me, my defeated husband. No, I can't wear them, because he has sent them to me. If I wear them I have to accept him as my husband and how can I? Before that I have to kill the dream that I have of him which is based on our life that we had together. I must kill the husband that I once had and loved. That time we had no money to buy nice dresses. We had to spend our money to produce underground papers and I was happy. He would warm me more than all warm dresses and being with him was more precious that all these nice dresses. But now he is not the one that I loved. Though he has the same name and the same face. But his eyes are empty now, there isn't fire burning in his eyes any more. I don't desire his hugs any more, I'm not sure I can bear his touch any more.

They watch me, they laugh at me, even when I go to the toilet, they come and check what I am doing. They don't understand that it is my business to decide whether to live or die. It is true that to enter this horrible world is not in one's hands but to stay or to leave it is in one's hands. I'm sure I wasn't the fruit of love. Maybe I'm the outcome of a rape on the wedding night? I didn't choose to come to this world but I have the right to leave it. For a while I kept banging my head against the wall when I went to the toilet. They came and told me to stop it or they would come in, so I had to stop. Another time I was going to break a glass to use it to end my life but they took it by force. Now I'm going to cut my blood vessel with a pencil sharpener when I have a shower. I will hold onto the shower pipe until I die, I won't let myself sit on the floor like last time, when they checked me from under the door and saw me sitting down watching the water washing my blood away. Next time they won't be able to catch me, I know what to do. Though they watch me even during the night, I know what to do now.

Lately my teeth have been talking to me. They tell me everything that is happening. They tell me that the guards

29

are talking about corpses and that some of them feel sick from the smell of blood. They are the bodies of our fellow prisoners. My teeth tell me how to kill myself so that they cannot take me to be tortured. Today I told my leader that my teeth are talking to me and she smiled at me kindly and told me to pull them out so that they cannot do it any more. What a clever idea, why didn't I think about it? So now I'm looking for some pliers to take out my teeth. I found some but they took them away from me by force. I am watched by my cellmates all the time. I have two kind of guards now, the *Pasdars*[3] and the prisoners. Sometimes I cannot tell the difference because they are all here to stop me being free from myself.

Donya's Story

Today is my turn to watch Pary. She takes her bag and goes to the shower, I'm worried. Every five minutes I check her from under the door but I cannot see anything unusual. It seems she is standing under the shower. The last time she cut her wrist under the shower she was sitting on the floor, watching her blood washing away. So the person who was watching her understood quickly and we could rescue her. How about now? It is about fifteen minutes since she went in. I feel there must be something wrong. I'd better bring a chair and climb on it and look over the cabin. Now I can see her better. She is standing under the shower, while holding on to it firmly. I push myself up to see more of her, she looks pale, she is not washing herself, and she is just standing there. Oh no, she is holding the shower and the water is washing out her blood which is running out of her wrist. I scream and call for help; I'm shaking like a leaf. Some prisoners and one of our fellow prisoners who is a doctor come to help. We pull her out of the bathroom and we tie her wrist with a cloth. I can't hold on to my tears, they are running like a river that is free from any barriers. The doctor tells me to go and have a rest; I go in a corner and watch her. They lay her on some blankets. Different from the other time. Pary

30

doesn't resist them. It seems she has no power any more to push them back and escape. The doctor says that we have to send her to hospital to stitch her wrist. We have no choice; the blood is running from her wrist, though it is tied with cloth. If she doesn't receive medical attention she will die. If she is sent to hospital she will still be left to die. Yet we can't leave her here to die, we have to send her to hospital for stitches. We call for the guard and she takes her to hospital to leave her there to die.

Pary has been in hospital for two days now and we have no news about her. We don't know if they did stitch her wrist or left her to die. Or did they stitch her wrist but left her alone to kill herself? Now the guard asks for her clothes to hand in to her family. The guard says she is dead and she was when we sent her to hospital. We knew that she would die. She managed to do what she wanted, but if the cruelty of this year, the year 1988, hadn't taken place, she would be alive now and maybe have lived for many years.

I miss her very much and I cannot forget her attitudes after Grave. She came back quite different from when she was taken to it. When she came back I felt that she did not see anybody around herself. Perhaps she didn't realise that the Grave situation in which she had no right to walk or talk to anybody or see anybody is changed. In the Grave she had to live and even sleep blindfolded. Perhaps, when she was there, she had to switch her mind in that way to bear the situation and she could not get rid of the habit when the situation changed. Most of the time she was walking alone with her thoughts and sometimes she could be seen smiling as she watched the sunset. I wondered what she was seeing or what she was thinking of. Her husband? Her mother or her family? Dawn and sunset have different meaning for prisoners, but for her it was even more than that. After coming back from the Grave every day she was sitting face to the wall for a few hours, doing nothing. Sometimes she was face to wall hugging her feet with her two hands and with her head on her knee, sitting for hours. Lately sometimes after a shower she wore a pretty dress for a few minutes and then changed it again to her old dark dress. Part of her wanted to wear the pretty dresses that her husband was sending to her and most of her didn't want to wear them. Didn't she want to wear beautiful dresses or didn't she want to wear the dresses that her husband was sending to her? I could see the conflict that she was facing over everything and all the time. The conflict that drove her mad. Many times I tried to talk to her to establish a friendship again, but she wasn't interested and put me off politely.

I was her friend for years and she would tell me about her feelings. Everybody needs someone to talk and she would talk to me about her defeated husband. She had no visit, no family to care about her and I would give her money when she needed to buy things. Her husband was in prison and sometimes she had a visit at her husband's request. After each visit she was upset, and in two minds. In the early years when she talked to me she would say that he was a different person from the one she married. That he was denying all his principles and was asking her to repent. She knew that he was wrong because he was broken but she hadn't the guts to tell him. After all he was the one that introduced politics to her and by doing that gave hope to her life. Hope to fight for a world of equality and liberty for which she wanted to donate her life. Every time after her visit she told me that she wouldn't meet him on his next visit, but she couldn't carry it through and she was still going to see him. She was divided between her feelings for him and her idea that he became a penitent. She could not tell him that she believed that she must persist in refusing to make a confession, and the contradiction was eating her from inside. When she was in the Grave, once *Haji* went to her and asked her opinion about Marxism, and she replied, it is the working class knowledge of emancipation. If *Haji* asked her more she wouldn't say more, because she didn't know much about it.

Now it is about a couple of years since she first wouldn't talk to me. One day when I went to talk to her as usual when she was walking alone with that strange smile on half of her face, she told me that she would not continue our friendship because I had talked to some other prisoners. She told me that all the other prisoners except the Jahan group, of which there are less than a dozen in prison, are counter revolutionist. I asked her how come? But she didn't want to talk to me any more. It seemed I could be with them or against them. It seemed she liked to identify herself with them. The only person she liked to have communication with was Jahan who wouldn't pay much attention to her. Perhaps Jahan's mind, like Pary's, was too busy from all the suffering she went through in the Grave. Pary praised Jahan as a leader though she used to ignore everybody not only Pary. She ignored even her friends and her followers. Such an attitude by the leader made the followers more desperate to make themselves visible to her, by doing things that she might like or not doing things that would be forbidden to her. Pary always looked on her as a hero. She used to stand in front of her door and look at her with joy of seeing her. Sometimes she just liked to watch her and you could see that the great joy for her was to talk to her hero.

Seeing Pary and some others looking at their leader for approval for whatever they did made me think of relationships. Why do some people possess the upper hand over others in a relationship? Isn't it that people who like to become a leader find those who need a leader? Why is it that these two types of personalities make themselves complete together? Why can't people build up an equal relationship among themselves? Doesn't it mean these two kinds of personality need each other? However some of the Jahan followers try to be a leader in some other relationships too. What do they get from Jahan relationships and what do they get in other relationships? Isn't it a circle of need that makes such relationships exist? I look at Jahan, she is pretty and she talks very well.

She is confident, which is something here. However if we were not in prison and if these people didn't need to identify themselves with a tendency, would Jahan become a leader? The reason is that she is one of those few (about fifteen people out of one hundred) who didn't break in Grave, unlike many others who recanted their past; the reason is that she doesn't want to engage in the struggle at the same time that she doesn't want to recant; and that there are prisoners who are tired of torture and struggle too. Prison conditions made her a leader. However one cannot stay neutral in prison, one must oppose either the regime or the revolution. To escape torture Jahan drew her line against the revolution and since she can justify it well so that she doesn't fall into the hands of the regime, some of the prisoners identify themselves with her. Here the situation is like any other community that causes improvement in some people but not to others. Relationships are such that some people become more educated and find more emotional support than others. Here too, people are not free to achieve the goals they need. People are not in mutual harmonious relationships but instead, differences are highlighted. Therefore those who have some quality, it doesn't matter if it is good or bad, can lead the others.

A couple of years ago Jahan and her close friend asked the guard to transfer them downstairs, to the penitents' ward. The ward in which most of the prisoners are Mojahed and in the early days of prison many of them treated people like Jahan as untouchable. Prisoners like Jahan had no right to wash dishes and if they did a Moslem had to purify it with water at the end. Most of them don't act the same now because the situation has changed and acting as a penitent is not fashionable any more. But still one must have the nerves to live with them and here one of the heroes prefers to identify herself with them than us. The guard asked them to be ready behind the ward bars. Jahan and her friend packed their belongings and waited with a *chador* on all day behind the

34

bars. But the guard didn't turn up to take them to heaven! By now we should have got used to the guards playing on our demands. While all Jahan's friends were waiting for her transfer to go and demand the same thing, she and her friend came back to their room and unpacked their belongings.

Lately when the regime started to kill prisoners, Pary's attitude changed. Her face was full of terror and she could not eat most of the time. When they killed all the Moslems who were in our wing and started to call our prison mates for torture, she tried to kill herself several times. I don't know if she knew that our prison mates were beaten at every Muslim prayer time, while the torturer was calling for God or Mohamed. I don't know if she knew that they were beaten to accept Islam and pray. For a while she could not manage to kill herself, because of us watching her every moment. After all it wasn't only Pary at that time who wanted to kill herself, and we had to prevent their action. Because we knew when the situation changed they would be fine again. For a while Pary used to bang her head on the wall while she was sitting in the toilet and it was so terrible. I could hear the noise of banging when I was in the corridor some distance from the toilet. Many times we took glass from her hand before she managed to use it.

Once she told Jahan that her teeth were talking to her and Jahan told her to pull them out to stop them talking. Then she looked for pliers to pull out her teeth. At last she found some pliers to pull her teeth out to stop them talking to her. Though she hadn't eaten for days, there were five of us to take the pliers out of her hand. Pary was shaking from anger that she could not defeat us and keep the pliers. She went and sat in the corner of the room in her usual place and in a low voice swore at us as counter-revolution. At such times her leader wouldn't do anything to ease her. It was obvious that only her leader would talk to her and she would only listen to her. If she wanted she could even save her life.

1. *penitents* (Tavab in Farsi). Prisoners who have repented of their dissident activities against the Islamic Republic and have pledged to work for the regime as born-again Muslims in return for a cessation of torture.
2. The orthodox Muslim concept of *najes* categorises non-Muslims as untouchable, and the objects they have come into contact with as defiled.
3. *Pasdar* are guards in support of the Islamic Republic

Death by Stoning
Ziba Karbassi
(Iran)
Translated by Ziba Karbassi and Stephen Watts

little morning star
     are you here with
          your star-gaze gone?
little wren
     are you staying in the bushes
          when you go to the skies?
little silver coin
     are you coming up heads
          when you fall down tails?
my always-greening pine
     is it winter when it's spring
          will you tell me?

your sisters are here
     and your brother too
          and I am still here but
where are you?
     where
          are you?
why don't you?
why don't you
     come and see
          the red little shoe I am knitting
               for the
          apple of my closing eye?

and from the petals
            of my heart
the red little shift
        I am making
and from his deepest bones
        the cradle that your brother's
                            shaping
                baby roe deer, just
                    for you,
and from their hair
        pillows that your
                weaving sisters
                    make

everyone today is looking at me kindly
they are looking at me with coloured eyes
and their shy withheld charities
        are killing me and are
            making me
                break

little baby roe
        deer

everyone is here excepting you
who the flower meadows of my broken
            mind are craving

and I want to make of my holding
        arms a hunter's pit
            for you
so you would never
            ever leave
                your mother

what am I saying
                little baby roe deer:
        I don't want anything, anything
                        at all
I want you to always be free and to go
                wherever you will
to sit by with whoever you choose
        my free-flying bird,
                my up-starting startled
        baby roe deer of the white and
                        running feet

everyone is here
        everyone, but who
                I do not want
                        to see
        but who I do not
                        want: no one
        not anyone,
                excepting you,
                        only you
I want to see

                who is not here

why doesn't anyone say anything
                any more
why is no-one talking at all to me
such silences are sharp needles to
                        bite me
and to knife me through my heart
such silence is
        the deepest scar
                        of my body
and you are not coming
        and the sadness
                is a cloudburst
                        valley-flooding
                                me

39

and I am not a scaffold to be toppled
not a felled tree to be sunk in the flood
I am only a bag of bones and skin
                smashed about
and the only thing left of me is the tiny
                scared beast of my heart
that quite simply
        does not believe
                that this flood
                        has taken you

and look
this is the sun shining
        and this is the white lily you used
                to pour away its water
and this the red little fish
        that last night a neighbour's
                cat broke the bowl
                        of
        that I wish no harsh omen
and this is the small flower-edged scarf
        you bought for me last
                New Year
and this is your notebook
        that always was half-
                way open
and when I was closing it
        a star jerked out
                and pierced the throat
                        of my speech
and the word-route of my inspiration
        closed up forever

last night wolves were howling
            I heard their voices
                  last night
they brought me your torn clothes
the blue shirt your auntie made you
I wish her dear hand had been
                              broken
your blue shirt is red with blood
and I cannot make out its print
            or pattern

they said their skirts were filled with stones
their hands were full of stones, their skirts
everywhere stones were being rained down
            the world was become a world
                  of stone

I wish
      I wish
            I wish
  your mother were dead
                  I wish I were

your sisters' skirts
                  are filled with blood
your brother is burning
            the cradle of wood, can't you
                  smell the smoke?
look, I am not
            scared any more
the wolf of my fear is hunted
            by the tiger
                  of my venom
and I've become a fire monster
            if I open up my mouth
                  the whole earth will
                        burst

41

I was the out-breath
                you were the in
now these words are only words
now my breathing
                is hardly half-done

out — there
        out — of me
                out — where
there is no inspiration of reply
        there is no in reply
                there is no
because you are not here now
        and because you will
                never now
                        come

        I know

and everything
        like my breathing
                will stay half-done

and I will stay like that
        until the earth brings you
                if ever back to
                the fullness
                        of my arms

CONFLICT AND OPPRESSION

Buttons
Sherko Bekas
(Kurdistan)
Translated from Sorani by Kamal Mirawdeli

This mountain is like that.
It looks like a tall man.
It feels cold twelve months a year
Wearing a grey narrow coat
Buttoned with four large rocks.
This mountain happens to be like that.
Today at dawn there was
Heavy bombardment.
I was only worried about that tall man.
When I looked at him later
He was the same
Standing upright.
Only a button from his coat
Was slightly undone.

Land

Sherko Bekas
(Kurdistan)
Translated from Sorani by Kamal Mirawdeli

When I touched the bough of a tree
It trembled in pain
When I held out my hand to the branch
the trunk started to weep
when I embraced the trunk
the soil under my feet shuddered
the rocks groaned

this time when I bent down and collected
a handful of earth
all Kurdistan screamed

Mother You Are Not Winter

Kamal Mirawdeli
(Kurdistan)

*To a mother who spent one year as a captive
in the deserts of the south of Iraq*

Mother, you were not so frail last year
Your hair was long and black.
When did this never-melting snow
fall on your head?

How did this inextinguishable flame
rage in your heart?

Mother you are not winter
To bring together snow and ember!

How come you are drinking
the last sips of yourself?

As if you have come back from hell
in the company of a black cloud:

Your pink lips are full of wrinkles
in which smiles are buried

Mother are you looking for yourself?
Who stole you from yourself, Mother?

Your eyes search for your sight,
Your ears yearn for a sound,
Your tongue pines for your voice
Your lungs for your breathing?

Your soul, as you breathe, looks for your life?

I wish I had never seen you like this
You were not frail last year.

This is I, mother
Please recognise me.
I am your sight, your hearing and your voice.
Breathe me in with your deep sighs.
Let me give you the blood of my heart.

Mother, please don't go away!
Wait
Wait with me
Wait until the next dawn.

In the Name of Kabul

Berang Kohdamani
(Afghanistan)
Translated from Dari
by Suhaila Ismat and Jennifer Langer

My presence is here but
My heart reposes in the alleyways of Kabul.

My tongue utters its name
My lips sing an anthem of Kabul.

Trees shrouded in inky-blue
Years, months, weeks, days, mourning Kabul.

Oh traveller! Traverse my town silently
For in mourning is Kabul.

He who knows its streets, its palaces
Murmurs "Where am I?", Kabul.

Oh God, you who are both benevolent and wrathful,
Your munificence is disposed elsewhere, your anger vented
    on Kabul.

Mother of Rostam undeserving of this cruelty,
Undeserving of this affliction, Kabul.

It groans, screams, shouts, this was not pre-ordained
Dark days, dark times, sombre days, the destiny and
    misery of Kabul.

The plant of sadness alone grows in the deserts of its
    memories,
Mourning is the morning of Kabul, lamentation is the
    night of Kabul.

47

All ventures are with beginning and end
A venture without conclusion is Kabul.

The hand of God must surely intervene
The hand of Satan powerless to assuage the agony of Kabul.

The living are miserable and wretched
The sorrowless are the deceased of Kabul.

Died before their time, without healer, without remedy
The sick children and orphans of Kabul.

It should be unshackled from destruction and annihilation
My permanence, your permanence, is the permanence of
    Kabul.

At dawn, the water seller bears his parched goatskin
He dreams of water, the water-seller of Kabul.

From annihilation, liberate Kabul, may its citizens survive.
If I live out all my days, so too surely will Kabul.

The yellow trees of the tall and gracious poplar
Rise up – a hand praying for Kabul.

Years, months, weeks of destruction. How can you destroy it?
From the dawn of time, God was omnipresent in Kabul.

As tyrants Yazed and his followers spill the blood of
    innocents
Oh Hassan, oh Hassan, is this the Karbala of Kabul?

The Taliban surged forth, broke down the gateways of
    knowledge, the windows of learning —
They who are illiterate, now become the spiritual teachers
    of Kabul.

We are plunged into the abyss of the Stone Age,
The painters of vanity now come forth as leaders of Kabul.

Dah Afghanan transformed into the abode of strangers,
The age slides relentlessly backwards, these are dark days
    for Kabul.

Dahsavaz now the grazing land of primitive beings,
The privileged the heathens of Kabul.

In Zandabanan the clock ticks as the keepers of life await
    the grim reaper
Alas, my poem is an elegy for Kabul.

Dah Mazang and Baghqazi, Shahemow with Takhtapol
    razed to the ground
All these places obliterated, the Jeljta of Kabul.

Soil and ashes overlay Pamanor and Chindawol, a
    celebratory place, it once was —
Now transformed into purgatory for God's people of Kabul.

The avenging sky spilling the blood of the Innocents,
The descendents of Ashequan and Arifan of Kabul.

Unyielding sky, even Mount Asmaye has relinquished its
    pride
Wise statesmen degenerated into beggars of Kabul.

From Polmastan, joyful voices resound no longer —
Grief, disappointment, moans, pain, commonplace in
    Kabul.

Shaher-I-Ara, Bagh-I-Bala, Dah Dana, Chil Soton —
Their tears flow constantly beneath the feet of Kabul.

Where is Ghobar, where Khalili, what the fate of Hazret
    Shaiqu —
Ashquairi in his grave yearns for Kabul.

Kocha-I-barana the rain no longer falls,
Wearing impure garments is Khowja Safa of Kabul.

Joie Sheer the stream of blood, Bala-I-Hesar site of
    lamentation.
Looting, slaughter, fear, reside in the house of Kabul.

Musicians no longer dwell in Kharabat.
Before the Judgement Day, observe the punishment of
    Kabul.

The leader of looters strips bare Afshar,
Abode of the poor of Kabul.

The alleyways of Khawbgah do not slumber, for
    everywhere is warring and dread.
Cries and howls emanate from Kabul.

And the back of Peer-I-Boland is bent double,
Alas in the robes of Satan is attired Kabul.

The river of Kabul has shed tears of blood.
Oh God! Unseal your eyes for swimming in blood is Kabul.

They are embattled in the forests,
Armies of anguish, striving to conquer and destroy Kabul.

From Gozarga marches the army of strangers,
Flag and throne crushed underfoot by the enemies of
    Kabul.

Neither Hindu nor Muslim pass through
Doors of cinemas locked tight in Kabul.

Destroyed by Jihad and discordance,
A judgement laid down to solve the problem of Kabul.

If God one day pours forth his wrath on this Earth, spills
blood —
That would be the retribution for Kabul.

Banned Poem

Yang Lian
(China)
Translated from Chinese by Brian Holton

To die at thirty-five is already too late
you should have been executed in the womb
like your poem no need
for a sheet of white paper to be your grave

children not permitted to be born
lock up their hands in crime
fingers rot like snakes coiled in winter sleep
eyes rot escaping the tempest that bites
your face at first touch is a current of water
bones tracing out white scars line by line.

It's a shoal of eels down in the deep water of the flesh
threading through white seaweed
among still-paler shouts you hear only darkness
coldly wiped clean by another hand
coolly turned into a misprint
placenta wrapping you ever tighter
your last words dying with you

to die today
is to be turned into a stinking news story.

The Battle of Algiers

Hadi Khorsandi

(Iran)

It was a boring day, so I thought I'd go to the movies. I flipped through the paper and had a look at the entertainment guide. *The Battle of Algiers* was playing at the Martyrs' Cinema. "It must be a good film," I said to myself, "otherwise they would not have shown it forty times in the four years since the Revolution."

I turned up at the Martyrs' Cinema at three in the afternoon. The first thing I saw was a piece of white cardboard with a note which said: "Children under five not admitted at all, but they can, in fact it is their religious duty, turn up at the war fronts – Imam Khomeini."

I went to the box office. There was a note on the wall, above the window, saying "Balcony Seats for Sisters Only". Next to it there was another notice: "Sisters are requested to abide by the Islamic code of dressing, otherwise they will be strictly forbidden from entering the cinema."

I went in after a full body search. Inside the cinema, there were two grey loudspeakers, blaring out a distorted recitation of the Quran. Some of the men in the lower seats were waving and signalling to their wives and kids up in the balcony, and girls wearing the chador were throwing date stones at boys downstairs.

Before I had time to overcome this initial shock, a waiter turned up in the hall with a tray in his hands shouting: "Nuts, Pepsi, Dates, Halva, Sweets, Rosewater!"

A minute later, the Quran recitation was cut off, and a commercial still was projected on the screen, advertising 'Holy Henna' with the picture of a huge mullah with a thick curly beard. That was followed by an ad for an undertaker offering long-term credit, another one for "Shark" cream for the removal of pubic hair, another one for an Islamic, interest-free finance house, and so on and so on.

At last the promised moment came and the Anthem of Islamic Unity blared through the loudspeakers. Everybody stood up and when it got to the part where it says "Allah-o Akbar, Khomeini is Our Leader", the entire audience repeated it three times.

Then the lights near the screen were turned on and a fundamentalist-looking man (with a beard, a military overcoat and a pair of trainer shoes) went to the microphone and began talking.

"In His Lofty Name. In the Name of Allah, the Compassionate the Merciful Sisters and Brothers! Welcome to the Martyrs' Cinema, a cinema which under the previous filthy regime was a centre of corruption, and its ungodly owners, under orders from their dirty masters, had been promoting a policy of corrupt, Western culture. But now, thanks to the efforts of the brothers from the Foundation for the Deprived, it has become one hundred-per-cent Islamified. By the way, there is a room next door for those brothers and sisters who would like to say their prayers."

The man had barely finished talking before some of the audience got up and headed for the washroom to prepare themselves for saying their prayers. Others, feeling embarrassed, followed behind like a flock of sheep. The hall was left almost empty.

Now the hall was dark and the ushers having run out of batteries for their torch-lights, were showing the people in with the aid of kerosene lamps.

A film appeared on the screen with the title "Soon In This Cinema"; then a voice, which sounded like it was coming from inside a grave, announced, "Martyrs Never Die, Allah is the Greatest", and finally said that the presentation next was going to be "Imam Khomeini's Collected Speeches 1963–83." O my God!

Children were not supposed to be in the cinema, but a crying baby was driving everybody crazy. Then all of a sudden a mullah-like voice boomed over the loudspeaker: "Sister, will you please see to it that the baby is silenced?"

Just before the film was supposed to begin, the lights at the front of the hall were turned on. A revolutionary guard turned up in front of the screen and said: "In His Lofty Name, Sisters and Brothers! The road to the liberation of our beloved Jerusalem passes through Kerbela – Imam Khomeini."

The audience shouted "Allah is the Greatest" three times and then the revolutionary guard went on: "I would like to ask our disabled brothers to come in here."

The doors were flung open and a group of invalids came in – some walking with crutches, some with sticks, others in wheelchairs, and still others carried on people's arms; they lined up in front of the screen.

The audience welcome them with shouts of "Allah-o Akbar", and then broke into a mass rendering of the anthem "O Khomeini, Our Imam" and then began chanting "We Are All Your Soldiers, O Khomeini."

The revolutionary guard asked everybody to keep quiet. When that didn't work, he fired his machinegun into the air, showering plaster and bricks on the audience's heads and forcing them to shut up.

After everybody had gone quiet, the guard said: "Take a look at these people and that should be enough to put you to shame. These disabled brothers have offered their lives to Islam, with their own hands, but unfortunately were not lucky enough to be martyred. And you lot have the cheek to come to the movies! Is this the time to go to the movies? I mean, really!"

He then pointed to me and said: "Hey, brother! You... yes you, the gentleman with glasses in the fourth row."

I blushed with embarrassment and wished I could crawl under the seats. Everybody was looking at me. Then the guard said: "Don't be scared, Brother! I'm not going to do anything to you. I just meant to remind you that our country is at war. The superpowers are fighting us, and we must be self-sufficient. We must meet all the costs of the war with the criminal superpowers until Saddam is overthrown and the beloved Jerusalem is liberated. This is every Muslim's religious duty."

Then, turning to his sidekick, he said: "Take that collection box over to the doc!" The boy came along, with a box marked: "Imam Khomeini's Special Account Number 100".

There was no way out. Hoping I'd get it over and done with, I took out a ten-*tooman* banknote, all the money I had on me, and shoved it into the box. Then all hell broke loose, and money started pouring into the box from every direction. A woman's voice shouted from the balcony: "Send another box over here!"

At last, *The Battle of Algiers* came on and everybody was trying hard to make out what was going on in the movie. Halfway through, the film was suddenly cut and a sign came out, announcing the intermission. "My goodness," I said to myself, "What can they be up to this time?"

I Fear for Freedom

Agim Morina
(Kosova)

I'm afraid freedom will come one day
And I will not know her
I will not notice her.
She will sit next to me in the bus,
Get off in some distant land,
And I will be told:
"There goes freedom! Didn't you recognise her?"
Freedom will come, like my father's death,
That I could never believe...

I fear freedom will come very bright,
I fear freedom will come quiet, very quiet
I fear I will die
While she is in the hall taking off her shoes.
I fear freedom is a beauty
I will never make love to,
I fear freedom, poor freedom,
Will come and I'll have her in my hands,
But I will lose her like the most loved photograph.
I fear freedom will fail to stop, rushing by.
The train driver will fall asleep
Or she will not see me, like the sailor
Missing at sea, shipwrecked.
I fear I'll say to her "Get lost you dirty whore!"
Or "My dear, where have you been until now?
How could you come to Kosova this late?"
I fear she will miss her plane, terrorists will kidnap her
Or she will lose her ticket.
Something unexpected will happen.
An Irish dancer will try to teach her to dance in Dublin.
Some Italian will take her to Rome,
Or some Eskimo will freeze her under his igloo
Trying to make her smile while giving her smoked fish.

I fear I'll be very happy.
Too happy. When I see her come.
And I will be very sad when I realise she won't come.
I might get run over by some fast train
While confused and delighted I greet freedom,
I fear the building will collapse,
While under its shadow, with a little flag in my hand
I wait for freedom to pass by.
Both God and The Devil I will thank,
One day when I've seen freedom.

I fear someone will hand freedom to me,
And I will be polite and not take it,
Or, I fear, I'll take it, just to be polite.
I fear it will be cold,
And freedom may freeze on the road,
Or it will be too hot
And she will die of a stroke or thirst
(I haven't got good neighbours who would help her).
I fear freedom may eat an apple
And it will get stuck in her throat...
Or may fall from a bicycle
On a Sunday
When the ambulance drivers are off duty...
I fear freedom will have a faulty passport,
With a stamp from Qafethana or expired!
I fear I might eat freedom in some sweet shop
Or swallow it like a kebab,
Never knowing what I have eaten.
I'm afraid that freedom might pop,
In some kid's balloon,
Where she has suddenly fallen asleep.
I fear freedom might be caged
In some zoo, as a rare species,
Very rare.
I fear freedom will come disguised as a rabbit
To amuse the children
And some hunter will fire at her, before I get to say

(just like in the movies) "Don't shoot!"
I fear freedom might be a bear
Some Gypsy is pulling by the nose
Making her dance from village to village;
I fear freedom is a nail
Some villager has nailed into some beam
And now it is going rusty from sadness.
I fear freedom might phone me,
While shaving and whistling in the bathroom,
I will not hear the phone ring.
Or she will knock on my door,
And I'll be with Haqif or Luli in some café,
Discussing peppers I never eat.
That's why I fear when I leave my flat
I fear when I'm in my flat,
I fear while walking or eating.
I wonder if she has lost the address or the phone number
To some pickpocket who had no idea whom he was robbing
And what.
I fear I might go blind or deaf,
I fear I might get sick or die
Since I could not give slavery its due,
I want to welcome freedom with everything
Ready as a broom.
Smiling. Combed. Neat. Perfumed.

When I go out, I look at people carefully,
I say, I might see freedom amongst them, or its herald.
I look carefully at the loaded donkeys,
The wandering dogs
The river currents
And the train timetables
I explore the beehives and cuckoos' eggs.
I open my mailbox every day,
And scratch behind my house.
I follow the cow and the birds flying
Anything could happen
That's why I fear everything

I wonder if tired
Sick or thirsty,
She is somewhere.
Waiting for me.

"Ova, Signora"

Reesom Haile
(Eritrea)

When the Italians occupied Asmara
We saved a few chickens
In the old district four.
They got fat on the cheap barley,
So we weren't totally poor.
We sold their eggs
White as fine plaster:
"Ova, Signora. Ova, Signora,"
Till our throats were sore.
Thanks to those chickens we survived
While General Baldisera, fortified for war,
Ate omelettes.

Kazenga

Antonio Joaquim Marques
(Angola)

And the tin house is invaded
By the pleasure of music
Unconciliatory voices choking
In vain forgotten dreams
Disputes and rebukes over glasses of beer
Faces at variance with each other
Elucidating despair in every gesture
But the music invites indulgence
And the occasion responds
With Kanjica with *mufete*
And *funji* with dry fish in hot sauce
Oh the music invites hope
And the dance syncopates now
In the girl's wriggling waist
And Kalunga's ecstatic eyes are fireflies
And the smell of sweat coagulates the air
The movements of bodies punctuating
And oh the scent of sex as the music growls
Suspicion erupts at first glances
Raising disturbing questions of the day:
Who is stealing somebody's wife?
Who is the sorcerer, why did Mbele die?
Why was the Minister smiling nervously on TV?
And the answer is muffled in exasperation
Of everyone talking without listening
The elements of purpose are deviated
The truth is muffled with fear of betrayal
And now the smoke of tobacco
The *semba* and the *kabetula* dance
The chattering and the gossiping
Deprecating laughter pours in once in a while
Provoking the stubbornness of raw-rapprochment

And the sun lumbers west in resignation with music
The evening interferes with the day
A charcoal light lamp intercedes
And it's time for everyone to go home now
To face the nightmare of a country at war
With itself.

Kazenga = A township in Luanda — Angola.
Kanjica, mufete, funji = traditional Kimbundu foods.
Semba = A dance of the navel from which Samba of Brazil originated.
Kabetula = folk dance (Luanda).

Operation Water Reservoir

Ahmed Omar Askar
(Somalia)

The soldiers rushed into two flanks in opposite directions
and in a few minutes the village was surrounded. Sergeant
Godgod and his friend Lugogod dashed into the village
instead of going with the other soldiers. They had to be
there for the hunt for gold, before anybody else. They ran
down the only street in the village. Godgod in the lead. As
he ran, he turned his head from side to side, looking for a
glimpse of a woman. When he saw a woman disappear into
one of the huts he shouted to his friend. "Let us go to that
hut, a woman has just entered it. She was wearing nice
clothes; she must be rich." They reached the hut and
rushed in with drawn guns. The woman seeing the two
soldiers with their guns pointed at her, uttered a loud cry.
Sergeant Godgod slapped her hard on the face. Her one-
year-old child was sleeping on the floor and the startled
child crawled towards its mother. The mother scooped the
child into her arms and pressed it to her breasts, sobbing
in terror. "Guard her and do not let her make the slightest
movement. I will search the hut," said Godgod.

He started turning everything upside down and inside
out. He turned over the mats but there was nothing under
them. He tore the pillow open and flung its contents onto
the floor. He could not find any gold in that either. He saw
a wooden box in one corner of the hut. That would contain
all her important possessions, he thought. Hurriedly he
carried the box to the centre of the hut. It was locked. He
prised it open with his bayonet. He lifted the lid off the box
and started throwing its contents onto the floor. He
opened a tin and on finding that it only contained some
incense, he threw it away. A small cloth bag caught his
eye. He immediately picked it up and he could feel that it
contained jewels. He opened it and poured its contents

64

onto his palm. His eyes lit up at the sight of the gold. Greedily he gazed at the golden necklace and at the two earrings in his hand. The woman in her desperate plight had collected her wits and said "Please don't take that gold, it's all I've got in the world."

Godgod lunged at her with the butt of his gun and hit her hard on the jaw. The woman and the child collapsed on the floor. He shouted to his friend, "Let's get out of here." The two soldiers emerged from the hut leaving the child crying over its unconscious mother. They met up with their friends in the street who were guarding the villagers who were now their prisoners. Nearby lay a collection of loot, sacks of food, clothes, cooking utensils and water pots. They had no intention of leaving anything of value in the huts before setting them ablaze. This was a disappointment for Sergeant Godgod and Corporal Lugogod. There was nothing left to loot. Their friends had made a neat job of it. They had wasted their time on one hut. "We were slow in searching that hut. The other soldiers had better opportunities than us. They have looted all the money from the teashops," said Godgod.

The first explosion from the water reservoir shook the ground. Water and earth erupted into the sky like a volcano. The wet particles from the blast obscured the skyline of the village. The blast cleared slowly. The villagers knew, the army was blowing up their water reservoir, the most precious thing in their lives but they could not defend themselves whilst sitting in the hot sun in rows, surrounded by the soldiers. The blasts continued mushrooming over the village one after the other, until all the water reservoirs had been destroyed. The villagers were counting the number of blasts and judging from the direction of the explosions which water reservoir was being destroyed. Dego Bayr returned from the direction of the water reservoirs and shouted orders to his soldiers. "Take the prisoners and the loot to the trucks and burn all the huts in the village."

The soldiers drove their prisoners to the trucks. Some of the soldiers laboured under the weight of the loot. Godgod and Lugogod ran to burn the village. They poured petrol on one hut in every street and then set fire to them. The soldiers then left the burning village to join the others who were doing the same job in the next village.

That day Saleban Ugas had taken his camels to the distant hills which lay eastwards of Tuulo Buur, his home village. Herding camels being a most difficult job for a nomad, he was wandering with them to make sure they did not stray. It was the breeding season and the large camel was after the she-camels, not giving them a chance to feed. He was also driving the younger camels away from the herd.

At noon when the herd was feeding peacefully, Saleban sat in the shade of a tree to rest his aching feet. Suddenly the thunder of a distant explosion brought him to his feet. Frightened, the camels ran up the hill. He pursued them until he managed to stop them at the top. From there, he could see a grey cloud over his village where the explosion had occurred. Another explosion followed. He could clearly see the smoke mushrooming over the village.

A wave of alarm ran through his whole body. He felt he had to get to the village without delay. He had left his one-year-old child and wife there. He started driving his camels home as explosions continued in quick succession. The camels were rushing back and he had to stop them with quick lashes of his long stick. The narrow path, along which he drove the camels, zigzagged between patches of acacia tree and then rose over the hill. From the top of the hill, he could see that his village was ablaze. He rubbed his eyes and then looked again at the burning village. It was reality — dense smoke hung over it like a cloud and the flames looked like an infernal fire.

Leaving the camels, he ran down the hill towards the village, regardless of the thorny bushes tearing at his clothes and skin as he brushed against their branches. Finally he reached the open land of the village. He continued running, turning right to reach the tarmac road since the direct route to the hut had been blocked by the fire. He could now see that the fire had not yet reached his hut but the flames had started to lick the adjacent one. He ran down the road like the wind, arriving at the hut gasping.

At the door he heard his child crying and hurried inside. He found his wife lying on the floor holding the child to her breasts. She was conscious but too weak to move. He said "We must get out of here. Can you walk?"

"If you support me," she said weakly.

He lifted the child into his arms and told his wife to lean on his shoulder. Painfully she rose to her feet and leaning on him, they walked away from the flames to the bushes. There Saleban told his wife to sit down for a while so that they could rest before continuing their slow walk. She sat slowly on the ground while he seated himself on a rock and asked; "Who set fire to our village? Where is everybody?"

"The soldiers."

"Which soldiers?"

"The military."

She started sobbing and it was hard to question her any further. He had to make a decision. Their only chance lay in crossing the border into Ethiopia at night.

When You Called On Us

Hilton Mendelsohn
(Zimbabwe)

When you called on us,
With head sometimes bowed,
sometimes held erect, proud, unbroken.

When the guns fell silent at Sharpeville
and we all counted the cost,
the high price of freedom's demands.
Did we quietly decide we would
engage in silent diplomacy
or stand calmly by,
still
Respecting those who only sought to kill?
Did your cry fall on deaf ears?
or did we not all scream

AMANDLA!

with you?

They are trying to kill us, Thabo
Unless we agree to ignore incompetence
and to accept tyranny.

They have promised to kill us, Madiba
We who wrote songs
Prayed to our Ancestors and to God
Free Mandela!
We who believed
our singing pierced prison walls
and gave some strength
or comfort
or solace.

They are trying to kill us
Bantu beNkhosi
We who were reduced to uncontrollable sobs
when Biko was arrested
When we heard that he was dead.

We are calling on you
South Africa
Just like you called on us
And for you not to hear us
would simply be wrong
It is just wrong
for you not to hear us.

Sarajevo
Semezdin Mehmedinovic
(Bosnia)

1. Death by Freezing

When Sarajevo lies covered with snow, when pine trees are cracked by frost, bones in the earth will feel warmer than us. People will freeze to death: a fireless winter approaches, a sunless summer is past. The nights are already cold and, when somebody's pet dog barks from a balcony, a chorus of strays barks back, in tones as sorrowful as a crying child's. Only in this city does an Irish setter — normally an unusually cheeky dog — howl dismally in the night like Rutger Hauer in the final scenes of *Blade Runner*. Snow will bury the city as war has buried time. What day is it today? When is Saturday? I don't know. The daily and annual rituals are dead. Who will print calendars for 1993 in December? There is day, there is night; within them there is a man whose existence is defined by the end of the world. He knows that the fullness of life would be diminished were it not for the looming global catastrophe. Therefore he strikes a light at dusk; a wick threaded through a metal ballpoint refill, fixed to a piece of cork wrapped in tin foil, so that it floats on the surface of the cooking oil which burns in a lamp made of an empty beer can. The cheerful flame allows him to see that objects and the faces of dear ones have an earthly glow; and that there is no plight but the failing of light.

2. Wounded Parks

Driven by fear of winter, the inhabitants of Sarajevo have been felling trees in the parks. The prevailing sound in the city, apart from that of shelling, is the noise of chain-saws. Everyday scenes: men pulling at a wire rope, the poplar resists, swings to and fro, children run around it, some cheering the men on, some rooting for the poplar, and when the crown has fallen the view opens on to the woods of Mr Trebevic, a very tall man, with neatly cut greying hair, in a new lustrous suit and shiny shoes, bow-tied, carrying a briefcase in his left hand, and in his right, a hefty chestnut branch chopped off in a park. He drags it with difficulty through the street door.

"The city's trees are under attack. They are being felled in parks, in the streets, even in cemeteries. We call on all citizens to protect the city's trees. Failure to comply will incur severe punishment." These lines from a daily newspaper tell me that if I fail to protect the city's trees, too busy with my own affairs, I shall be severely punished. Nevertheless the plaintive wailing of a chain-saw is heard to the north. People in the city are desperate, as thin creatures always are at the approach of winter.

3. Chetnik Positions

First the excavator arrived. It dug trenches in the ground and a lorry brought concrete slabs to line them with. Tanks were dug in at the sides so that only their cannon protruded. Guns as well. Our rifles cannot reach them. Perhaps they could spend the winter in such trenches? It is August now; they get tobacco from Nis, brandy from Prokuplje. I don't know where their women come from but I have seen them through binoculars. One of them has placed an inflatable mattress by the trench and is sunbathing in a swimsuit. She lies there for hours. Then she gets up, goes to the cannon, pulls the cord and fires a shell on the town at random. She listens briefly for the explosion and watches for its source. She even stands on tiptoe innocently. Then she goes back, coats her body with suntan lotion, and surrenders herself to serenity.

The Walls of the Bazaar

Afshin Babazadeh
(Iran)
Translated from Farsi by
Afshin Babazadeh and Abol Froushan

In the bazaar
Next to the walls
They're all
Standing
Stunned...

Windows looked down like the unsure feeling of making
    poetry
Walls stood like chapters of all that mattered
and the summary of death
        gapingly passed me by.

The passage of walls alongside the bazaar
Walls of:

> Stone
> Cement
> People
> and Emotions

The bazaar revolved round the writing
Every book repeated hundreds of pages
And any possible thing passed along the walls.

The bazaar
        over and above the stone
                and
                        Steel
        and
                        Emotions...

And wall after wall showed the strength of weakness.
The walls stood
The bazaar and the writing were passing by.
And chattering heads
Hanging from windows
Were watching.

Heads headed for separation from the body of windows.
The people of the bazaar glanced up at the sky
Passed under the windows
And everyday the morning sun with its broken light
Poured into the bazaar.
I stood for a moment
Next to a shaft of shattered light.
The blood of my veins
Was shining in the colour of dried flowers
I stuck my head, as yet not detached from my body,
towards the window

I was frightened by the sounds inside the windows
The fear that I always see in the sunlight and windows.

                    I felt my laughter was not loud enough
I covered my face with cement
                    and stones.

I stood next to the walls.
All that there was passed by me.
Till where
The bazaar and
                the walls and
                        their anthologies
Roamed in search of the dead bones of words.

At the heart of the bazaar
Gamblers in sonnets and lyrics
Were busy caressing lambs.
Dice rolled on the floor
As I leaned against the wall
Busy with torn diaries.

I pulled my hand out of the sunlight
My footsteps alongside the walls
Up to the heads hanging from windows
Went in search of cool shadows
Shadows far from the deceit of the sun.

All that there was passed by the walls
All that there was cast a shadow in my eyes.
I could see drops of red
Dripping on indigo

I saw no alternative
But to pour wine over my hands
A wine that in poets' images, could not be inscribed.

The bazaar and its walls like chapters of all that mattered,
were written on my lips with a smile and the bazaar
mistook me for a whisper. Windows passed me by,
overhead, like the unsure feeling of poems and blank pages
in waiting. I got up and looked at the flat landscape, that
was tired of tombstones of the same shape. Small windows
with no hanging heads were shut in an everlasting silence.
Far from the windows the rain lost its willingness to fall.
Wet coffins were piled up on each other. Bodies were laid
alongside the bazaar walls.

Windows looked down like the unsure feeling of making
    poetry.
Walls stood like chapters of all that mattered.
A beautiful shadow.
A cool shadow fell from the sky.

I stood in the shadow
By the wall.

Everything was cool
Like the coolness of a corpse.

Bombardment

Mohammed Khaki
(Kurdistan)

Ex...plo...sion
A child's severed arm flying
Delicate deer legs breaking
Poor butterfly through the dust crawling

Ex...plo...sion
Houses collapsing
Schools flattened
Corn alight with a thousand burning nests.
Bridges blasted
City destroyed, in ruins.
Explosion
 groaning
  wailing
   agony
Nearby the wireless bulletin howls "success!"
"Enemy target attacked and destroyed."

The Knot

Gulay Yurdal Michaels
(Turkey)

the sea sleeps rain-dimpled
like a child
talks in plain tones uncomplaining
of the deeds of man.
how did it put up with
our passions
small as a fig seed
how will it erode say —
the shame of continents
and conscripts
with movements small
as a fig seed one day

RESISTANCE AND FREEDOM

The Road of the Gun
Rafiq Sabir
(Kurdistan)
Translated from Sorani by Kamal Mirawdeli

I had a small blue sky
The occupiers brought it down over me
I had a little stream of dark blood,
a bundle of honey dreams
and a collection of books
they plundered them all.

But when they came
to change my skin
deform my face
I wore the snow and thunder
carried my homeland on my shoulders
and took to the road of the gun.

Liberty

Hastie Salih
(Kurdistan)

Whoever thought liberty was dead?
It's just mountains ahead!

Watch the silver-streaked streams
Bouncing freely through fertile fields so bright,
Awakening dreams
Of liberty, of life.

Inhale the dew of the meadows
Inhale the sunlight

Whoever thought liberty was dead?
It's just mountains ahead!

Ravaged rivers may be tainted with blood
Watch them wriggle though the tiniest crevice of sun-
baked mud!
They say they see contorted bodies
In a sea of despair
But even these defy
The piercing sun's glare.

Whoever thought liberty was dead?
It's just mountains ahead!

As jagged mountains emerge
Sliding shadows are cast
Upon sleeping sheep, ready to graze
Kissed gently
By the sky's boundless rays.

Of all the battles in the past
Of all the passages through time and place
Of all the trials of our human race
Freedom has always been achieved
Humanity eventually retrieved

Whoever thought liberty was dead?
It's just mountains ahead!

People Dancing in Moonlight

Sofia Buchuck
(Peru)

I saw you my people
Dancing in moonlight
Dressed in red
Blood of innocent Indians.

Your wound
The exploitation
The loss
Of your children.

I need to paint your hopes
To dance with you in the wind
With the reason to exist
To keep alive your colours.

People of the Amazon
Lungs of the world
Dressed with pearls, sapphires and emeralds
With gold and silver.

Wild flowers on your head
Warm hands of brotherhood
Your jewels of secret legends
Not yet defiled.

Sweet perfumes of lilies
Mountains of corn and quinua[1]
Dressed in icy skirts
Rivers and sea at your feet.

I saw you my people
At the frontiers of man, waiting to see the far end
Grasping to understand their ownership
Hanging the sky with both hands.

I saw you my people
Hanging from the thread of life and death
Singing water cascades
And dancing as no one had ever seen.

1. *Quinua* = South American seed

TRAVERSING SPACES

Refugee for Life
Parniyan Zemaryalai
(Afghanistan)

All of our belongings were packed and we were ready to go, my mother had informed her sisters of our departure, and they were both there to say a tearful farewell to us. We were driven to a tourist centre and then loaded into a coach that would be going through the Hindukush Mountains.

Other families who were attempting to escape the country surrounded us. Each of them wore the dreadful expression of lambs that knew they might be slaughtered. The atmosphere was so heavy with the sensation of anxiety that you could taste it on your tongue, feel it on your skin, and smell it in the air.

I rocked against my *Madi* (mother) as the coach rode over a dent in the uneven road. By this time I had already realised that this coach did not belong to the centre; it was a smuggler's vehicle. This system of smuggling people out of the country was something the government was aware of, but had turned a blind eye to. Only the people who were rich enough to pay for these people's services were able to escape the country.

We had been travelling for a very long time, and my fear was beginning to be overpowered by sleepiness, when our coach came to a lurching halt. My heart rate began to increase and I could feel sweat beads forming upon my brows as I heard the rough voices of men outside the coach. Our luggage had been hidden under a secret compartment in the bus so as not to make us look suspicious.

"Bang, bang, bang!" came the sound of one of the men hitting the end of his rifle against the side of the coach. I think he was checking whether the inside of it was hollow or not. My parents had sprung into action, my mother covered herself, my sister and I with large and unattractive Burkas: where the eyes are, small holes are placed in order to make vision possible. Looking through those holes, I could remember a couple of sleazy men talking about them, when I went to the market with my mother...

"I don't know what has come over the world!" he bit out, looking at a Western magazine. "Thank Allah, we know how to control the women in our country!" the other one boasted, his yellow teeth showing through his greasy beard. "If I saw my wife showing her hair, the way this woman does, I would burn every single one individually to its roots!" he added, the other men shouted their encouragement. "Women do not know what's good for them! That's why Allah created men like us! To place them back where they belong!" "Yeah! In our homes and in our beds!" one man shouted. The rest of them laughed like hyenas and smacked his back in approval. I frowned because I did not know what he meant.

Then a young girl walked past with her mother, she may have been thirteen or fourteen, I cannot recall. As she walked past, she pressed herself closer to her mother, who was also attempting to move away. All the men grew silent, occasionally a snigger could be heard, all their eyes turned into those of a predator. The one who had been doing most of the talking, waited until the girl's back faced him, then he reached out with his scrawny hands and grabbed her by the back of her shirt. She let out a terrified scream, as he pulled her against himself, his friends let out laughs and shouts of exhortation. The mother was frantically pulling her by her hands. The hairy man grabbed her hair, smelt her neck, and then violently pushed her away. She stumbled into her mother's arms, sobbing uncontrollably. The mother who was in hysterics, but also knew she was grossly outnumbered, grabbed her daughter, and they began to run away. "Bastards! I hope you rot in hell! Allah shall never forgive you for this!" she screamed. The man laughed in reply. "Allah approves of this! If you don't want me coming after your daughter, then cover her filthy body with a Burka!"

My legs were shaking with fear and I could not move. The man caught sight of me out of the corner of his eye, mistaking me for a boy because of my clothing and hairstyle, he turned and barked. I ran away as fast as my legs could carry me. When I got home, I could still hear their mocking laughter in my head...

"We want to inspect the people inside!" ordered one man outside.

"Is it necessary? They are tourists. No need to scare them," the driver suggested smoothly.

"You are going through the bloody mountains. I will see them!" he commanded.

"Do I have to wear a Burka Madi?" I asked my mother in a whisper. "Please, they won't know I'm a girl. I look like a boy."

"Oh! So they can take you to be a soldier!" she whispered reprovingly. I became silent.

Men dressed in rough, torn clothes with little vests on top, walked in, each wearing an Islamic hat and a large gun, around their necks hanging low. We were ordered to get out of the bus, and made to stand in a row. Every man was asked for his name and occupation. My father gave a fake reply, like every one else standing with us. Then they checked for any people who were Pashtuns; they are one of the biggest tribes in Afghanistan, unfortunately the Mujahedin hated them, and if any were found present they would be taken as hostage or killed on the spot.

After that strenuous procedure, one man produced a Qur'an and each person was ordered to say one of the prayers. They did this because they wished to ascertain who was a bad and neglectful Muslim; we all knew what would happen if one of us had not been able to read the Qur'an: they would have been shot on the spot.

From the back of the hill, a man appeared, he walked

towards us at a comfortable speed, which informed us of his status.

"What's the problem?" he growled.

"Nothing sir! I am just checking these people, who are trying to pass through the mountains! The driver claims they are tourists!" One man replied. The newcomer looked at the driver.

"They are tourists! I heard about their visit yesterday. Stop hassling them and go back to your positions!" The men hesitated. "Now!" shouted the bearded man. When the retreating men were no longer visible, the driver stepped forward, to shake hands with the intruder. As their palms met, a small amount of white powder floated out. I believe it was heroin. The bearded man grinned, as he placed his hands in his pockets.

"Thank you," said the driver.

"Till the next time we meet," was the man's only reply. We then returned to our seats, the colour was beginning to come back into most people's faces. I removed my Burka with great relief, and then finally managed to drift into a troubled sleep.

Fleeing

Abdirahman Mirreh
(Somalia)

And as we walked
we crossed
the Golis Ranges
Wadis and the
Ununuf plain.

Fearing the soldiers
who killed my sister
and a thousand others
too.

We walked by
night stumbling
on volcanic rocks
sharper than
butchers' knives

The feet bleeding
we had to walk
I touched a
stone with my lips
as I fell
the moon didn't
shine, it helped us.

Getting Ready for a Trip

Igor Klikovac
(Bosnia)

Getting ready for a trip. In a borrowed sports bag
you pile clothes upon books. Paltry things which are out of
    sight,
you deliberately forget. You sing to yourself.
Unbidden haste — a Czech tourist's itching feet — spurs
    you on.

You'd like to go as far as possible, but zipping up the bag,
you feel you've already arrived somewhere.
Opened scissors on the table, small change in the lee-side
of a pocket.

Outside the mortars are thundering — the distance you
    are now,
you'll never make it.

In Hiding

Zuhair Al-Jezairy

(Iraq)

I chronicled time in my diary step by step. But how to
return from the sunny Alamawi courtyard scattered with
pigeons, to my hiding place there? I will make a beginning
of these events. It was when through prior arrangement, I
met a man who seemed in haste; he moved and spoke
rapidly like a bird. He placed the false passport in front of
me saying briefly:

"As from now, you are no longer who you are. Forget
who you are and assume your new identity. You are a
Jordanian merchant by the name of Nadhim Kamal,
passing through by chance and in a hurry, huh?" He did
not look at me as he spoke, nor did he wait for me to ask
anything, but continued, pointing as he did so, to a page in
the passport:

"The task is quite simple, just sign and write the date
here in this triangle and place your trust in God."

I examined the passport many times. I wanted to feel
the delicate fingers that had made it and placed my picture
on it. Happy and yet scared, I was now in possession of the
instrument of my salvation, or possible downfall. This
passport put an end to my hesitation and delays and left
me with one route to take, a risky one. As I turned the
pages, I also wondered about the cruel, doubting eyes that
would be examining it at the checkpoint. The guard would
slowly come up to me to make the fatal statement:

"That is not you!" However, I warded off this possibility
with an irrevocable decision. "What does it matter? Hiding
is a greater risk!"

In this new, secluded house on the edge of Baghdad,
time was a burden which was painful and humiliating.
Every morning the couple would leave for work saying
their goodbyes to me with some pity. I read and read, my

mind deranged by the multitude of words and depravity of life. Like a caged animal tormented by the need for space, I roamed the rooms of the house. Every other minute, I opened the fridge to eat or drink but not out of hunger or thirst. I smoked and drank coffee endlessly and later on would stand under the shower to calm my nerves. On television I watched the series *The Boat of Love*, a paradise which enticed me. I was a prisoner of the secluded house and of the concept with which I had conspired to create another life.

When the wife returned from work, I welcomed her with overwhelming joy; there was a human being to talk to. I asked her with great persistence about news from the outside world. I was a victim of confinement and illusion imagining many things going on in this city where I was hiding. However, I was saddened by her boring interests; she neither read the newspapers nor was concerned with politics.

"What do you expect to happen, other than that the price of eggs has gone up and the New Zealand meat has arrived?" Her husband returned home exhausted bearing a bottle of Arak and always starting his conversation with the remark:

"People are almost exploding with impatience." I was content with this feeble remark. It crystallised my illusions.

Every now and again the owner of the house received "unsafe" friends. I would then disappear to another room with a novel. However, my attention was diverted from the pages of the book as I found myself ashamedly eavesdropping on people who were unaware that the walls had ears listening to their passive conversation. They discussed the recent football match and real and fictitious sexual adventures during their recent visit to Poland. With nervous pleasure I listened to the voice of this friend I used to meet frequently when I was "alive". He sounded more coarse to me. I could not see his face but could imagine his eyes protruding whenever he was involved in serious discussion. Their conversations were fleeting and constantly changing, not allowing room for silence, as if through words they were hiding something horrible within themselves. I felt their voices become hoarse with fright when the discussion moved to me. One of them spoke of his last encounter with me and my son at the market, but I could not recall such a meeting. Another fabricated a lie to invigorate the discussion. A third alleged he had seen me the day before my arrest, torture and probable death, while I lay there hiding behind the walls. I smiled in disbelief that the person they were referring to was me.

Before leaving, I began to practise the role of the new identity I had assumed with my new passport. During my roaming in the house where I was hiding, again and again I would stand in front of the mirror, staring at the tense veins in my face, which had become more sullen and gaunt. My voice hissed:

"You are not you, you are a Jordanian merchant named Nadhim Kamal!" I bit my lips to take a grip on the rebellious scream within me, against this self-denial. I drank Arak and read a poem by Elaur. The broken being emerged intact but hypersensitive and with tearful eyes.

"You are me, why deny it?" Again I repeated the exercise, I roamed the house with steady steps like that of a determined man and within weeks I was wearing my mask: a moustache I had grown, a shaven head and the narrowing of my eyes to fit the dark, medical glasses. I had trained my voice to speak with the accent of a Jordanian Palestinian and simplified my words to suit the style of a salesman eager to persuade a customer. As I took on the role of the other person, my face became more pale and gaunt. I noticed as I stood in front of the mirror to chase away what remained of me.

"Remember well. You are not you!"

When the date of my departure had been determined, I left my hiding place for the city. For the first time I joined the stream of workers heading for work. I wore an old, grey jacket and carried "his" briefcase, with a packet of cigarettes in my pocket and I imitated "his" cautious walk when I crossed the road. Yet I committed the first error of a man in hiding. I was unaware that during my absence, the road had been made one-way.

When night fell, I entered the house of some friends who were horrified to see me — a dead man brought back to life. We drank, chatted and laughed to delay the horror that awaited us. The strong alcohol had liberated the frightened man hiding behind the mask of a Jordanian merchant and level-headed worker. I emerged reddened, angry and sarcastic to announce to my reflection in the mirror

"I am no-one but myself!"

Too Many Shooting Stars

Miroslav Jancic
(Bosnia)

The mighty white ferryboat Slavia
Ploughs through the ever bluer Adriatic Sea
In the middle of a blessed late summer night:
The sky has displayed all its jewellery
Ulysses marvelled at the same.

Yet the usual romance is missing
An elderly singer is delivering messages
Over the loudspeaker:
Thrust love/Love is almighty, or so
Whilst the ship's engine is definitely throbbing
Love-is-gone/Love-is-gone-for-ever
As a refrain.

Whilst cruising into the unknown
I'm alone on the deck
Keeping my eye on a shooting star
Which is tearing the horizon over the mainland
By its long, long tail;
Before I succeeded in expressing any wish
Another appeared from the opposite direction.

The sky is shattered
All of a sudden there are so many shooting stars
That one simply doesn't know what to wish
As his homeland is vanishing for good
In a deep, deep night.

How we Fled from Angola

Sousa Jamba

(Angola)

In February 1976, the civil war came to Huambo. It was one of those lovely African afternoons when it is neither too cold nor too hot. Rumours were spreading that the Cubans were at Acmol, a suburb of Huambo. I came home from school and found my sister packing.

Everyone was on the move. I had never seen so many anxious people. The next day we reached Silva Porto, where my aunt Teodora had an orchard with gigantic pears. All the townspeople were preparing to leave.

Serpa Pinto had been one of the most beautiful towns in Angola. Astride the River Cubango, the Portuguese had built some magnificent hotels, but they were already bullet-riddled and so filthy that people preferred to sleep in the open. Most of the people who had come this far supported Unita and the young men were enthusiastic about going as guerrillas to the war.

It was decided that we drive to Cuito Cuanavale and walk from there to the Zambian border, 180 miles away. It was at Cuito that I first saw a Mig fighter. It glinted silver in the sky, flashed over us menacingly and emitted several terrifying thunderclaps.

We were now in the forest, guided by an old map of Angola someone had plucked from a classroom wall. This map was to prove disastrous. The older people, whose map-reading left much to be desired, argued continually as to whether the stream in front of us was the river on the map. It often turned out that the river in question was not a river at all but a huge swamp.

The squabbling continued and our group, which numbered a thousand, broke into factions. Our faction was led at first by Alfredo Sachipangele, a medical assistant who thought that he was a doctor and bored us all with the stories of the operations that he had performed. He had also read so much of the Bible that he thought that he was a priest. He navigated by the position of the sun. I will never walk so far again.

Our reserves of food soon finished and we had to turn to nature. Fortunately, it was the rainy season and there were many caterpillars. There was one variety that was delicious when properly cooked but another furry kind which I detested, though it was reputed to have medicinal properties. As we moved deeper into the forest food became scarcer, and no living creature that could pass through fire was spared. Many of our group died after eating wild mushrooms. One man died after eating an onion-like plant which caused his stomach to swell. My brother-in-law used to tantalise us by describing *kapenta*, a kind of fish available in Zambia.

Alfredo walked the whole journey with a stethoscope round his neck, telling people to stick out their tongues, and looking beneath their eyelids to see whether they had enough blood, as he put it. Among those who died was Elder, a boy whom I had never liked because he was cleverer then I. He used to correct my Portuguese pronunciation. Unlike me, he had been brought up in comfortable circumstances in which milk was not a luxury, and therefore found the hardships of the forest harder to bear. He scarcely ate anything, while we obeyed the Portuguese proverb: *come sujo guarda a vida* (eat dirt to save your life). He died of diarrhoea and vomiting. He was buried in a Unita flag (the only cloth available) in a shallow grave by the banks of the River Quembo.

During the funeral, I voraciously eyed the pot of caterpillars. Alfredo, of course, preached a sermon and the women begged the exhausted men to dig the grave deeper so that the hyenas would not dig up Elder's body and eat it.

Water was another hazard. We had to drink water contaminated by mud and animal droppings. The banks of one of the rivers that we crossed had reputedly been mined by the Portuguese during the war of liberation and we had to follow the animal tracks for the sake of safety. As we were walking across a swamp I saw a woman lose two young children who were sucked downwards into the swamp and whose only tombs were a few transient bubbles breaking the surface.

Crossing the River Quembo was a problem. The men, who now numbered 30, were too weak to swim. One man, however, made it across the river, but his skin was lacerated by sharp reeds. Covered in blood, some villagers on the other side thought he was a messenger from God, because they had never known anyone swim the river before. They sent canoes to fetch the rest of us.

After crossing the Quembo, food was easier to come by because there were more villages. In one of them I was treated for worms by the local herbsman in a way I found repulsive. Five strong men, however, ensured I took my medicine and I was too weak to resist.

At a village near the Zambian border we were surrounded by a gang of men with grenade-launchers and automatic rifles. Their leader wanted to take my sister as a wife. She wept, I wept and trembled. My brother-in-law argued that we were simple peasants without political opinions or significance; but later he told us that he was thinking of grabbing one of their rifles and killing them all. The gang belonged to the Chipenda faction of the MPLA.

A member of our party tried to escape, but when he was caught he said that he was only going to relieve himself. The gang told him that he would soon have all the time in the world to relieve himself for they would kill him; but the chief of the village, who had seven wives and fifteen children threatened the gang with witchcraft if they spilt blood in his village. They released us instantly, except for the pair of platform shoes that my brother-in-law was carrying.

When we crossed the Zambian border, three months after we set out, there were eleven of us left. I spent the

97

rest of my childhood in Zambia. While there, I received a letter from a man in Huambo who had helped me when I was knocked down by a Portuguese taxi-driver. He asked me to send him a pair of shoes because it was impossible to find any in Angola. Afterwards he wrote to thank me for the shoes, but said they had arrived a bit late. Both his legs had been blown off in a land-mine explosion.

Over Europe

Fatmire Kocmezi

(Kosova)

Evening. We are in flight,
Plucking at the world of the clouds.
Beneath us a white kingdom,
Azure triumph.
We speed on and pay no heed
To borders, armies, herds.

As if on the century's crest, we push aside
The mildew of history, the wars.
A lady shakes the sighs from her handkerchief
Somewhere over Mauthausen.

Evening. We are in flight.
Beneath us pensive
Europe drowses over serious matters.
Sleep on, wise lady,
Never bothered about your whims.
Which were not mine.

1. Over Europe by Fatmire Kocmezi, by kind permission of the
   Refugee Council from *My Name Came Up, Kosova — War,
   Exile and Return. Më doli emni — Kosova — lufta, dëbimi
   dhe kthimi.* London, 2000.

The Journey

Karim Haidari
(Afghanistan)

08:59 Heathrow

The plane manoeuvred. I looked out of the window; little signs of activity were becoming visible on the ground below. I said to Suson:

"I think we are getting there." She turned her face away. Like a scholar reading verses. The plane descended. I was the authority, giving myself the right to come here. But soon the power shifted to the voice of a man behind the immigration desk:

"Passports please!" Suson was not bothered. She did not speak English. I pretended not to either.

"Which airline did you travel with?" The advice of the agent rang in my mind: if they know the airline they might send you back on the same plane.

"No... Anglish," I hesitated. Oh, my first conversation started with a lie. How many lies should I tell before I could prove the truth? Why do reasons fail against the system?

The officers started to search our bags. Groups of passengers were passing by, casting us puzzled glances. I felt humiliated, as if I had committed a crime. In my luggage the officers found a tiny bag with the Emirates logo on it and a Swissair pen. There were other items with airline names on them. The tallest of the officers asked me something in German. I wished I could tell them about the woman I knew who used to work for Areana Airline in Afghanistan. She had valued this collection so much. When she was no longer allowed to work [because of the Taliban] she was generous enough to give me the collection.

The officer added another harsh-sounding comment in German and gave me a serious look. I looked into his eyes.

I was on the brink of saying in English: "Listen to me, I'm screwed up by the system of my own country. I need shelter and food for now. I'm capable of putting my own bread on the table. So please let me in. I wouldn't have left my home if I didn't have to. I understand your concerns but my reasons are strong. Can't we sit and talk as human beings?" But I remained silent. Humanity is not the superpower in the real world.

My wrist-watch was ticking towards a late afternoon in Afghanistan. The officers asked us to sit on chairs in front of the desk and wait. I was expecting a thorough search so I checked through my things. I found a visiting card belonging to Angela, a woman who worked in the Geneva office of the organization I had quit twenty days previously in Kabul. I asked Suson if she knew how to get rid of the card. She took it from me, put it in her mouth and chewed it.

Every limb of my body was shaking. It wasn't just the fear of going back home and getting into trouble again. It felt as if a nightmare was about to repeat itself. At times of extreme emotional disturbance sometimes writing helps me. I opened my blank diary and without thinking I wrote a few lines which turned into a letter to my mother:

> Sitting here is not easy. This is making me feel like once again I am accused of an offence, a treason. Dear mum, these guys have the same rough attitude as the people who were interrogating me at the beginning of my imprisonment. Do you think I will survive a new life with such a start?

One of the officers came and took the diary from me and tried to read it. I had written in Dari script using the Arabic alphabet. He never gave it back. They asked the same questions again. Perhaps our appearance confused them. I had a tourist T-shirt on, a money belt around my waist and a stylish haircut. Suson was dressed like a Western Asian returning from her motherland. The officer gave us each a form to fill out. "I wish they would take us somewhere private, even a prison cell," I thought, when another group of people passed by. Suson and I were separated.

"For the last time, I'm asking you: which airline did you come in with?" I shrugged. Another officer banged his bunch of keys on the desk:

"We need to put it on this bloody form. If you want to be difficult you will stay here even longer," he shouted. The other gave him a disapproving look. I was helpless and exhausted. After a long search of body and luggage, I was led to a waiting hall where I met Suson again. The air-conditioned room was cold. I found an intimacy with the other people from various cultures. Like us, they all had fear and fatigue on their faces. I looked at Suson, her eyes filled with tears, her shoulders hunched. We had known each other barely a day — only since becoming travelling companions. But I felt a wrench in my heart for her. I was twenty-five and had survived harrowing moments; I knew uncertainty. But she was only sixteen and had grown up in an era of total male domination. "She's such an innocent," I thought. "How is she going to make it?" She noticed I was looking at her.

"What's going to happen?" she asked. I sighed:

"I don't know."

"Are they going to prosecute us and send us to jail or will they send us back home?"

"Which one would you prefer?" I asked, as if we were given a choice. She became breathless for a moment; silent tears ran down her cheeks. "How stupid of me," I thought. "She can't handle it." I grabbed her arms.

"You are a silly girl. This is a civilised country, we both have strong reasons to be here. You know a family who will look after you. Someone will marry you one day, and you'll have kids, one after another." I was relieved when I saw her face brighten again. I told her that her name, with a slight change in pronunciation, was Western, that a character in a famous novel was called Susan.

There was a Sikh immigration officer sitting near the

door behind a small desk. He had done nothing throughout the hours we had been waiting there. He came to us and handed out parcels of food. He gestured towards the free drink machine. Suson was hungry and started to unpack her food.

"Don't you want some?" she asked. But I didn't have the appetite for anything but getting out of there.

"They give rations to refugees all over the world," I said. She glanced at me, pausing while biting the plastic with her teeth.

But I was delighted with a discovery. I had found my new identity: I was a refugee.

ROOTS AND MEMORY

To the Memory of the Thirst of the Southern Mountain Slopes

Shadab Vajdi
(Iran)
Translated from Farsi by Lotfali Khonji

I can hear the rain
I can hear the rain
It has been raining all night,
and my heart has been singing all night
in the memory of the great salt desert
thirsty as ever for every drop of rain
in memory of southern mountain slopes
in memory of droughts and their heart-breaking
    remoteness
in memory of the innocence of the familiar soil, so close to
    my heart.

It has been raining all night
the whole town is filled with the melody of rain
my whole memory is submerged in your distant voice
the tiniest particle of your soil
is my dearest jewel.

I can hear the rain
Behold! Here, in memory of your soil
I rain in unison with bountiful clouds
rise in loving hope of greener spring-times
moments of budding are the dearest ones
and the springtime yields
springs of uniform, clear water.
rise in loving hope of greener spring-times
your spring-time will be mine too.

My Ancestors' Fire

Faziry Mafutala
(Democratic Republic of Congo)

During the night of Africa
Shining and black night
I have learnt the deep mysteries of the god of my ancestors
The first breath of humankind

It is a tradition among my people
To settle around the fire made by the ancestors
To hear a talking drum
To sing and dance
To hear legends and myths from the lips of a griot
While he communes with the night spirit

Every night
The griot gives birth to words
A truth of deep mysteries
The sea that fills my stream
That raises me high above all

I pass the words on to my children
As father told them to me
Who was told by his father's father
To fuel the ancestors' fire
My words are silent
No-one can steal them
No-one can destroy them in my mind
My words have power over any other thing

Let me play a tune on the soft wood Likembe
The art in my heart
Listen to my first words as Likembe talks
From my ancestors
Who lived among the Bantu in the tropical rain forests
Among the Pygmies in the deep bush
I gathered the mysteries
How the strongest ancestors sank in the sea

In my mind's burning
Into chaotic dreams
My memory is as dry as the Sahara desert
I want to drink from the old calabash
To remember my ancestors' history
In the nightmare of the monster city
Stranger in the intoxicating beauty of the swarming city
Where crowds flow over high-rise islands of power and
  wealth
I get lost under the brown fog of a winter dawn

In the dark night of winter
All the dogs bark
The stars are dead
The moon, queen of the night realm has lost her memory

Time seems to stand still in my brain
But it does not halt for those outside
In the splendour of the public gardens
Where streets in full daylight confront the passer-by

My grandchildren ignore how the old calabash was broken
Tomorrow the words will cease to fuel the ancestors' fire
My grandchildren won't drink from the old calabash
The first breath of humankind will drift away.

Dying Young

Shirin Razavian

(Iran)

My friends
    Are all dead
The souls
    I used to write with
        Sing with
The songs of freedom
    On the mounts of Esfahan

Those familiar smiles
Knowing sparkles in their eyes

Souls who knew me,
    Are now wandering at night
Hovering over the blue mosques
Brushing away the sound of Azaan
    From the navy sky of a suffocated town

The sounds
    Which throttled the songs of freedom
        In our mind
And why would god
    Play the devil's advocate?

Was he not merciful?
Was he not kind?
Did he not whisper softly
    In my ears
Sweet lullabies of Erfaan
    From the silver throat of the moon?

Did he not gently
                    Stroke my hair
          Through the kind hands of the midnight breeze?

Where did I leave him behind?
Where did the devil hide my mercy?

In the grave of some rotten corpse
                              Of ignorance and need?
In the lethargy of decayed beliefs?
Or in the fire of lust and greed?

My friends are dead
                    All beautiful and young
But through the silence of the night
                    Lives on the whisper of their song.

To This Brown Sugar Dawn

Mir Mahfuz Ali
(Bangladesh)

I will never return to this brown sugar dawn;
no more dusty play for me on this lush lawn.
How can I forget this land of fish and floods,
While death squirms around me, catfish in the mud.

I may wish to come home on a long boat,
carrying my pride on a summer day tide.
I hide no cruel ambition or revenge for those,
who sent me out from my country in disgrace.

A war later, water may still flow over the ruin,
and the flute-shadows lean into the monsoon wind.
My bright eyes may one day turn dim like a silted stream
but first I must rise against this blue rifle dream.

Asmara by Night

Reesom Haile
(Eritrea)

After work I like to stop
At Rita's Bar Gurgusum.
The fighters who won the war drink there.
"My heroes! Good evening."
The men greet me back.
But where are the women who fought!

"Ciao, Rita." "Amore!"
"Please help me out.
A White Horse or a cold one
With the old-style Melotti cap!"
"Amore! Do what you like. Don't ask me.
Peace. It's a free country."

Animal Joy

Abdirahman Mirreh
(Somalia)

On the mountain slopes
I herded my horses, camel and sheep
As a nomad son;
I blew my flute,
Jubilant they grazed
with swinging tails.

As sunset came, I
drove them home,
and on the way,
they did spring trap,
trap, trap,
here and there.

I knew what it meant
their jolly jump, and
all it said thank you
for the day.

Dawn is Imminent

Fawzi Karim

(Iraq)

Translated from Arabic by Lily Al-Tai

Pastures are bedewed this Sunday
I will drink straight from the bottle
A piece of cheese is enough
enough a spark in your pipe
to keep you warm

No café this Sunday
I will drink out of the bottle
till my shirt dampens
while the dawn spreads
Frightened by my footsteps will be
the squirrel
Through the mists of dawn — a door opens
I enter "Who are you?"
the doorman asks
"I am he who writes in metaphysical verse" I reply.

Thereupon, the dewy leaves are swept
   around me.
This Sunday, I deserted the house
crossing the crucial boundaries
between dreams and awareness
I deserted the house
crossing paths to reach a myth
no one else has crossed but me.

I drink out of the bottle
my hands fatigued
resisting a desire to roam in the pastures
for dawn is imminent
Through the mists of dawn — a door opens
I enter "Who are you?" the doorman asks
"I am he who writes metaphysical verse" I reply.

Like a cotton fountain
embittered, muffled silence,
My feet so flickering
vanish almost in my footsteps.
Waves of water
Propellers of palm on the banks
How to answer your call?

I will drink out of the bottle
till my breath smells bloodied
and spirit is cured
from the flesh.
I will toast to this ill-fated land
vanishing from the sight of days a house in Karch.

A friend melting in a pool of acid.
Another, like a scarecrow shepherds
the mine fields
What splinters and skulls
shanks
the mire giving them a dense presence
Sight of abating spirit
endless
Is this the resurrection of the lame or
is dawn imminent?

A piece of cheese is enough
enough a spark in your pipe
to keep you warm
No café this Sunday
I shall return home
and listen to the radio.

Beledweyn

Maxamed Ibraahim 'Hadraawi'
(Somalia)

The poet accompanied a troupe of actors to Beledweyn, a country town, where he met a girl for whom he composed this mock-romantic poem.

Love! May you live for evermore!
It can't be true — it's a lie, I say,
That it was you who killed Bowndheri!
Love! May you live for evermore!
It can't be true — it's a lie, I say,
That your piercing iron-hard thrust
To liver, heart and flank
Is a wound no physic can heal
Nor nursing mend — it can't be true!

When I went down to Beledweyn
The times were blest and prosperous.
The river had overtopped its banks
And bestowed its water on the farmlands,
Grass fit for grazing covered the ground
And trees and bushes were bedecked with blooms.
The maize and millet were threshed and winnowed
And the grapes were now all ripe.
There was a *bullo* dance, and others, too —
People danced and danced till dawn's first light
As the homesteads rejoiced in the season of spring.

Now, in that town, on the eastern side,
There lives a queen!
Resplendent she is as sun-gilt water,
And the beauty and charm of womanhood
Are found in her to true perfection.
Her long hair falls as far as her heels —
I could compare it only with ostrich plumes —
And on the crown of her head there are auburn shades
Which evenly sweep to right and left.
Her locks are anointed with scented *ghee*
And they serve her even when she sleeps
For does not her body rest on them?
Are they not a pillow for her head?
Does she not spread them as a coverlet?

And when I met her —
Ah, what a fervent longing,
What joy she planted in me!

It was in the morning, early,
On the eighth day of the month,
In Beledweyn, halfway across the Swaying Bridge
That spans the water, swinging to and fro —
It was there we chanced upon each other,
Beerlula and I.
I stopped and spoke to her in greeting
And she returned me words of welcome.
We arranged to meet — it was fate —
She said, "Be here tomorrow!"
Didn't she?

"I can't face the journey home —
I'm desperately ill —
Please cancel the departure —
Consider the state I'm in!"
But the news of my affliction was not welcomed —
"We're off today!" was the troupe's response.
The director even thought that I was lying —
That harsh and wicked man ignored my plight
And didn't want to know about it, did he?
Then most of the troupe got on the truck —
Quite blatantly they did it —
They all climbed up from one side
And I had to climb up from the other.

When strong feelings get out of hand
And longings overpower the mind,
One prays sometimes for evil things to happen
And did I refrain from this? I didn't, no!
I prayed that some part inside the truck,
Some metal part, would cease to work,
I prayed that the petrol-tank would spring a leak,
I even prayed that the driver would get ill
And not recover before departure time.

At dawn, and through the first hot morning hours
Far on the horizon we could see a giant shape,
The massive tree that all Beledweyn knows as Baar.
The wind rushed through its withered pods —
We heard it calling out to us —
We heard it whistling, didn't we?

117

The truck went rocking on its way,
Back and forth and side to side,
And grievous illness gripped me again.
The evening heat rose towards me from the dunes
And I fainted.
Beerlula seemed to be at my side
A green meadow lay beneath our feet
The season was prosperous, the times propitious,
And together we danced the *beerrey* dance —
But now my senses returned to me
And what had it been but a deluding dream?

Like a bird of prey on the wing
The truck sped on and on
And climbed to the top of a lofty hill.
As I gazed around me,
Peering now to one side, now on the other,
It came into my mind to jump —
I cared nothing for the risk of death!

I am a man who has been bewitched
I long to be not here, but there —
Not in Banaadir, where I'm living now,
But in Beledweyn — that is where I want to be!
I look for her, I call her name — Beerlula!

Oh God — make Beledweyn a garden of solace and joy!
Oh God — make Beledweyn an abode of happiness!
Oh God — turn aside from Beerlula any threatening
    harm!
Oh God — let her live in peaceful and prosperous times!

Permission to reprint kindly granted by Sheila Andrzejewski

There is a House

Choman Hardi
(Kurdistan)

There is a house with four bedrooms
where a couple live with their three children
one, is seven years old,
and the other two are three

There was a house with four bedrooms where seven people
    used to live,
And they ate around a flowery *sufreh* every day
and a young man used to play his flute until the women
    would cry
for what there would be
and a father was torn between politics and poetry
and a little girl who believed that there was a bell in her ear
and managed to avoid wearing slippers
even when the floor could burn her feet

there was a garden where the brown chicks would grow big
    enough to be killed
and it snows to let you know that another winter has
    arrived
and every death was cried over,
where a lonely fish was swimming around a blue pot
    aimlessly,
and a little goat once spent a night

there was a place, before the marriages taking place,
before the mountains attracting the men,
before buying one-way tickets
there was a place where seven people lived happily in the
    four seasons

There is a place
where you can smell the satisfaction of the land
when the first rain falls
And you can hear the fat rain-drops

there is a place where it doesn't rain continuously,
where you can sleep on the flat roofs on the hot evenings,
and a little girl who kept dreaming about chicks, goats and
    rabbits.
may be for what there was

Through the Vast Halls of Memory 2

Haifa Zangana
(Iraq)

Zino is the brightness of light and its crystallisation; the many colours of the mountains, the red mountains with their black summits. The colours seem to be unlimited. The huge caves invite you to leave the mountain trail, to enter and discover the cool darkness, dripping water, the scent of moss and the hanging plants. Routine has its own richness. Tobacco fields and pellucid views. It is a refuge, a conscious longing for the mother's womb and father's lap. Snow and mountain top; snow sold by children during summer. The rugged mountain tracks. Nature radiant as if behind glass; springs are crystallised moon and snow. Pomegranates and vines. The moment of meeting a shepherd and his goats on their way home of an evening; the blue water washing the coloured rocks, the beautiful faces of the women and their colourful dresses. What sadness had those women felt when they were forced to leave their homes and live in tents in another country?

Zino was just a long, muddy road surrounded by houses built of rock brought from the mountains nearby. In the village there were a number of alleys starting at the muddy road and ending at the foot of the rugged mountains. The main road in the village was narrow, not because of any error in the original plan, but owing to the shopkeepers' persistence in displaying half of their wares on the road. Thus, sacks of rice, wheat and barley, sat besides children's clothes, rubber shoes, fabrics, sewing needles and cotton together with heaps of old magazines, religious and Marxist tracts in Arabic, Persian and Turkish, with a few publications in Kurdish. In small wooden boxes were knives, forks, spoons and kitchen utensils. Next to these were all kinds of pills, including pain-killers and pills to combat indigestion. And, believing

Zino to be one of the most popular resorts, visited by thousands of tourists daily, the shopkeepers insisted on exhibiting postcards and local handicrafts. Each day at 5pm, the shopkeepers hauled their goods back into their shops, to re-exhibit them the next morning. Zino women are always in a hurry. On their shoulders falls the responsibility of looking after husbands and children and taking care of sewing tapestry and weaving. Bedspreads have to be ready for winter, so little pieces of material are carefully collected and arranged in beautiful patterns to make sheets and bedspreads for young brides. Women also have to gather wood from the mountains, load it on the backs of their mules (or their own backs, if they have no mules), help their husbands at farming and in building temporary summer huts from leaves and branches in the hope of letting them to tourists.

I was eight years old when my father took me with him to Zino. He was proud to see me reading and writing Arabic, to the extent that he forgot to teach me his mothertongue. Although he was fluent in Kurdish, Persian and Assyrian, Arabic remained a closed book to him.

We arrived in the village at noon. The road was empty and the shops open, with half their contents outside on the street. It was the time for prayer, lunch and siesta. We headed for a half-built house, passing an incomplete fence, and went through a room with no door or window. As we reached the wooden door, Mam Mahmoud opened it, welcoming and hugging my father and me in turn. The room was almost empty except for a huge wooden box in one corner. On it there were blankets, cotton covers and round pillows. From the other corner, there came the smell of tea brewing in a samovar, and the scent of burning coal. I was fascinated by a beautiful, multi-coloured Persian rug which added its warm, welcoming atmosphere to the room.

A few minutes later Mam Mahmoud's wife walked in, carrying a tray with four tea cups. She put it beside the samovar and shook hands with my father and then hugged me. As I could understand very little of what they were saying in Kurdish, I occupied myself in watching the cubes of sugar as they dissolved in the tea, which I stirred continuously, making enough noise to attract the adults' attention. I expected my father to be angry, as he would have been at home. Instead, he remained silent and relaxed, sipping his tea as if time had lost its importance.

In that room, my father's presence was different from in the city. He questioned Mam Mahmoud about relatives and what they were doing and he talked about the city. Mam Mahmoud talked about problems with the border guards and how times had changed. Mam Jin was silent most of the time and when she spoke , she asked my father to make an appointment with a gynaecologist. Mam Mahmoud said nothing until he commented that the time was getting late... I whispered,

"Why can't we stay in Zino?" In the way he sat and in his green eyes, I could see the meaning in his coming back to a place where he could stretch out and touch familiar things and feel that oblivion could not reach him.

And I felt the urge to touch him, to make sure it really was him, the man who was lost to us in the big city. He sensed my feeling and stroked my hair tenderly. I whispered, "Why can't we stay here?"

He did not reply. The city was his dream, being married to an Arab woman was his dream, and being proud of a daughter excelling in her studies and politics was also his dream.

"The cold weather has arrived early this year," was a phrase of Mam Mahmoud's as he quietly stepped out, on the outlook for the last birds of summer. He walked ahead of us, towards one of the shops, which unlike the rest, was locked up. He unlocked the door and, from the darkness within, came an unforgettable smell. In the years that followed, and in moments of despair, that smell turned out to be the only window open on the sky: the smell of darkness, humidity and mounds of Persian carpets rolled up in a certain way to keep them safe from moths. I jumped on them and as my father gave instructions, I helped Mam Mahmoud pull one out. Mam Mahmoud unrolled the carpet in front of the shop. How beautiful it was! Fascinated, I stood there gazing at the endless patterns and bright colours. Moving closer, I felt the woolly texture, trying to imitate and upstage my father in savouring its smell. Mam Mahmoud laughed and hugged me again. That day we bought two carpets. Then we started our journey back to the city.

Kin The Beautiful

Mabiala Molu
(Democratic Republic of Congo)
Translated from French by Jennifer Langer

O Kin! Beautiful town so coveted
For you, Blacks and Whites made war,
Both claimed their right to fortune
And you, Ebony Princess, cast your spell on them.
Who did not succumb to your charms?
Who did not sing your praises?
For your love
Kallé became great,
Manu played the Cha-Cha
Senghor stopped at Léo
Césaire made himself loved
Fanon lived out his destiny
From the Maison Mère to the Congo Bar
They danced the Independence Cha-Cha
Kin the bold
Who can forget Dendhal with its maze of streets?
Who can forget the little "Mbongo and the Bills"?
Your lively lanes
Where women and girls bustled about
Gaily singing with breasts in air
Your beloved roads
Where the men swaggered past
Your enchanting roads
Where Mbéleketé was shown off skilfully
Your sunny roads
Where the street musicians strolled up and down
Your beautiful avenues
Where the other people grew rich
And Angualima defied them
Your roads where once
Black men and women danced the bamboula

And now, misery plays its game of fate
Kin Malebo, Kin the promise
Town of leaders, town of light
Kin the beautiful, become the playground for miracles
Great city, devastated by those cockroaches
Jewel of an epoch, destroyed by those ruffians
O Beautiful Widow, cry for your heroes.

1. *Kin* = Kinshasa, capital of Zaire.
2. *Whites* = in the French, Toubabs is used. This is a term used for Whites by Africans.
3. *Kalle* = a popular singer.
4. *Senghor* = one of the founders of the Negritude movement, writing that draws heavily on the African past and identity rather than the colonial European tradition.
5. *Léo* = Leopoldville, the former name of the capital.
6. *Manu Dibanga* = Cameroonian musician.
7. *Césaire* = another founder of the Négritude movement, originally from Martinique
8. *Independence Cha-Cha* = dance at the time of independence
9. *Dendhal* = area of Kinshasa with bars and clubs.
10. *Mbélékete* = a dance.
11. *Angualima* = a famous burglar who was never caught.
12. *Malebo* = port area of Kinshasa.
13. *the tombola* = lottery; many people were duped into selling property in the belief that they were certain to win with many losing everything.
14. *playground for miracles* = life is so difficult and miserable that the inhabitants hope for miracles to make their lives bearable.
15. *Fanon* = an Algerian writer who was involved in the anti-French colonial movement in the 60s.

Ma Terre d'O — My Land of O

Muepu Muamba
(Democratic Republic of Congo)
Translated from French by Denise Ganderton

No
Not only a trigger at the ready on the gun Africa my
undulating country I come from the land of fruity water-
laden like a pleasant orchard and in my heart surges
dream upon dream endlessly the hope of regaining my
forfeited country.

Zaire was once the realm of singing trees and shimmering
dreamy waters my land of O like a twin fairyland crescent
of tenderness the laughter burst forth corollas of flowers
like a bohemian seduction of pleasure

but
today my destitute *likuta* land is enthralled by misery how
can I tell you of the enchanting metamorphoses of my
ancient proud land when tears and mourning constantly
cast deadly shadows onto its azure bed

this
landscape of sweetness one day I may speak of the divine
bewitchment of *munkamba* and of *kivu's* proud gaze my
watery land of reflecting rivers softly caressing my watery
land an infinity of joyful rivers and smooth streams.

the
springs of airborne melodies are not exhausted yet so I
cannot really belong elewhere I who so long have lived
elsewhere my land of O.

Efasa' Moto

Simon Mol
(Cameroon)

My Mammy and Papa
are themselves children of the great *Efasa' Moto* —
half man, half stone
eternal flame/ash,
coagulated lava-remains, that once and always course from
the volcanic womb of Mount Fako

Invasion of unripe changes
is questioned with earth tremors echoing His voice
from His sanctum where He rests...
on a hot-bed of coal —
there, where no one will forever dare.

I am a child of the Bakweris —
theirs and His son — myself as old as the Sun.
and as young as Yesterday.

Efasa' Moto is a deity of the Bakweris... the coastal and
mountainous tribe that lives at the foot of Mount Fako, otherwise
known as Mount Cameroon. They believe that Efasa Moto lives
on the top of the active volcanic Mount Fako and that he is partly
made of flesh and stone.

The Nightingale

Mahdad Majdian
(Iran)

In the shameless dark,
  In the shadows of the night,
    In my deep brown eyes,
        There's a nightingale, a nightingale, a nightingale

Inside the waves of the sea,
  In reflections of tormenting dreams,
    In the congregation of a million migrant starlings,
      Someone is singing continuously,
          It's a nightingale, a nightingale, a nightingale

In the flow of sorrowful joys,
  Inside the agony of daily chores,
    Whilst planning these futile roles,
      You recognise something is missing,
          Isn't it a nightingale, a nightingale, a nightingale?

Then I look to the flickering flame,
  To that grand candle which burns,
    Looking inside my heart,
      I find a burning nest,
        And that's just the right place,
            For the nightingale, the nightingale, the nightingale.

Fingers

Dursaliye Sahan
(Turkey)
Translated from Turkish by Aydin Mehmet Ali

As Zilan fed the thick material rapidly into the machine her left hand reached for the next piece in the bundle. With every piece the rattle became a little quicker. The beat of the wash stick against wet clothes would also quicken as the pile on the rock by the side of the stream rose higher.

She had always liked the sound of the wash stick and she also liked the rattle of the machine. She sometimes stopped and straightened her headscarf as she watched her reflection on the water and dreamt of which boy she would marry. Zilan had no time now at the machine to stop and think, but occasionally she would slow it down and wonder who her children would marry when they grew up, what work they would do and, most of all, try to figure out how much Miho had lost gambling the previous week.

She would often think of the small hamlet where she was born. She missed its air, water, grass, earth, animals and the smell of dried animal dung. In the last years before she had come here the smell of gunpowder seemed to cling everywhere. Even the plants had turned a different shade of green. The earth had become a cloudy yellow as if in protest. Summer and winter had merged into one. There were village guards[1], soldiers, Apocular[2]... They had gone short before but now they were poorer than ever. They would spend the winter half starved.

Zilan burned inside for her mother and sister. She also felt sorrow for her elder brother, Siho and her old grandfather but the loss of her mother and sister had burned her heart in a different way and left her insides knotted and twisted. She had never thought it would happen to them, even though there were funerals in the hamlet most weeks. Why hadn't it occurred to her that her mother and sister might die?!

She had cried for days. Then she had thought God was punishing her. Two days before her mother died she had heard that her betrothed Huseyin had been killed while doing his military service. She had suddenly felt great relief. She had not told anyone apart from her sister. She had not said anything when everything had been agreed, but she had never liked Huseyin. Zilan had seen him from a distance. He was stocky. She had looked at her mother about to tell her, but her mother cut her off before she could start and snapped at her: "What are you saying, girl? What more do you want? Of course a man should be large, what will you do with a small one? Who better would have you? People can't be without governments and women without owners." She and her sister had wondered if God would be offended, but she had been relieved anyway.

She had her eye on Miho. His family had three oxen and his mother didn't like any of the girls in the village.

One Friday her betrothed Huseyin's body was brought to the village. An NCO had brought the body and four pieces of paper to the headman of the village. They were documents of martyrdom for Huseyin's mother, father, betrothed and for the other villagers. His mother pushed away the certificate, saying:

"I didn't give birth to my child for him to be a martyr. I didn't bring him up to be the target of stray bullets," as she wept at the head of the coffin, too small for her well-built son.

Zilan had also cried into her headscarf as it was not considered respectable for young girls to laugh or cry publicly, or to speak in a loud voice. Talkative, laughing, shouting girls and newly-married women were frowned upon. "Women should not speak, they should remain quiet," her mother would say.

A week had not yet passed before Rustem Agha[3] sent an envoy asking for her hand in marriage. Her heart had pounded. Rustem Agha had two wives and fourteen children. Seventeen people lived in his little two-room house. He was called a landlord on account of his sixty *cediklik*[4] of land. They also would only just make it through the winter. But it was apparent that the oversexed man wanted a new bride, a young woman. Her father had said," We'll think about it," in a reluctant way. He had obviously thought that the bride price would be low.

Three days later her elder sister had been shot when taking the sheep to the meadow to join the other flocks. The crops had yet to be reaped.

It was not clear whether the Apocular or the village guards were responsible. Zilan had frozen when she saw her sister lying lifeless facedown on the grass. The image of her bent body would always stay with her. The edge of her baggy cotton trousers could be seen from under her dress. She had a pair exactly the same. Their mother had made the trousers for them for the *bayram*[5] before she died. When her sister's body was being washed on the funeral slab she had taken her sister's trousers and her own without washing them, folded them up as one and put them away in her chest. She still had them. Whenever she saw them her eyes would moisten. On every Ramadan festival she would take the trousers out of the chest without showing them to anyone and press them to her face, breathing the smell in deeply. She remembered the long winter nights they spent together. How they had laughed as they had chewed the thin sheets of *pestil*[6] and worked the embroidery canvas by candlelight. While her mother had knitted socks from goat's wool they had prepared cushion covers and sheet corners for their *çeyiz*[7] darned with plant-dyed red, green and indigo threads. They would string row after row of beads. They learned together how to count to ten on their fingers. If her sister hadn't died they would have learned to count on their toes too. "Counting to ten is no small feat," her sister said, "if we learn to count on our toes that will be enough for us."

132

How she had cried. After they had died she had counted the days one by one until she reached ten. Then she had gone out of her mind, as she could not count any more. Her pain grew. It was as if she had lost even the memory of her sister. Zilan struggled to count her toes. She couldn't ask her father and her grandfather couldn't count either. She asked her nine-year-old brother but he could only count to five. She told him to ask older children but he didn't.

One day while beating clothes at the stream she found a new method for counting her toes. She would give each one a name, starting with her little toe; husband, bride, child, earth, millet, food, fire, soldier, gun, corpse. While joyously counting, she saw the village guard Husam. He was watching the bare toes she was trying to count and looking strangely at her face. She had not been frightened. What could Squat Husam do? Still, her hand slowly gripped the stone beneath. Suddenly Miho appeared from behind the bushes. When Husam saw Miho he was startled, saying:

"I thought you were the Apocular," and hurried away. Miho asked

"Did he say anything to you?" Zilan's mind was on her toes as she asked excitedly:

"Miho, do you know how to count?" Miho was surprised, but still answered: "Of course." Sure of himself.

Zilan looked around and seeing it was clear asked him:

"Miho, my brother, could you teach me. Tell me once and it'll be enough." She wanted to be able to count the nights since her sister and mother had died and to know how many days had passed. In silence Miho started to scratch the surface of the earth. Zilan's heart sank. Miho, too, could only count to ten.

The next day by the river Zilan had worked out using her own method how many days had passed since her mother and sister had died when Miho again appeared from behind the bushes. He had learned how to count to fifteen, and said there wasn't much use in learning more.

133

The day after that Miho came again. Zilan was intending to ask him if he had learned to count when he said:

"My mother wants to arrange a marriage for me with Gulizar." Gulizar was a pretty girl. She was a very fast weaver. Her elder brother lived in Istanbul. No girl in the village had a bottom drawer like hers. Zilan said:

"Congratulations."

Miho looked Zilan in the eyes and said:

"Zilan, I'm going away from here." He mentioned far away places. He spoke rapidly. He swore that those who left were not infidels. As Zilan collected up her washing and was about to rise he took her hand and said:

"Come with me, Zilan. They'll soon marry you off to someone like Rustem Agha in any case. Your betrothed has been shot. I won't come back until Gulizar has been married." Zilan was about to say, "It's impossible" when she felt the warmth of Miho's palm in her hand. A man's hand had not touched hers before. How nice it was... .

What would they say if she left? It wouldn't be right. Moreover, Gulizar was her friend. But Rustem Agha?

Miho spoke even more rapidly:

"Tonight they're coming to collect me... the ones in the mountains."

So Miho too. If her father heard she had talked to him he would kill her. "No good will come from them... The state is powerful... They kill the villagers... It is wrong to go up in the mountains." The previous winter they had come to take her elder brother. He had been scared and did not want to go. Her father had given them half their winter provisions. Her mother had complained all winter that they would starve and not see the spring. Her father had looked up at the mountains, saying, "They are hungry, too. What can they do? Keep quiet and be thankful for what you have." He would also secretly warn her brothers: "Keep your distance from the ones in the mountains. When they come we'll feed them of course, as they are our people, but keep away from them." If he

134

heard now that she had run away with one from the mountains... Was Miho one of them? It wasn't known in her village. If the military heard they would take her away immediately.

Miho shook Zilan by the arm:

"When night falls and everyone goes to bed go down below the village and wait at the edge of the old grazing field. Don't bring anything heavy, we have a long way to go. Wrap up warm, eat a lot of bread and drink water on top before you leave."

They had met up with the ones in the mountains towards morning. They had walked for a night and a day before reaching the camp. How lovely it was, how they had enjoyed themselves. She and Miho had got to know and love each other in that camp. They had stayed there for three months. Their wedding had taken place there. Miho was as happy as a child. Had her sister's spirit seen her then with Miho? In the camp a girl called Berivan had taught them how to count to a hundred. How easy it was.

By the time they had arrived in London in *Zemheri*[8] she could recognise the letters. Eight years had passed so quickly. How much she had learned. She had met so many people. She had had three children. Miho had learned to gamble and had taken up smoking.

Betul, the Cypriot woman working on the next machine would ask her:

"Why do you give your husband money? Let him go hungry then he'll work. Don't let yourself be used." How could Zilan do that to Miho? Who apart from Miho knew her sister, mother, brothers or the taste of the plants they had gathered from the lower slopes of the mountains in spring to make soup? Or the story of the two pairs of cotton trousers from the hamlet? If Zilan lost Miho what would she do all alone in London?

1. *Village guards*: Villagers employed and armed by the government to fight against the Kurdish PKK alongside the security forces and to act as informers in their village.

2. *Apocular*: Supporters of Abdullah Ocalan, leader of PKK, which waged a guerrilla war against the Turkish Government from 1984-1999.
3. *Agha* = Landlord.
4. *Çedik* = A unit of measurment of land.
5. *Bayram* = Religious festival.
6. *Pestil* = Fruit pulp, usually apricots, grapes or mulberries, squeezed out into thin sheets. Eaten as a dried fruit.
7. *Çeyiz* = Bottom drawer. Items in preparation of a girl's married life.
8. *Zemheri* = Old term for depth of mid-winter, month of January.

Homesickness

Mohammed Khaki
(Kurdistan)

If one day
your jasmine sweet memory
came with the zephyrs of spring
ruffling the pages of my poetry —
Which drop of rain
would wash away my homesickness

My Wish

Mohammed Khaki
(Kurdistan)

In my dreams
I come to your tent
filling my shepherd's basket with
the songs of mountain starlings.
I am making a bed of sweet violets
entwining my arms as honeysuckle
for you.

EXILE

Return to Neverland-upon-Rupture
Ahmad Ebrahimi
(Iran)

English version dedicated to
Esmail Kho'i and Karina Zabihi

What would be the point of departure
to return to Neverland-upon-Rupture
at this or any other juncture?
After cycling on for years in different circles
breaking up and going round in a loop,
turning all the time, pedalling away exhaustion
turning away, from friend and foes,
yet giving way to the nostalgic impulse
in our toes.

What would be the point of departure
even now that we have to stop altogether?
Watching each other's hearts retire,
searching but not finding the magic glue
to repair this odd yet very old puncture
with blow job
hardly meant for the tyre
to arrive, finally, in the future.

Spared from the firing squad and torture
but not from the fire of one burning wish,
yet knowing deep down that it will never come true for us,
a new wheel, a ready tyre and a gun to fire.

Dorothy didn't know that her shoes
could have always returned her to Kansas
we somehow knew, but discarded ours long ago,
to walk away from life barefoot
on the fire of only one exclusive desire.
Eventually we are bound to understand the impasse,
our limited resources and the power of black satire.
Even if the world is not burning with
our exclusive desire,
we must be thank thankful for our stay —
a stay of execution you may say.
But in this mix of lifeless love and crossfire —
OK — call it the purgatory of leave to stay in the UK,
we have to find a way before we retire
to be able to entertain all kinds of interests, desire:
retaining the Ashes, Dad's Army and
England, your England as George Orwell wrote after
reluctantly shooting the elephant — maybe as a farewell
    to the British Empire.
Then the world around us would have a chance
to understand our unnurtured nature
and we take it to be our true home
— whether London, Karachi, Ankara or Rome.

Neverland-upon-Rupture
from a distance, one can see the landscape
inviting as an intoxicating mirage, a dead sea of flesh.
But when one closely inspects the texture
it turns out to be a mirage of shimmering wine
which nevertheless makes you tipsy
as long as you are asleep and dreaming.
But the moment you wake up, there is little mercy.
You have to run from one corner to another
tracing the footprints of "the testifying Goddess of Youth"
in vain, only to see in yourself
Hagar, abandoned by the Prophet Abraham,
running the seven hills of despair and thirst
carrying the almost dead baby of hope

in search of the bosom of water,
but to no avail.

And the Motherland
an empty dessert-bowl of breast
that does not answer
the desperate call of your pitiful heart.
And roots
that strangle you without haste.

What would be the point of return?
A return
to Neverland-upon-Rupture
even for the sake of dying there
too late to contemplate victory,
too exhausted to surrender.

The blue sky is no longer in the air
when you set foot on that particular part of the sphere.
We are trapped in past continuous.
For us there is no longer a future to share.
Why then, tell me
you still care
to return there
to Neverland-upon-Rupture
at this or any other juncture?

Whine

Dubravka Ugresic
(Croatia)

Sometimes I wonder whether what drove me out of my country was, in fact, music. That is, the reasons for going into exile are often far less serious than one imagines. After all, if someone can go mad because of their sensitivity to sounds, I don't see why a similar kind of sensitivity (a sense of taste for instance), could not be the reason for someone to leave their homeland. Be that as it may, every exile often feels that the state of exile is a special kind of sensitivity to sound; sometimes I feel that exile is nothing but a state of unconscious musical recollection (which may be agreeable or disagreeable).

One day I went into the centre of Munich to meet my acquaintance Igor, but some way from Marienplatz I stopped, drawn to the sound of music. An elderly Gypsy was playing Hungarian Gypsy songs on a violin. He caught my passing glance, gave me a smile that was at the same time deferential and brazen, recognising me as one of his kind. Something caught in my throat, for a moment I couldn't breathe, and then I lowered my eyes and hurried on, realising a second later that I had set off in the wrong direction. A couple of paces further on I caught sight of a life-saving telephone box and joined the queue, pretending that I had to make a phone call, what else. There was a young man standing in front of me, tight black leather jacket, tight jeans, high-heeled boots, a kind of insecurity and impudence on his face at the same time, like colours running into each other. A second later, I knew that he was one of "us", my countryman. The way he slowly and persistently dialled the number — looking neither to right nor left, like a waiter in a cheap restaurant — filled me with a mixture of anger and pity and put me on the side of the people in the queue. And then the young man finally got through (yes, one of us, of course!). My countryman's habit of talking for a long time about nothing, as if coddling, pampering, mutually patting each other's backs and jollying each other along, that habit filled me again with a sudden mixture of anger and pity. The violin was still whining sorrowfully, the young man was talking to a certain Milica, and in my head, as at an editing table, I was joining the whine to the young man's babbling. The black-eyed violinist was staring persistently in my direction. For a moment I wanted to leave the queue, but I didn't, that would have given me away, I thought. That is why, when the young man finished his conversation and smoothed his hair with his hand, (a gesture which filled me with the same mixed feelings as before, because of its unexpectedness), I telephoned Hannelore, who was the only person I could have telephoned, thinking up some urgent, practical question.

I was late for my meeting with Igor. We went to a Chinese restaurant and as we chatted while waiting to be served, I observed that I was restless, absent, that my eyes were wandering. I felt as though I was covered with a fine film, like spectacles on a winter's day. At one moment I was conscious of a sound which I had not registered at first. There was pop music playing, Chinese or Korean, or at any rate, pop music from some eastern part of the world. It was a soft, elegiac, sweet crooning, a love song presumably, which could have been from my home or from Igor's Russian home. Just then there was a sudden downpour of rain which streamed down the restaurant window, behind Igor, and finally I broke down, let myself go, reacted properly, exactly, according to an ancient, well-practised reflex, of which I had not been conscious until that moment. In a word, I salivated at the sound of the bell, that universal, sweet whine, the same whine no matter where it came from. I struggled inwardly, resisted, grumbled, almost glad that I was in its power, almost physically satisfied. Quite softened, I splashed about in the warm invisible puddle of tears...

"What's happening, Igor...?" I asked him as though apologising.

"I understand," he replied. "I myself belong to a provincial, tango culture," explained my friend, a Russian Jew from Chernovitsa, an exile.

Permission to reprint kindly granted by Erewhon

A Letter

Himzo Skorupan
(Bosnia)
Translated by Damjana Finci

My dear sister,

I am writing to you from afar. I have found myself in this godforsaken place where the snow would not melt. My granddaughter told me the other day that the North Pole (whatever that is) is not far from us, but heck if I am gonna check that one out.

Word has it we are in Norway, some say we are in Sweden, so I truly do not know who to believe. Wish you were here to sip coffee with someone dear and near. To tell you the truth, I have never heard of your whatchamacallit Malasia. Do tell me if it snows there, I will send you some wool socks and a warm jumper. How are you doing? I — poorly. At least days go by, somehow, but nights drag on forever. I don't know what is worse: when I stay awake all night long, or when I fall asleep and dream. During the day I make myself busy, and old as I am, I have to learn this darned language. All three constituent nations from Bosnia attend out language course, and there is also a Jewish woman from Sarajevo, so it is widely thought that we could communicate better with each other after we have learned their language! The fact is, once we all return to Bosnia, we'll have to talk through a translator, or by sign language. We'll look pretty much like the UN Assembly on the East River. Mind you, this language of theirs won't go through my thick head, but I am relieved when I think of the wretched souls who ended in Japan. I reckon Japanese is mighty hard to learn.

Apart from the language course, I have found yet another pastime — philately, that is, stamp collecting. I correspond with our folks from six different countries, and every time a letter arrives, I take off the stamps first. I bought an album and a magnifying glass. If you want me to, I can send you the spare ones. Do tell me, if you're interested.

Neither Here Nor There

Translated by Damjana Finci

from Diary of an Exile, London Notes

I had my trepidations for a long time.

But yesterday, I could wait no more.

I went to the phone and dialled a number: my number!

At the other end of the line, in my house, I heard an unknown voice saying that I wasn't there. I asked him if he knew what had happened to me, where I was, and he said that he had moved in recently and that he didn't know.

I know perfectly well where I am, but I wondered whose head was on my pillow, who was browsing through my books, who was looking at the pictures on my walls... I wanted to know who was picking fruit in my garden and what had happened to my plants.

And I started thinking.

What does he dream about while resting on my pillow?

Is he afraid he might choke when biting into apples picked in my garden?

Is he enjoying the scent of my plants?

Does he feel uncomfortable in my bed?

What does he say when he hears someone knocking at the door?

What does he see in the pictures on my walls?

My books, he doesn't read, I know that!

God have mercy on him!

And this is the way things are: I am not really here, and over there, I am no more.

Lone Lorn London

Sousa Jamba
(Angola)

Sousa Jamba finds that it is not easy for an
African to meet a girlfriend.

When I was told in Africa that people in a Western
metropolis could be lonely, I did not believe it. I
imagined London, for instance, with ten million people,
which was double the total population of Zambia, where
I grew up. I imagined that if anyone felt lonely he would
simply walk out and talk to people. After three years in
London, I have come to discover that it is not that
simple.

One of the first things I wanted after a week in
London was a girlfriend: someone I would write poems
for, take to films and symphony orchestras. I had once
read a short story by an African writer in which he
described a romantic walk with a charming white girl on
Hampstead Heath. I too hoped to take my girlfriend
there.

I went to the local McDonalds in search of a girlfriend. I
ordered myself a King Burger and a family size orange
juice and settled beside two girls. As I ate the burger and
sipped the orange juice, my eyes switched from the *Sun* to
the two girls. I noticed a funny story in the *Sun* and
showed it to the two girls. I thought this was a way of
breaking down the barriers between us, in order to start
conversing. The girls giggled over the story and left, not
wanting to say a word to me.

I had to think of a strategy. In Zambia, my contemp-
oraries and I had adopted what we then considered an
impressive way of starting a conversation with girls in the
street. On approaching an interesting girl the proper thing
to say was: "Hello Baby, did I see you somewhere in

Washington or was it in Tokyo? Paris perhaps?" The girl would then allow herself a little titter and say she had never been out of Zambia. Of course she knew that the boy had never been out of Zambia, either. But that was part of the game. The next thing to say was how beautiful she was. The line for this was: "If roses were black they would be like you."

I tried this strategy in London; just the first lines, that is. It failed. The girls would simply answer no and give me an angry look. I befriended a Nigerian student who claimed to know the way out of my dilemma. He said he knew the way to ingratiate oneself with British girls. His line was: "Hello, I come from Nigeria."

Whenever my Nigerian friend repeated how sound his advice was, it was as though I became seized by fits of jingoism. I told him that nothing short of death would make me say that I was not an Angolan. He would look at me, shake his head, and say: "It is your problem, my friend. These people here are very stupid. They've never heard of Angola, so they will think you come from one of those countries where people walk naked. But Nigeria, they all know it. I mean these people fear Nigeria. Tell a girl that you are from Nigeria; the first thought that comes to her mind is money. I mean, we have money."

I told this to a British girl who just wanted to be a friend of mine. She said my Nigerian friend was a Male Chauvinist Pig. British girls, she said, went for love. I asked her how I would come into contact with them. She said night-clubs. But before going to these night-clubs, she said, I was to divest myself of some attitudes which, she suspected, were common to most African men. British girls, she said, hated sexism and men who were too proud to show their emotions.

I went to a night-club ready to dance attendance upon my would-be girlfriends and to break into tears once overwhelmed by love. The Empire in Leicester Square was filled on this night with Japanese tourists who danced with their cameras strapped to their necks. At the entrance, a few steps from the cloakroom, couples were kissing passionately. I saw a few black boys — I took them for African — kissing British girls. Soon, I hoped, I was going to join them.

In Africa, people never kiss in public. A woman who allows herself to be kissed in public is said to have loose morals. Everything (moral or immoral) is supposed to be done indoors. But we considered ourselves civilised. At the school I went to, for instance, we used to kiss girls at the back of the hall when films were being shown: and at night after prep, we escorted them to their dormitories and kissed them goodnight, in full view of the junior boys, who, it was said, were "cryptic voyeurs". So if I found myself a girlfriend, there was nothing wrong in kissing her in Oxford Street, for it was admissible in the Western culture of which I considered myself a part.

I asked several girls to dance with me: they refused and walked away. I went back to my British friend and told her that I had tried my best at the Empire to no avail. What was I going to do next?

She said the Empire was not the right place for someone like me (I had presented myself as a poet); that it was full of tourists. She gave me a list of proper clubs. But there was another drawback — my clothes. It is very easy to tell an African man by the clothes he wears: they tend to be bright-coloured and oftentimes baggy. My British friend told me that London girls prefer duller colours. If, however, I was to present myself as a student, then a ragged pair of faded jeans were preferable. My friend is what I later came to be told counted as trendy. I declined her advice and stuck to my checked trousers, bright shirts and bright shoes.

I never gave up the search. One day I saw a beautiful girl who enthralled me. I went to her and said "Hello, have I seen you in Washington before?" She looked startled. "I was actually born there. Where in Washington did you see me?" I began to scratch my head and confessed that I had never been there. That night, I went home and wrote a poem in which I compared her beauty to that of the mighty Victoria Falls. She was to become my girlfriend for over a year. And then we split. I was once again back to square one.

At Amsterdam Station

Kamal Mirawdeli
(Kurdistan)

How nice to be a stranger
In a stranger town, a stranger time,
meeting total strangers!

How beautiful is ignorance, illiteracy,
The lack of language!

Now you can play the game of being a child again

I signal with my fingers to the drink.
— That one. Coke!
Emmm!

Like a child I pull out a handful of change
Put it all on my palm
And stretch my hand to the beautiful lady
Is this enough?

She looks at what is in my hand with excitement
One by one she picks the coins up
Counts them with primitive pleasure
As if she too had turned into a child with me

She picks some very, very tiny bits
She holds a 25 coin as small as a shirt button
With her very, very slim fingers
And breathes in a sigh of relief!

She completes the game with triumph:
Yes, yes, you have enough
In fact, you have a 25 too much

She looks m in the eye and gives me a smile!
She gives me the coke.
I take it.
I am sad the game is over.
She is now busy with another customer.

But I look around.
Thank God. I do not know anyone.
I do not understand anything.
The streets, shops, cafes, telephone boxes, trains
All are new to me
I am a total stranger!

How beautiful to be a total stranger!
How pleasant to be an idiot!
How wonderful to play the game
of being a child again!

Gift

Esmail Kho'i
(Iran)
*Translated by Ahmad Karimi-Hakkak
and Michael C. Beard
London 1990*

This package arrived today, from Iran.

No, there is nothing much in it
what it holds
is hidden in the mood it evokes.

Its cloth wrapper...
stop, don't open it —
smell it, look at it!

Among the stitches of all the balmy scents it emits
there's a stench, half-hidden
that is not of us
    that works against us:

do you smell it,
see it?

The cloth wrapper intends to smell of spring
   and of friends
and of my humble sister's habitual refrain:
   "just a little something — some green herbs!"

Instead, hidden in its folds
it brings the stench of a shroud.

I know, yes I know well
the dried up herbs in the package
with their lasting harvest of cunning fragrances
are harbingers of springtime.

Yet,
these are the ashes of my spring,
ashes smelling of the green lawn.

I just won't open it.
It's no use to me.

When the green herbs are no longer green
the message they carry from the fields, from spring,
is writ upon a yellowed sheet
    crumpled
        by the hands of autumn.

It is scissored to pieces by the censors of the cold wind
until all you can read
is the smell of its drying up.

No, I won't open it.

The cloth of this package
    the package made from this cloth
spring wrapped in a ragged shroud
spring
rags
shroud
camphor
camphor
death
death
ah
when the stench of death
comes from far away
it sets to flight the birds
    of sudden recollections
in the air over my homeland.

She Shall Not be Moved

Shereen Pandit
(South Africa)

I swear, if it hadn't been so late, I'd have done something about it. Or if the previous two number 201 buses hadn't vanished into thin air. Or if it hadn't been so cold. Or if I didn't have Mariam with me, her almost turning blue with the cold. Yes, I would definitely have done something about it, there and then. I would have given him a piece of my mind. And them.

But the thing is, it *was* late, and the buses *hadn't* come for more than an hour. And this being London, it *was* pretty darned cold *and* there was Mariam, shivering next to me. So I was highly pleased, I tell you, when that bus finally pulled up. I paid. That's another thing, it was the last change I had on me and I couldn't afford to get chucked off, could I?

Anyhow, this bus finally comes, I put Mariam up alongside me, while I pay. Then I try to move her along into the bus ahead of me. Only, we can't move. The aisle's blocked by this huge woman, with a pram in the middle of the aisle... She seems to be Somali, from her clothes — long dark dress, hair covered with a veil, like what nuns used to wear, arms covered to the wrists, nothing but face and hands showing. The driver shouts at me to move down the bus, only I can't because of the pram. I'm about to say to him, well get this woman to move out of the way — it's one of those modern buses with a special place for prams — when I see what the problem is.

There are these two women, sitting in those fold-up seats in the pram space. White, fiftyish, wrinkles full of powder and grey roots under the blonde rinse, mouths like dried up prunes, both of them. One of them's wearing a buttoned up cardie like Pauline in East Enders. The other one's wearing a colourless crumpled and none to clean mac of some kind. The big-breasted, big bottomed type. Both looked strong enough in the arm to lift a good few down the pubs every night.

They're sitting right under that notice which says: "Please allow wheelchair users and those with prams priority in using this space". Which means, these two are supposed to get up so the Somali woman can put her pram in the space left when their seats fold up. Only, they're staring hard out of the window, pretending they haven't heard a word of what's going on, and if they did, it's nothing to do with them.

As I said, they didn't look like the kind to tackle unless you wanted a real scene. I wouldn't have put it past the likes of them to use some pretty rough language regardless of whether there were kids around. Me, I don't like exposing Mariam to unpleasantness. So I turn to the driver, who's still yelling down the aisle from behind his glassed-in box. I reckon it's his job to tell the women to move. I mean why should I do his dirty work?

There're two empty seats right opposite the women. They can just move over the aisle. I look hard at them, trying to will them to look around. They finally can't resist looking round to see the havoc they've caused. They're still trying to be nonchalant but you can see this gleam of satisfaction in their eyes, their mouths growing even thinner as they jam their lips grimly together, as if to say: "That'll show you who's boss!"

I take the chance to point the empty seats out to them. Politely. I'm doing as my mum said when I was young, always show them we're better. So, even though I've got a small kid with me, I'm not scrambling to grab the seat. Usually I let Mariam sit down because buses jerking around can be dangerous for kids, especially kids like Mariam, small for her age and skinny to boot. But do these old so-and-sos take the seat I'm pointing out to them? Not likely. They look at me, then look at the seats as if they're a pile of dog dirt I'm offering. Then they mutter something to each other, turn up their noses and stare out the

157

window again, like it's nothing to do with them.

The Somali woman, meantime, has squashed herself tight up against the side of the aisle, just below the stairs. If anyone really wants to, they can squeeze past and go on upstairs. Her face is tight too. Lips set. Eyes blank. Head held high. She looks like a haughty queen. She's done her best to accommodate other passengers by leaving them what inches she can, and now she just shuts off and looks into space.

Through all this, the driver's been yelling on and off. Finally, his door swings open — the glassed-in bit leading into the bus, I mean. Right, I think, here he comes, he's going to make the old witches move. He's not scared of them, big strapping bloke, he doesn't have to be scared of anyone or anything. Besides, he's got right on his side. They can't even complain amongst themselves, let alone to his employers that he's taking sides with the Somali women just because they're both black.

But oh no! He comes at this Somali woman and yells at her that either she folds up the pram or she leaves the bus. He's all over her, leaning right into her face and shouting. I reckon he's going to hit her. I hate violence and I turn Mariam's face away. I don't like her seeing ugliness like this. The Somali woman doesn't give an inch. Except to turn aside disdainfully because this bloke's spit is flying in her face. Pulling her wrapper more closely about her, she says scornfully that she's not doing either. And you can see why not. Her baby's asleep in the pram and she's already got another small one hanging onto her. One hand on the pram, another on the toddler.

Her face is full of contempt for this driver, but her voice isn't rude or loud or anything. Just firm. She's paid, she's got these kids, she's staying put. He shouts and storms. Eventually he gives up and goes back and starts the bus so it jerks and she and the kid and the pram nearly go flying, except for the pram being stuck. Me, I'm totally shocked at his attitude. I'm really building up a head of steam here. If it wasn't for all the stuff I said before, at this stage I really would have given him a go. But he's gone back and there's nothing I can do about him.

I tell the Somali woman to sit down in the empty seat, thinking she can at least hold the small one on her lap and maybe I could steady the pram while Mariam sits next to her. She shakes her head wordlessly. It's like she's used up all her words on the driver. I reckon maybe, in spite of her looking so proud and firm, she's too timid to give the women a go. Maybe she's worried, being black and a foreigner, probably a refugee and all. Maybe she also doesn't like a scene and is already embarrassed enough by the women. Maybe if she'd said something to them directly, I would have backed her. But how could I go and attack them out of the blue, make them move, if she's not saying anything to them?

The two women, deciding that they aren't having enough fun, start a loud conversation with each other about how they're not getting up, no way. Cardie reckons to Mac that "they" — meaning women with prams, or does she mean black women — just pretend "they" want to park the pram and then snatch the seats. "They" want everything their way. Definitely black people this time. And on and on they go. I'm fuming, amongst other things, because Mariam is being subjected to all this racist hogwash. But what's the point in having a go? It'll only lead to a row lasting the whole bus ride and I probably will get chucked off then for stirring. Even if I'm in the right. They can say what they like about anti-racist laws, but I've yet to see them stop people like these two slinging their poison around.

I look at the other passengers in the second half of the bus, past the stairs. All white. No-one's saying anything, no-one's seeing anything, no-one's hearing anything. Not their business. Mariam starts to nudge me and whispers to me to tell the driver to tell the old witches to move. She doesn't call them that, though. Calls them "those two ladies". Ladies my backside.

Mariam's language is polite, but this is a kid with attitude. Got it from me, I guess. I used to be known as a kid with attitude too. They can have our seats, she says loudly. I nod, but say nothing. Mariam decides to go on, so I feel like really nudging her hard, only I don't hold with hurting kids. They are the problem, she says even more loudly. I look at them again, still saying nothing. I'm still thinking that with the Somali woman saying nothing to them and the driver on their side, I'm going to end up outside in the cold with Mariam, minus the fare, if I take them on.

This is what I'm thinking, but not saying to Mariam. Kids, there are things they just don't understand. I mean, Mariam would definitely not get to her dance lesson on time and then she'd be right miffed. And then there's the bus-fare and the fees and the time and everything all wasted.

Mariam glares at the women. She glares at me. I know what she's thinking. How many times have I told her to stand up against wrong-doing. How many times have I pushed her into standing up against bullies at school, whether they're bullying her or someone else. And her only such a small kid for her age.

We try to bring her up thinking about right and wrong. Like how many times have I told her that I'm only living in this miserable country because I'd got into trouble back home, fighting for our rights. There are political posters and slogans all over the house. One of them's got Pastor Niemoller's speech: "First they came for the communists..." and all that. She knows, alright. She knows that I should be speaking up for this Somali woman.

And here I'm saying nothing, doing nothing. Every once in a while, when people get on and mutter about the aisle being blocked, the driver shouts at the Somali woman. She stands there like a rock. Cardie and Mac have restarted their loud conversation about "them" wanting to take everything over. I laugh in their faces and start agreeing loudly with Mariam, but I don't say anything to them. The

160

bus is filling up. At a couple of stops some pretty yobbo looking types get on. You know, tattoos, earrings all over their faces, hair sticking up. The type that I can't afford to get tangled with. I don't fancy a boot in my face. Or in Mariam's. While those two probably watch and cheer. The yobbos just squeeze past the Somali woman. It's a couple of blokes in collars and ties that swear at her before they force a path upstairs, nearly making her let go of the pram and fall. You can't always tell by appearances can you.

Then the bus empties a bit. Another middle-aged woman gets on, about the same age as the two troublemakers. But this one's sort of frailer looking. Now my mum, when we were kids, she'd only have given us what for if we didn't get up and offer our seats to older people. I've still got the habit drilled into me. I don't like Mariam getting up, like I said, in case she falls, so usually I give up my seat. But this time, I sit tight. Mariam gives me a questioning look, then makes to get up for this new old lady, but I pull her down. Call me a reverse racist if you like, but if those white women won't get up for the Somali woman, then I'm not giving my seat or my kid's to one of their kind. No way. I didn't start this.

Now they start a loud conversation about "their" manners. Meaning me. I glare at them and say nothing. I can feel Mariam wriggling with impatience for me to mouth off at them. But I reckon with the driver on their side, even against this poor woman with her pram and her kids, what chance have I got? He'd probably call the police for me, if I gave them lip. And guess whose side the police would be on! So I glare and sit tight. I stare straight ahead, like this old lady standing is nothing to do with me. I can feel my lips tighten with satisfaction at getting back at the other two. See how they feel when it's one of their kind getting a dose of it.

But I'm feeling right small inside. I feel like a real sod. Not only for not standing up for the Somali woman, but for not giving my seat to the old white woman. Plus Mariam starts hassling about getting up for the old woman. I almost blow my top at Mariam. I mean, can't she see what I'm doing? Standing up to them? I pull her down again and glare at her, whispering "No!" fiercely at her as she struggles to stand up and give her seat to the old woman standing.

Then I feel like a right idiot, getting upset at Mariam. The kid's only doing what she's been taught. I make my excuses to Mariam, but she's not taking any notice of me. She doesn't exactly look like she wants to cry, like when she's mad at me, though. Her face is just the same as usual, not swelling up and going red like it always does before she starts to cry, but her eyes have that sad, lost, grief-stricken look. I sit there feeling right helpless. I'm trying to remember where I know that look from.

The bus is coming to a main shopping area, people are walking around with holly-printed plastic bags full of goodies. That makes me remember when Mariam had that look on her face. She had it when she woke up in the night last Christmas and found her Dad stuffing her stocking. I feel sick at the thought of what she's thinking of me. The thing is, what can I do? You can teach kids to stand up against bullies, but sometimes they've got to learn discretion is the better part of valour. I start to explain, but Mariam isn't taking any notice. She looks again at the old woman swaying about on the bus, trying to hold on to prevent herself falling. Then she gives me a look — like I've chucked away her favourite teddy bear.

At last we get to Wood Green and the troublemakers get off, slinging a last few barbs over their shoulders. At that, the Somali woman finally snaps. She lets go of the pram and leans out the doorway and shouts "racists!" after them. They're still hurling abuse at her, as if they were the injured parties, as they disappear into the crowd, everybody staring. But thank god, it's Wood Green and the sea of faces staring interestedly at us is as much black as white.

The Somali woman starts to struggle to turn the pram so she can get off too. I offer to help her, muttering to her that she should report the driver. What's the good of that, she says bitterly. But why do you think he's taking their part, I ask her, because I am truly confused. I mean he's a black man. The black woman is clearly in the right, so, as I said before, he can't get into trouble with the company if he tells the white women to get up or get off.

The Somali woman gives me a long look:

"Because he's a slave," she says. "He is a slave," she repeats loudly through the still open back door of the bus, at the driver collecting fares from passengers boarding at the front. I realise from her attitude that they probably already played it all out, she and the women and the driver, before I got on the bus.

"But me," she says, looking at me hard again, "I am not a slave. I would rather die than be one." Her voice is like granite, hard and unmovable. Every word falls heavy as a stone between us, cuts into me like a diamond.

I feel my face turn red as I take Mariam's hand. All through Mariam's class, that woman's words go round and round in my head. I reckon it's me she's called a slave too, for not sticking up for her. And the thing is, I'm not even mad at her if that's what she's saying. I'm just upset at myself for not doing anything.

And then there's Mariam. People reckon kids forget things quickly. But I know Mariam. All afternoon I sit there watching her. I want to tell her she still shouldn't let people walk all over her, just because they're white, or stronger, or richer, or anything. I don't want her not to stick up for other people if she sees wrong done to them. But I also want to tell her that you can't always do that — you've got to pick your moments. Then I ask myself what's the good of raking it all up again? What's done is done.

After her class, Mariam asks to go to the bagel shop for a hot buttered bagel. This is our usual routine, our little treat. I suggest an extra special treat instead. I take Mariam for a pizza and let her have coke as extra, extra special. She looks puzzled for a moment at all this, but then she's yakking away, back to her usual bouncy self. I reckon there's nothing like a special treat to let kids forget bad memories. Soon she's blowing bubbles into her Coke through her straw. She's got a smear of pizza tomato on her cheek.

So why can't I forget the whole thing? Is it because I imagine a bit of Mariam's look of this afternoon still about her every time she looks at me?

The Circular Nature of All Roads

Nazaneen Rakhshandeh
(Iran)

Why was Holloway Road hollow?
With its barbershops of shortcuts
Holloway express dry cleaners
At a discount too.

When is the time that runs smoothly between other times?

I dodge the depressed and lonely suicider under the
   Archway arch
it's like a tradition between all those who choose not to be,
today white lilies were
attached to the fence
in memory of the one who had dared.

one night,
in a dream;
I was in for some crime
not sure quite what
for hours I paced that cell
the thing was that
the guards were extremely gentle
They kept bringing cups of tea.
Early Grey.

Freedom is that which has a taste
On Holloway Road of Holloway prison.

KissFM with its Marlborough lights
is beating
echoed with the calls of street vendors
selling illegal cigarettes
here's where Holloway and Angel are loosely connected.
Driving through Holloway
smoothly listening to the tune
Filled with that *je ne sais quoi*
On this heavy but unruly road.

A Woman

Saadi Youssef
(Iraq)

How will I drag my feet to her now?
In which land will I see her?
and in which street of what city?
should I ask about her?
— and if I find her house
(let's suppose I do)
will I ring the bell?
How should I answer?
And how will I stare at her face
as I touch the light wine
seeping between her fingers
How should I say hello...
and how will I take the pain of all these years?
Once —
twenty years ago —
in an air-conditioned train
I kissed her all night through...

Flowerheart

Simon Mol
(Cameroon)

I ate its egg, am watching it — The Pheasant.
It reminds me of potentials,
flying across Vistula.
It squeaks, flaps, flies North.
When it returns
a gift is mine;
fragments of Africa...
in images of You.

I Got Drunk at Home Alone Today

Hilton Mendelsohn
(Zimbabwe)

I got drunk at home alone today
After a few weeks of popularity
Like I have never known.
Well perhaps not never
But it's been a while since I have had
A stream of young nubile girls call
And say 'hey bro…
What u doing today'
I even got kissed
and more.
There was one girl,
ordinary.
who I will wipe clean
and place on a pedestal
amongst the gods.
Tell all my friends
how fine she was
and how I could have been in.
I got drunk at home
And remembered how very, very alone
I am here.

Seventeen Lady Teachers and a Professor

Mirza Fehimovic

(Bosnia)

Extract from the novel
Ms Edwards

I got up early, as usual. It was still dark outside. It was pitch dark outside. I could see nothing but an odd tree immersed in the darkness. I didn't see it. I imagined it.

It was dark outside. I think I've said this before. I've hopefully repeated a correct sentence. The ones that I don't trust I don't repeat. If the word *repeat* has been appropriately used and not misspelled. Or misspelt; maybe — mis-spelt? How do the English spell the word?

I knew the window was facing the park, though nothing of the sort was I able to make out. I was just staring into the darkness, imagining a forever-abandoned field as it spread into the distance: a space untouched by humans. Across the space a fierce wind was blowing, a fierce wind and dark too.

In the dark dark space there was a dark dark house.

In the dark dark house there was a dark dark room.

In the dark dark room there was a dark dark corner...

But in the corner at least the newsroom on the screen was brightly lit; the South-East Newsroom as flooded with light like a shiny lab cleared of all obsolete equipment.

Perhaps I'm wrong. Perhaps the place rather gave an impression of a spacious ground-control room at some distant air base where the alarm was about to go off any minute. Perhaps it did give that impression. It was five to seven anyway. She was reading the news.

As ready for the news as ever, I was expecting something or other must have happened. That was what I had been doing all the time. One morning a journalist might say, "The war is over. And on to the travel now."

The newscaster looked as if just a minute ago she had had a shower she enjoyed beyond description. Ms Edwards herself was like that — beyond words. Beyond words are the deities of the omniscient pantheon that could do nothing else but flood you with joy.

So I was watching you, Ms Edwards. I watch the news very often, never missing those at six am, seven am, eight am and one pm... Will there be a TV set at our new address if we were to move house again?

Every morning I'd turn on my wife's friend's TV — my wife's friend's landlord's TV, and then take a bath in the milky light that pervaded the room so effortlessly.

What I found out was that there was nothing as refreshing as the sight of a newscaster early in the morning. I liked the milky light all right, but it was the newscaster who finally proved that the people who wanted to believe they're better off by watching TV than by sleeping were right; the ones who looked forward to watching you smile; who, unlike me, probably felt desperate; who were so keen, Ms Edwards, on seeing your face that hadn't given up yet.

Indeed, the face of a newscaster is more radiant than that of the colonel who's about to address his ranks, "The war's over, folks, and the party starts seven sharp." Even more radiant than the face of the soldier hearing the news. But no matter how radiant it is, I for my part, who have to admit: whenever I felt down, Ms Edwards, I turned on the TV to see you smiling or else I'd take up reading Walt Whitman.

Or I'd go for a brisk walk.
Or indulge in nail-biting.
Or chain-smoke twelve cigarettes.
Or go out running as fast as I could.
Or stand up and then flop down on the floor again, throwing my head back against the wall while sinking into oblivion.

It struck seven o'clock. There was a wall clock above our mantelpiece; our friend's mantelpiece; our friend's landlord's mantelpiece...

It was an old clock the owner was probably proud of. It kept perfect time, too. More than its precision, my wife liked its chimes. It reminded her of her family clock that she had left behind; of her father that she had left behind. Rather sentimental that.

Her family clock survived several generations. I don't know how many the one above the mantelpiece had survived, but its chimes had the same sound as my wife's father's clock. That's why my wife has become so fond of it so quickly.

The clock hung high up on the wall. It looked like a majestic master over all the bric-a-brac on the mantelpiece. Though if I were writing a better book I'd never use the simile. Not that simile, no. Rather pompous that, I think. But my wife would probably like it. Neither sentimentality nor pomposity is my cup of tea. If by using the phrase I'm really telling you Marta's different from me.

Be that as it may, she joined me in the drawing room at five past seven. Marta, that is. She got up, went to the toilet, and came back after some time slowly taking her seat on the floor. That was how the bedroom changed back into our friend's lounge. The three of us slept on the floor, Benjamin, Marta and I. Sara and Hasan were in the bedroom.

While still at Hasan's I realised how good the hard floor was for my spine; the backbone that now, I feel, cracks too often for my age. There was nothing either pompous or sentimental about the floor. It was flat and hard, and that's probably why I don't think I can remember anything else to which I'd taken such an immediate liking.

We were on the floor, ready for the news: I, wearing my friend's striped pyjamas; my friend's landlord's striped pyjamas that the landlord was so generous as to unwittingly leave behind; and next to me was Marta, wearing my friend's wife's night-gown; my friend's landlord's night-gown; my friend's landlord's wife's night-gown that the landlord's wife was either so negligent as to leave behind in the chest of drawers beside the window or so compassionate as to give to Sara to wear. I mean — a wonderful nightgown it was: large, brand-new, with a lovely floral pattern that any homeless or night-gownless person that would happen to have it on would like.

The nightie was actually too large for my wife. That was why the beauty of the scene — her landing on the floor as if she were a gigantic snowflake that somehow didn't get melted once on the ground — had a strange, unreal touch. The graceful touching of the carpet lit by the screen was like a soundless slow motion of a parachutist landing on the ground, her colourful parachute folding all over.

The parachutist kept silent, touching me gently with her palm as if both of us had landed in the midst of the enemy's territory, where any sound could give us away. I acknowledged her arrival and continued staring at the screen. I noticed she was shivering. We both had someone's nightwear on, and in spite of that she was cold. Was she going to cry again?

The temperate sound of water filling the cistern was dying away while I pictured for myself our friends' pale green low level WC, our friend's landlord's WC, dirty and stained, with plastic lid and seat, and a chrome flush, and I wondered if I should ask the landlord to fix it... if I should ask Hasan to ask his landlord to get it fixed.

"I've just been to the toilet," Marta interrupted.

"What?"

More time than I was aware of elapsed before she answered.

"I mean, I didn't realise..."

I expected her to say something. I thought she'd say she was surprised how little of the programme I was able to understand.

"What do you mean you didn't realise?"

"I didn't realise how old I'd got."

173

Whitewashed Houses

Abdirahman Mirreh
(Somalia)

What a pleasure to be
in such a whitewashed city
watching the fishermen
mending the nets.

Standing at the quay from
where the Vikings rowed
their boats through morning
mist.

What a beautiful rainy day
sitting in a bus after the
sunset, the mountains
on the left, the fjords on
the right.

Here comes the spring a
few days early to touch
the trees to awaken the
flower, seeds beneath
the earth.

The Mailed Parcel

Ibrahim Ahmed
(Iraq)
Translated from Arabic by Lily Al-Tai

On that day they did not have any lessons at the language school. They were busy with the domestic chores when the mail-flap clicked. He remarked to his wife that this time they might have dropped through some coupons for flour, and quickly went to find out.

On top of the usual colourful papers he found a dark-coloured parcel. He examined it calmly. He thought it must have been delivered to him by mistake, but discovered that it was addressed to him in vague handwriting as if the sender was not entirely certain of his address. But where had the sender obtained his address from? He remembered, in the camps, he had exchanged addresses with Iraqi refugees, to keep in touch in the course of their long path ahead.

He was about to open it eagerly, but his fingers hesitated at the edges of the parcel; he was suddenly overwhelmed with fear. It occurred to him it might be a parcel bomb. He remembered what he had seen on television a few days ago about an explosion in which a Kurdish woman and her daughter had both been killed by a parcel bomb. What exacerbated his unease, was the fact that the parcel was from abroad with Czech stamps on it and no name of the sender only postmarks and some deletions and scribbles added. So this parcel had been on his trail throughout his wanderings through the camps. It might have been sent to his first address in Sweden. He thought it unlikely for a parcel bomb to pass through all those places undetected. His wife came up to him, prompting him and inquiring:

"What is this?" but he quickly signalled to her cautiously when she was about to pick it up. He distanced

175

her from it saying:

"It might be booby-trapped". She carried on looking at him disconcertedly and said:

"Who are we, for them to send us a parcel bomb?"

He had stopped his political work after they had had a child. When he worked in politics, he had been neither a leader nor a prominent figure. He said:

"And what were the Kurdish woman and her daughter up to when they murdered them with a parcel bomb?" The wife said:

"We have been forsaken to the end of the world." He said, staring at the parcel:

"Sometimes they murder people of lesser significance than ourselves to frighten others!"

He carefully placed the parcel in an empty corner by the door.

For a long time now, they had stopped expecting mail. In Algeria, almost a year after leaving Iraq, their first and only son had drowned at the seaside when they were on an outing. The shock had almost crushed them both. They were frightened of informing their families in Iraq who were attached to the child for when they were leaving, they had asked to keep the child. A cryptic letter had arrived from their families requesting that they did not correspond with them; but they understood. Their families, like others, received their mail from the party headquarters and security bureaus of their districts. Yet they still feared receiving a letter from the family asking about the child.

Their letter to friends abroad were spasmodic and reluctant and had now stopped for they carried no news other than catastrophes, tragedies and misfortunes which they could no longer bear to hear about. They now feared the postman and were scared when he appeared, repeating to each other that they "could no longer handle a letter".

They had had two children in the course of their migration to various countries. They had arrived in Sweden not more than a year ago, anguished by exile. Their savings had dwindled. They had been transported to various refugee camps and were sent to live in a small town by the sea.

In the first week of their arrival, they received a letter with a plastic green key from one of the supermarkets inviting them to collect two hundred and fifty grams of coffee, as a token of hospitality and welcome. It was a successful commercial and humane gesture.

The man held the letter fearlessly, remarking to his wife that no longer was coffee the Arab symbol of hospitality and magnanimity. In the many Arab countries in which they had found themselves, they had been received with annoyance, dejection and meanness. In Algeria, when their child had drowned, the father's spirit and health had been destroyed, and yet they did not renew his teaching contract but asked him instead to vacate the house and country within weeks.

Here they had found security, peace and a carefree life marred only when they saw in each other's eyes, the waves of the sea in the darkness of the nights carrying them to the vortex of that distant past and its devastating nightmares awakening in their hearts the vision of that beautiful child drowning and fading in front on their eyes in the nearby deeps of the sea, while they both stood helplessly looking on.

They busied themselves learning the Swedish language in preparation for work.

Everyday when the man heard the click of the mail-flap, his heart would throb; getting to the front door was like reaching a haunted place at night. But as he often found magazines, supermarket adverts and colourful fliers with attractive offers for food, clothes, cars and castles, mingled every so often with one or two letters from friends or the local authorities, he shook his head and laughed, remarking to his wife

"Perhaps all the junk mail has had one benefit. It has enabled us to hold a letter again."

Up to now, they had found opening letters in this part of

the world an experience that was not frightening. It no longer seemed to them, as it once had, like the opening of a grave. They now felt able to receive letters from their families and to reply to their questions. They did not, however, dwell too much on such hopes since their families had heard nothing from them for some years now. They too did not know what had become of them, or whether their address had changed since the Authorities and the Party still regulated everything.

The man was happy to hear the clicking sound of the metal mail-flap. It sounded like the rustling of two heavy twigs dropping their ripe fruits on the ground. The pictures of commodities and the advertisements with their bright colours and prices, consoled him as it made him feel that there existed a world immersed in benevolence and pleasure, not catastrophe.

But this parcel in the corner seems to him now something else. He approached it imagining that it might explode in the faces of his two children on their return from school. His wife told him to place it on the balcony, but changed her mind when she remembered that it was covered in snow. The man became irritated and said:

"Shall we call the police?" The wife was in a calmer state and replied:

"We will show it to the postman."

But the man thought it horrifying to spend the night with a bomb in the house. The wife sensed this through his anxious glances and unrest and said she wanted to go shopping and that he could accompany her to the post office which was on the way. He decided to risk carrying the parcel. As he walked on the snow, the chill winds penetrating, he feared he might slip and that the parcel would land on him. So he walked slowly, careful not to shape the parcel or collide with one of the pedestrians on the snowy, narrow pavements. He kept a reasonable distance from his wife thinking that at least she should survive for the sake of the two children. With the hand carrying the parcel stretched away from his body, he persuaded himself that the explosion might sever his hand, which would be a reasonable sacrifice, but would not affect the rest of his body.

At the post office, in a mixture of English and Swedish, they spoke to a beautiful girl who sought the advice of one of the officers inside who carefully checked the parcel and said confidently:

"It is perfectly normal and safe." When he saw they were both still apprehensive and looking at him in despair and sadness, he said to them: "Do you wish me to open it?" The man nodded his head hastily. The officer opened the parcel and passed it to the man. The man removed the contents of the parcel and found a letter:

I could find no resting place. I have moved about a great deal. I am now clearing everything to prepare to emigrate to Australia. I did not wish to lose your precious belongings. I am certain that both of you with your two beautiful children look upon the past with strength and courage.

He opened another old and faded envelope. He found between his now trembling hands, a picture of their drowned child and a lock of his hair. The Swedish officer could not understand why this man uttered a loud moan and why the woman broke down in tears. He began to look at them and at this place in which calm and order reigned, as if something had exploded which he had not heard.

The Street I See from My Window

Yang Lian
(China)
Translated by Brian Holton

on the street I see from my window it never rains
it lies by my windowsill
composed and calm as a comb
waiting for a silent woman
flying in from shore like a tired seagull
hands hugging herself as tight as a pebble
on her back in a furry grey satchel
a lemon quietly changing shape

the street I see from my window is white with snow
all winter on the street only
seven stray cats and a man sleeping in an abandoned car
or eight identical pairs of eyes
empty husks, utterly free of resentment
so affectionate I am convinced
they have promised to feed each other with their corpses
and, like a guarantee the gentlest of touching

'Think of Nowhere...'

Abol Froushan
(Iran)

Think of nowhere and you're freed from bounds of place
And think then of your face before inception
and you'll outgrow your name. And then laugh
as thunder witnessing terror in eyes far and wide...

Clouds pass and the rain	
does its work, and all	*man dar sama am*
individual beings	*dar asman am*
flow into their forms	*ab am*
forms	*chun abr*
form	*barun am*
as vapour turns	*man dar ab am*
to a drop and all	*dar sama am*
fall is a confluence	*dar asman*
of forms	*chun abry*
of energy	*barun am*
flowing in the universe	*man dar ab*
Its essence is power	*va asman*
or energy in motion	
(as an emotion)	
Its image is heaven.	I'm in esctasy am
Time is regarded	in the sky am
as the basis of this	water am
motion. Power of	like a cloud
Time and the power of	rain am
persisting in time	I'm in water am
the power to endure	In esctasy am
the strong creative action	In the sky
of the One in the	like a cloud
Universe or the action	'm' rain am

of the creative sage
through his power
the rulers and leaders of men
awaken and develop
their higher nature.

I in water
and sky am

Dog-Walker

Miroslav Jancic
(Bosnia)

After all is said and done
I'm about to apply for a dog-walker post
Advertised in the *Ham and High*;
But let me consult a fellow expatriate first
Who already has experience of the craft.

Well, it's so and so
It depends on the breed of the dog
And his master;
It's also much better
If these kinds of jobs
Are undertaken while one is young
As Rudyard Kipling or Jack London did,
Says the former theatrologist.

But hasn't everything turned upside down,
I argue
No one becomes a celebrity first
And finishes as a part-time waiter or so;
For instance
I have a lot of magisterial works
And to walk somebody's dog
Might round up my fruitful career nicely
In accordance with the alternative culture of the nineties.

What are we waiting for, then?
A friend from Sarajevo urges me
And he is right:
Whilst I had been buying a piece of advice
The post of dog-walker was filled up
Probably by a member of some academy of science.

Isis[1]

Jorge Jimenez
(Colombia)
Translated from Spanish by Erica Lewis

...and the lights play,
whilst an anonymous soul passes by
the cyclops who philosophises to the sightless world
and the salamander who contemplates me with immunity.

The future has already become eternal;
And a tear is a blue dream
A butterfly with broken wings
And one more child disappears in the silence.

The world is susceptible
When a silver halo covers it with its veil
A macabre allegory almost intense,
And hope twisted on the wings of dementia...

A symbol made up of stars,
an eternal labyrinth which I covered with time
a wilted horizon
and the absent boatman to whom I lie.

And magic is unheard of music
And a sigh of perpetual yearning
Crystals are mirrors
In which dumb innocence regards itself.
Absurdity is a certain mystery
And memory a presentiment
To believe in feelings is an uncertain game
And the inert past only a tale...

[1]Isis was an Egyptian goddess who according to mythology,
raised her husband Osiris from the dead and protected her son
Horus.

Poverty

Gulay Yurdal Michaels
(Turkey)

I strung the stars on my prayer beads
I sewed the leaves each to each
Braided the clouds
And hung them down untrimmed
And buttoned up the sorrows
I made life easy
With the poetry of beautiful things
Which never come about easily

Guess Who is Coming to Dinner

Darija Stojnic
(Bosnia)

Rich middle-class English housewives are so easily recognisable. They are in perfect shape, dress mainly in expensive trousers and flat golden shoes, have perfect hair, lightly tanned faces and beautiful nails. They smell expensive, are always polite and smiling, but are incredibly arrogant — a way to rid themselves of their working class origins, I dare to suggest. They do not know what to do with their surplus energy and time. They work steadily more on appearance than on education.

Having refugees for dinner is almost prestigious in the circle of these bored, rich, superficial women. I was delighted to have been invited to one such home. How naive of me.

"Sit, please," my hostess shouted, tapping the seat where she expected me to sit.

"Thank you very much," I replied

"Oh, you speak English," she put on her best smile, as if she was delighted with the discovery.

"A little," I answered politely.

"Your Russian must be very good."

"Why should I speak Russian?" I dared to ask back, and a brief thought went through my mind: 'Oh, help me Lord. I do not have any chance with her.'

"My dear, what was your name?" she asked reassuringly. "As far as I know, all communist countries were under Russia. Am I right?"

"I am so sorry, but we were an independent country. We did not belong to any Eastern or Western bloc, we were..."

"O, my dear," she interrupted me. "We know everything about your country and this dreadful war you have in Czechoslovakia, where you've come from. Don't worry, you are safe now in England."

"Yes, but... not Czech...." I tried. And again: "Not Czechoslovakia." I wanted to say; "I came from former Yugoslavia," but I did not have a chance.

"Have you ever been abroad?" she asked me, with the most emphatic facial expression you can imagine. "London must be a wonderful new experience," she went on.

"I used to travel a lot, and I spent nearly six months in the south-east of England, and in London of course." I replied.

"Oh, did you?" She lost her plot. The disappointed silence was broken by an announcement that dinner was ready.

I entered the most beautiful dinning room I have ever seen. Everything was perfect, from the stunning interior to the crockery, cutlery, the glasses on the table, and of course the remarkable guests. All of them rich, with a perfect image, chatty, full of self-confidence.

I was the only one who was not perfect. I was heartbroken, financially broken, dressed from a charity shop, feeling so uncomfortable, wanting to run away. But how could I? I was a special guest, although I felt more like the main course, invited for dinner as a great honour to show me — and to prove to each other — how much they cared about me. Did they?

My hostess touched me gently and whispered in my ear:

"Are you OK with a knife and fork?" The waves of humiliation swept through me like a thunderstorm, but I managed to use my last vestiges of wit and whispered back: "I'll try not to cut myself."

After this I had enough. I just wanted to faint and lie unconscious on the floor until everything was over. But I was not that lucky. I had to remain fully conscious all the way through dinner.

"Did you go to school down there?"

"Yes, I am a lawyer," I simply said.

"Oh, really?" Then a pause, to deliver a big thought. "Of course, you can be a lawyer here. Can't you?"

"No, I cannot because my English will never be good

enough and the British Law Society does demand..."

"Nonsense, dear. Your English is much better than my Croatian, or whatever the name of it is. But if you do not want be a lawyer, you can always be a nurse. Isn't that a good idea, my dear?" I gathered my strength in a desperate attempt not to say anything.

"Thank you for having me," I said to my hostess on my way out.

"It was a pleasure," she replied, then kissed me goodbye.

I have never ever been invited again.

Thank God.

Exile

Reesom Haile
(Eritrea)

Ethiopian women
Who are gorgeous
And wearing traditional dress
Wait in Cairo airport:
Beirut bound export
For restless lives
Of making beds
And little money.
Go with God, my beauties.
I don't envy you.

Exile Poem of the Gallery

Reza Baraheni

(Iran)

In the *Portrait of Appolinaire*
one eye of the poet is closed like Odin's
the double chin is lifted to one side of the face
the countenance is a moon blinded by its revolution   Yet this
is not what the Middle Eastern poet sees with both eyes
    Chagall has put
Over Vitebsk between the three eyes of the two poets
The year is 1914, when the 19th century ended
and human flight began in Vitebsk

In Rodin's *Adam*, the absence of divine clay hurts the hands
of prehistory   It is black and heavy   God moulding it
in the Age of Iron, with no touch of irony   Instead, you see
the organic unity of Rilke's sonnet to Orpheus   A pity
that Orpheus is not there with Rodin   *Adam*
would have been replaced by Eurydice, the woman in ashes
waving her soft hand, disappearing   Rilke the apprentice,
too timid to suggest it to the master, had to
go to the steppes of Pasternak's Russia and Chagall's
    Vitebsk

"Kiss my lips. She did." Whenever I see these words,

I run, then I fly, not freely, that is for Chagall, but
in a plane, to look down and see as Picasso
did the canvas, and Gertrude suggested that we should see
all his paintings as if looking down from a plane, since the
"war was the composition of cubism." Picasso inherits
The earth from the sky, dividing and blending frontiers
And Blake had said: "To create
a little flower is the labour of ages." This time, Eurydice
descends from the sky to lay her face on the double-mooned
face of the poet in the Gallery's Picasso
"Kiss my lips over and
over and over again she did."

But I am not talking of this flight, and this 1914

First, I have to walk to the biggest hall to wake up my son
sleeping under the legs of the draped female colossus, a
    Henry Moore
"I have feathers/Gentle fishes." And *Aba* Gertrude is my
    mother's title
in heaven Where I am watching a few Picassos in the
Art Gallery of Ontario "In the midst of our happiness
we were very pleased."

He sleeps there, the childhood of a long-haired deity
All around him children re-collapse and re-collect their
turbulent games, with parents and instructors

frenzied to educate them in the ways of stone and flesh
My son's dream is an education   Gallery objects wash him
in ether   He has a half-open, half-kissed moth
His mind gallery crowded with software of arcane material

And stone is a stone is a stone in Mr Moore. *Here* it is,
    copious,
but not to be copied And the game goes on Herculean
arms are needed to unhinge these stones, reclining on their
elbows, knees and buttocks Only a god could give you
a tour of these Moores in the Gallery, by lifting them all
on the tips of his fingers and nursing them by his lips
Male stones of stability cast
in female figures of needless heaviness
each posed, regular or irregular, like a sterile
island of desire, thirsting for passions of hammering rain
Round cavities, peopled by smooth half-shoulder and half-backs,
and single-fingered fists of female nipples, left untouched
    after
the first touch of their master mason Silent homes
of human members, each in search of an antediluvian desert
to live happily ever after with the rush of the sand
and the push of the wind The gigantic magic of curved
slabs rising musically to end in upturned faces
And how hard to say:

"I have feathers. Gentle fishes," in this hall Carry them all into
open air The zoo needs a breath of the forest
"I am waiting here... I'm tired of standing — let us fly
    together"
Chagall must have said these words
watching the uplifted toes of 19th century ballerinas in the
    next hall
"Ton visage ecarlate ton biplan transformable en hydroplan."
Appolinaire must have seen it in *Au-dessus de la ville*, lovers
flying freely over the city in colours, the spine of the woman
openly made pregnant by buttocks lifted by the insanity of art
to the top Two arms and only
three elegant shoes But they are flying and who cares?
I have also seen his *La promenade*, the horizontal beauty in
    the air

The lonely Chagall in the Art Gallery of Ontario has a date
I have gone through valleys of bronze and marble, and all

pastures of faces and lines and eyes and hips, and I have
noticed this: the epitome of my empathy   This: *Over
Vitebsk, 1914*

The crisis reflected in the flight of the doomed and the
    damned
The borders, as always, are closed
the wars are beginning, the pages of exile
are opening before your very nose   And Chagall
places my hat on the old man's head, hands him the cane of
    Oedipus
throws a beggar's sack on the man's bent shoulder
And make him walk in space, over the city of Vitebsk
In Gogol's   *Overcoat.*

We have to change the faces and figures of all coins
all the moneys And change all the flags There remain
Only three things: the epitomes of our empathy: the "Sketch
for *Over Vitebsk, 1914*; "Study for *Over Vitebsk*" and
"*Over Vitebsk,*
1914."   Three things in all three of them: the man in flight;
the schizophrenic gulf under him; and the city split in half:
the non-place of exile century
No one has a country

And the lonely Chagall in the Gallery keeps the exiled poet
    focused,
changing the figures, the notes and the flags
and even languages
Chagall inherits the sky as country
And the sky as language
And the poet looms over the precipice
with a dagger thrust in his throat
with his tongue caught between his teeth
performing the sacred duty
of writing this very poem of exile

1. Quotes are from Gertrude Stein, Marc Chagall and Appolinaire

RETURN

To Kurdistan
Choman Hardi
(Kurdistan)

It's June 2003. The war is over, I'm going home.
There are no direct flights yet
I will go to a bordering country and cross over.

I buy handbags full of little jewellery for my nieces
T-shirts and shorts for my nephews
gold earrings for my sisters in law
nothing for my brothers
two books and a dress for my sister
lipstick, nail varnish, perfume and jewellery
for friends who may remember me from secondary school,
for old neighbours, distant relatives.

My mother packs my bag with her things
her presents weigh 15 kilograms.
As part of preparing for her return
she adds some of her own clothes and a prayer mat.
"A PRAYER MAT?" I shout,
considering how many of them she can get back home
"It's a special one," she says
27 years ago she gave this one to her first daughter
when she got married.

I prepare to go home every day
can't sleep without dreaming of border guards.
I wish I could brings some books back
then I remember all the Kurdish alphabet books
that were torn and trod-on on that border[1]
"You teach your children Kurdish in the west
that is where the problem lies,
you teach your children Kurdish."

I will take the repeated advice
and will not say "to Kurdistan", when asked where I am
going
I will save myself the humiliation of being taken to the
world map
and asked, "Could you show me where that is on the map?
I don't remember having heard of it."

1. Turkish border

To my friend A.

Darija Stojnic
(Bosnia)

For years I knew nothing, nor heard anything about her, yet we were once good friends. I did not know whether she was still in Sarajevo or even whether she was alive. I cannot say that in all these years she had never been in my thoughts, but, as so often happens, I'd think of her for a while and then for some time I'd cease to think of anyone, including her. The people in Sarajevo with whom I was in touch had other things to think of, and it always ended in the same way: remember me to those who still think of me. I do not recall ever having received any answer to my greetings.

So, one Saturday morning, not too early, not too late, so I did not wake her, thinking she would be sitting having coffee. I made myself some, feeling a sense of excitement and happiness. After all, it had been a long time... I rang the number and then... a voice... the same:

"Hello" — I knew it was her.

"Good morning it is me," I said. Silence. I repeated who was calling and added the question:

"Are you pleased to hear from me?"... Silence... And then an outburst:

"Do you know what year it is? Seven years, and not a word from you and if you'd rung me a year ago I'd have put the receiver down, but now I've sorted some things out and it has given me the strength to talk to you. Not a note from you to let me know you've been thinking of me to encourage me, to give me strength to endure the horrible war. Do you know that I was living in the dark because we did not have electricity for four years? Do you know that I did not have a proper bath for four years because we did not have running water? Do you know that I was wounded? Do you know that Sarajevo was forgotten... Do you know all of that?"

Between these cruel sentences I tried to throw in the odd word, I even said sorry, but more in the form of politeness, since, to tell you the truth, I did not feel guilty about anything. Why should I say I'm sorry and for what?

I paid a heavy price for the war in Sarajevo and I am still paying it and I do not feel like apologising to anybody nor do I see what I've done wrong.

Thank God the conversation somehow came to an end.

When I put the receiver down I felt like someone had poured water over me, or rather as if someone had pissed on me. The first thing I thought was why did I do that? I'm just wasting my money, paying to get hurt.

A couple of days passed and I calmed down a bit and gradually came to see things more clearly.

My dear friend was angry and disappointed in me because I had not been in touch with her for all these years. Put like this, she was right. But how was I to tell her without hurting her that this was the first real chance I'd had of getting in touch. How to explain to her that I had had considerable worries while my mother was still alive in Sarajevo. How to tell her that I couldn't think of anyone, because I needed the energy to help me cope with life as a refugee.

Who wants to understand? Alas, there is no room for understanding the simple and decisive fact that she remained and I left.

My friend said to me:

"Did you know that my mother died in the war?" I said honestly:

"No." Then I asked her: "Did you know that my mother died in the war too?" Silence from the other end.

How to tell her that I do not know where my mother's grave was. How to tell her that for four days I did not even know my mother had died, because there was no communication with Sarajevo. Who wants to hear to understand the pain of being unable to help a sick mother or not to be able to be at her bedside till the end? Nobody.

They are deaf, since they probably think that when you are a refugee in London, the bright lights of the city make one's grief for a mother less and that life is so easy and pleasant that one does not spare a thought for the death of those nearest to one. How could they?

Common to the majority of people from Sarajevo, alas is the unity of being divided between: Them and Us, the ones who stayed and the ones who left. The war was terrible, but where is common sense. And this is another division which we refugees feel as a great injustice, which excludes us and we do not understand why, for God's sake. Why?

When I escaped after seven months of the hell of Sarajevo, with a child, penniless with two suitcases, I stood on the sea-front — stinking dirty, hungry, and at my wit's end, at three o'clock in the morning, without any idea where to go. Who wants to hear that? I have to keep quiet since my suffering, compared with those in Sarajevo, seems like a mockery, but I suffered hell. The end of my suffering was London, which seen from the abyss of Sarajevo, seemed like winning the lottery, but for me in everyday, bloody reality, this became yet one more curse to throw at those enemies who have torn our country to pieces. Still today, life is hard, but I have the strength to endure it and have set my son on a road upon which he will not be asked to die for somebody's holy national cause. My son will be a soldier in nobody's army.

Be that as it may. I made my decision. But still cannot, feel, recognise, why and before whom I should be guilty. Am I a traitor? To what? To whom? Because I refused to be a living target and because I was lucky enough to get on a list for evacuation and because my life meant more to me than my property? Was that my crime?

Clearly the neighbours thought it was, since they passed the sentence and carried it out immediately, taking everything from my flat which had made up my life there. What was the sentence? I do not know. I only see how it was carried out. Was it because shells were falling on Sarajevo? Did I send them from London? They fell on my mother, father, family, and friends and on my city. Would the siege of Sarajevo have been less criminal had I stayed there? Alas, no! Why didn't the neighbours mind looting my flat or friends not mind forgetting me and blaming me? Why? All because I left. It is a new crime, not written in law books, but in the hearts of people, yes. Which is worse? One simply cannot say.

Whether the division between Us and Them will remain for ever as a chasm between us, I do not know. I only know that one thing for certain will not happen. We'll never sit in the exclusive "Cellar" in Sarajevo and drink expensive Slovenian wine, nibble cheese from the island off Croatia and discuss our impressions of a performance by the Yugoslav Theatre from Belgrade. That time, when everything was normal has gone for ever. I think our friendship was sincere and valuable, while this evil war was monstrous and ephemeral. Is there any hope for us? I think there must be.

The Next Generation

Reesom Haile

(Eritrea)

Well travelled and knowing many languages,
The next generation arrives
Let's rise to the occasion.
"Welcome, *Vielkomen, Bien Venue, Ben Venuto*!
Let's bathe your tired feet with hot water
And serve the best *injera*[1], vegetables, meat and drink.
Take this warm, white *gabi*[2] to wrap yourself in.
Let's walk the mountains and valleys.
Given to us, we give them to you —
History and culture to read,
A legacy to satisfy your needs
And to share, even with strangers —
On one condition:
Don't give it all away."

1. *injera* = traditional bread
2. *gabi* = traditional blanket/cloak

NEW WORLD ORDER

Incomplete Anthem
Fadhil Assultani
(Iraq)
Translated by the author with thanks to Richard McKane

What will Iraq catch as she travels by sea for a thousand
    years?
Water in the veins? The peals of sons
sinking to the depths of the sea?
The world has returned, and Iraq has not.
No limits appear while she is travelling — what will she
    catch?
Will it be fish swimming in the sea?
Some oysters?
Shoes thrown overboard by people?
Shoes and papers roaming the sea for a thousand years?
The veins of the dead are her nets
our bodies with their necks cut are her fish-hooks.

What will Iraq catch?
An ounce of sand, a basket of Euphrates' water.
On the other bank creatures are sleeping, and life is born.
God is in the mosque and life is between the thighs,
while she travels the sea — what will she catch?
Basra misguided her land, and sold her Negroes.
A world collapses under a shout from the poet
    al-Mutanabbi,
A brick from Caliph al-Ma'moun's ruined house could
    rebuild it again.

Her sons are in the water and sky,
dead and alive who are dying
while she travels the sea.
What will she catch?
A sperm and a piece of clay drifting in the water.
A sperm and a piece of clay longing for life?

From my distant chair I see the dead rising
shaking off their sleeves the dust of graves
as if it were the day of Resurrection.

Have the dead risen
to draw something on the sand
and returned — to sleep?

Return, Iraq! You are not the master of the ship
nor prince of the sea.
There is no tower there,
no dam to keep back the tide.
You are naked like the waves.
There is no cloud to shade the caravan
and no tiny star to look down from your sky
no harbour calling you, and no houri to sing to you.

Everyone has returned
but you have been in the middle of the sea for a thousand
    years.
There is a dress of canes you spread out as a sail
and the wind rolls it up as tiredness envelops you
Are these your hands? Or two wooden boards?
Where did you throw the tower of Babylon?

Which god bought it?
Where did you hang the cities of gold?
On which neck have they become — necklaces?
Where is your first engraving?
Where is your first obelisk?
Where is your beloved Ishtar?
In which bed is she sleeping now,
to give birth to the legendary terrifying beast?

Iraq has come
and Iraq has gone
in her peace and in her war.
The water gulps her down
and the wind plays with her robe — it imagines it is a sail
sometimes, and sometimes it takes a rest
in her heart.
Delusion, delusion
all the times have passed you.
We knew you as a deity and wild beast
a house and a bier.
You were the obelisks high up, and the water-moss from
    Babylon.
A bed of Babylonian water-moss?
A bed of Sumerian stone so as to take rest?
A bed of love because the earth is narrow?
You have the sea, expansive like life
the columns of cities which have departed from you for the
    sea?
Pillows of books which have departed from you for the
    river?
Will your face return again?
Two steps to Astarte
two steps to the kingdom,
will you enter there?
You will reach it and die.

A bed of Babylonian stone?
A bed of obelisks high up?
A stair to go up?
Two steps to an apartment in heaven.
Will you enter it?
You will reach it, and return.

America America

Saadi Youssef
(Iraq)

God save America
My home sweet home!

The French general who raised his tricolor
over Nuqrat al-Salman where I was a prisoner
thirty years ago...
in the middle of that U-turn
that split the back of the Iraqi army,
the general who loved St Emilion wines
called Nuqrat al-Salman a fort...
Of the surface of the earth, generals know only two dimensions:
whatever rises is a fort
whatever spreads is a battlefield.
How ignorant the general was!
But *Libération* was better versed in topography.
The Iraqi boy who conquered her front page
sat carbonised behind a steering wheel
on the Kuwait–Safwan highway
while television cameras
(the booty of the defeated and their identity)
were safe in the truck like a storefront
on rue de Rivoli.
The neutron bomb is highly intelligent,
it distinguishes between
an "I" and an "Identity".

God save America
My home sweet home!

Blues
How long must I walk to Sacramento
How long must I walk to Sacramento
How long will I walk to reach my home
How long will I walk to reach my girl

How long must I walk to Sacramento
For two days, no boat has sailed this stream
two days, two days, two days

Honey, how can I ride?
I know this stream
but, O but, O but, for two days
For two days, no boat has sailed this stream

La L La La L La
La L La La L La
A stranger gets scared
Have no fear dear horse
No fear of the wolves of the wild
No fear, for the land is my land
La L La La L La
La L La La L La
A stranger gets scared

> *God save America*
> *My home sweet home!*

I too love jeans and jazz and *Treasure Island*
and Long John Silver's parrot and the balconies of New
Orleans
I love Mark Twain and the Mississippi steamboats and
Abraham Lincoln's dogs
I love the fields of wheat and corn and the smell of Virginia
tobacco.
But I am not American.
Is that enough for the Phantom pilot to turn me back to the
Stone Age!
I need neither oil, nor America herself, neither the elephant
nor the donkey.
Leave me, pilot, leave my house roofed with palm fronds and
this wooden bridge.
I need neither your Golden Gate nor your skyscrapers.
I need the village not New York.

Why did you come to me from your Nevada desert, soldier armed to the teeth?

Why did you come all the way to distant Basra where fish used to swim by our doorsteps?

Pigs do not forage here.

I only have these water buffaloes lazily chewing on water lilies.

Leave me alone soldier.

Leave me my floating cane hut and my fishing spear.

Leave me my migrating birds and the green plumes.

Take your roaring iron birds and your Tomahawk missiles.
I am not your foe.

I am the one who wades up to the knees in rice paddies.

Leave me to my curse.

I do not need your day of doom.

God save America
My home sweet home!

America
let's exchange gifts.
Take your smuggled cigarettes
and give us potatoes.
Take James Bond's golden pistol
and give us Marilyn Monroe's giggle.
Take the heroin syringe under the tree
and give us vaccines.
Take your blueprints for model penitentiaries
and give us village homes.
Take the books of your missionaries
and give us paper for poems to defame you.
Take what you do not have
and give us what we have.
Take the stripes of your flag
and give us the stars.
Take the Afghani Mujahideen beard
and give us Walt Whitman's beard filled with butterflies.
Take Saddam Hussain

and give us Abraham Lincoln
or give us no one.

Now as I look across the balcony
across the summer sky, the summery summer
Damascus spins, dizzied among television aerials
then it sinks, deeply, in the stones of the forts
                in towers
                in the arabesques of ivory
and sinks, deeply, from Rukn al-Din
then disappears far from the balcony.

And now
I remember trees:
the date palm of our mosque in Basra, at the end of Basra
a bird's beak
a child's secret
a summer feast.
I remember the date palm.
I touch it. I become it, when it falls black without fronds
when a dam fell hewn by lightning.
And I remember the mighty mulberry
when it rumbled, butchered with an axe...
to fill the stream with leaves
and birds
and angels
and green blood.
I remember when pomegranate blossoms covered the sidewalks,
the students were leading the workers' parade...

The trees die
pummelled
dizzied,
not standing, the trees die.

               God save America
               My home sweet home!

We are not hostages, America
and your soldiers are not God's soldiers...
We are the poor ones, ours is the earth of the drowned gods
the gods of bulls
the gods of fires
the gods of sorrows that intertwine clay and blood in a song...
We are the poor, ours is the god of the poor
who emerges out of farmers' ribs
hungry
and bright
and raises heads up high...

America, we are the dead
Let your soldiers come
Whoever kills a man, let him resurrect him
We are the drowned ones, dear lady
We are the drowned
Let the water come

The Terror Scenario

Mogib Hassan
(Yemen)

They are the authors of the myth.
At the same time they are the narrators, the directors and
    the producers of the movie of death.
It is they who wholeheartedly distribute the images
After production and editing.
And at the sales of the movie of death
On the market of fraud and bankruptcy
I apparently am accountable for the bill.

They prepared the theatre of creativity
And as usual they granted the roles to those who humbly
    begged for them.
And they said: "Oh Arabs, your roles are only those of
    extras."
Because they called us the sons of terrorism
While it is they who sow thorns
Near mines in the river of death.

And then the scene of terror starts
Bringing death to people and lovers.
Blood runs over the thresholds
And all spectators are stricken with fear;
Afraid of our Islam.
They forced us to go to the "house of justice" … as they
    screamed:
"That is the real terror, here is the terror!"

In the "house of justice" they are the judges
And I am the criminal.
They are the executioners.
They are the jury, the complainant, the journalists.
And the people screamed: "Hang them high, drag them to their gallows!"
"Hang them high, drag them to their gallows!"
And my picture was disseminated among people as if I were a terrorist.
But they have taken the picture, it is they who designed its frame.
They are the carpenter and the blacksmith.
They have enlarged the picture.
They have established the form, colour and size.
And at the end of the performance, at my execution
They will shout: "Highly esteemed spectators, we will meet again
same time, same place."

The Great Synthesis

Esmail Kho'i
(Iran)

Your Socialsim
      — Comrade East! —
goes for Social Equality,
leaving out Individual Freedom.
That is the problem.

And your individualism
      — Brother West! —
goes for Individual Freedom,
leaving out Social Equality.
that is the problem.

And the solution?
No!
Let us not argue
about the "true" kind of freedom
or "false" versions of equality.
That will not lead
to more of freedom
or more of equality.

The solution is Justice.
Equality freely shared
and Freedom shared equally —
Yes,
justice is the solution.

Thank you, Comrade East!
You have produced the Hydrogen of
                             Equality.
Thank you, Brother West!
You have produced the Oxygen of
  Freedom.

But now, Humanity thirsts
for the pure and purifying water of
                              Justice!
You have, both of you,
prepared the ground
for the great Synthesis.
You have, both of you,
paved the highway
for Humankind to reach
the non-metaphorical, non-metaphysical
                              Heaven
of the Humanity beyond you
on this Earth.

Thank you both.
You have done well.
And it is time,
          therefore,
for both of you
to go to Hell.

213

In Wonderland

Abdulkareem Kasid

(Iraq)

Literal translation by the author and Sara Halub
English version by David Kuhrt

extinct dinosaur
blind bat
frightened rabbit
crawling worm
eagle
(the aged eagle)
cunning fox
evasive serpent
all underway
up Alice's path to wonderland

***

"too late"
the frightened rabbit says
clutching his upside-down clock
on his run through the tunnel

***

fish-man
frog-man
man arriving with shadow
man departing with sun
man going two horned
the man coming with one
all at the same table

***

without magical potion
no fan
or gloves
no broom
or stick
we lengthen or shorten
shorten or lengthen
with no magical potion

***

the white rose
we paint red
the red rose
we paint white
and the roses,
the roses
we cut like heads

***

I'll tell you how mad I am
the tomcat says
and disappears
his laughter lingering in the air

I'll tell you how sad I am
the dog says
wagging its tail joyfully

I'll tell you how tired I am
the snail says
falling asleep again

we'll tell you
we'll tell you
all clamour

silence ... silence
the birds call
silence ... silence
the reptiles call
and for the first time
the first time
there is silence

***

Where is the house to be re-built?
One rat whispers to another
while going to hide

***

always
exultant words
conceal weaknesses
I don't see
always
preaches the wise fox

***

wonderland
all on paper
paper stars paper sky
paper gardens paper birds
paper soldiers paper queen
paper poem paper poet
everything
paper

Part 2

Readers in Exile

Mirza Fehimovic
(Bosnia)

How far are we conditioned by history and politics in our appreciation of poetry: an experience.

We think of the writers in exile as people who fled their country for a very good reason or were expelled from it for no reason at all. There are other types of exile, though. There is the internal exile too. You withdraw from interacting and spend your time locked up voluntarily. Those rare Serbian writers who remained in Belgrade throughout the recent wars in the Balkans while resisting to join the nationalistic euphoria also belong to the writers in exile.

I didn't remain in my hometown Sarajevo during the Serbian siege. I left and became one of the Bosnian writers in exile. I was not banished from Bosnia as the famous Roman poet Ovid was from Rome, for instance. There are also some other differences between Ovid and I but I'll leave that to the audience to figure out. Some of them are quite clear: Ovid was banished from Rome by the Emperor Augustus in the beginning of the first millennium to the Black Sea to live among the Scynthian people. I eventually came to London to live among the British. Ovid's hosts were welcoming and offered him wild fruit and the milk of a mare, the fact shown in the famous painting "Ovid among Scynthians" by the French painter Eugène Delacroix. At that time there was nothing even remotely resembling the welfare state and there were no state benefits for those who arrived. There was nothing like today's seminar either.

Joking apart, even today the writers in exile are in a precarious position. They lose the links with their language and culture that the writing feeds on. If they leave their country they are likely to lose their publishers.

At least for some time. But despite that they can still write. It is different with their readership, though. What is it that you can read with no libraries around, your books left behind the front line?

We read for various reasons and all of them work for us simultaneously. If one feels lonely one might read in search for a companion. One might read in order to get to know oneself better or to stretch and excite one's imagination. All of these reasons are valid. I'd subscribe to what Harold Bloom had to say about reading in his book *What and How to Read*: ultimately, reading has to do with strengthening one's self. But the pleasure of reading has no reason behind it easily put in words. The act of reading, in short, as Borges, the famous Argentinean writer and reader said, is far more refined than even the act of writing.

So if you have no books in your language around what is it that you can read in exile? You can remember what you learned by heart.

Several months into the war in Bosnia and Herzegovina I found myself in Greece. I took no books with me and the only contact that I had with my language and literature was the poems that I knew by heart.

Memorising poetry was intrinsic to the way literature was taught in my country, and I have never regretted it. It was different in kind from learning by rote. You internalise a particular poem until it becomes a part of you. This can prove to be a lifeline for those who spend a long period of time with no access to books and magazines. That is how the plight of readers in exile can be alleviated.

This brings to our mind the so-called oral literature. It is a term in literary criticism for forms of oral art in societies with no recourse to writing. The authors are unknown to us and Homer could have been someone else or more likely, as we believe nowadays, a group of people abiding by the rules of their shared tradition.

Oral tradition is passing on by word of mouth (from person to person and from generation to generation), oral art forms such as poems, songs, chants, and proverbs, often incorporating information of importance for culture and livelihood.

In the region that I come from the oral tradition was very strong and people are still familiar with a huge body of work that is generally known as epic poetry. Like the Ancient Hindus and the Greeks, the South-Slavs, too, have a vast and complex oral heritage. But it was not this kind of literature that I have in mind at the moment. It is the lyrical poetry that I am still able to remember; the poetry that I recited to myself while in Greece on my first leg of what is now a rather long life in exile.

By the way, I recently received an interesting proof that I still, it seems, belong to the oral tradition. I published a book of short stories in London and had it released in one of the Bosnian clubs. There were more than 30 people at the literary evening but hardly anyone wanted to buy my book. I was looking at them, the sign "We belong to the oral culture" clearly visible on their face, their wallets safely kept in their pockets.

The life in exile is rather solitary and reciting to yourself is one of the pleasures that solitude can afford. It is a healing pleasure for which you don't have to spend any money. If you recite in your language it brings you back to your people as well as to yourself. But what would be so peculiar about it in my example?

As you might know the war in my country lasted for almost four years and my town was under siege for almost four years. There are two major forces that bind a community together: language and religion. The people who waged the war were bound together by the same language, or almost the same language, and divided by religion. The language that the Bosnians call Bosnian, Serbs call Serbian, Croats Croatian and Montenegrins Montenegrin are the languages so akin to each other that I have no difficulties in understanding the most refined language nuances as easily as a native English speaker understands anything written in English anywhere in the world. So there are no linguistic obstacles for me when it comes to Croatian or Serbian poetry.

But there might be obstacles that come from the outside, so to speak. It could be that an ideology or tradition conditions the readership so that it is not possible for them to approach the work. A Muslim or a Mormon, who takes polygamy for granted, would find *The Heart of the Matter*, a well-known novel by Graham Greene, puzzling. The dilemmas of the novel's hero they probably would not be able to fully understand.

One's understanding of a poem could be conditioned by the climate one has grown up in. A South-African, though a native English speaker, would probably puzzle over the opening line of the famous poem "The Waste Land" by T.S. Eliot: "April is the cruellest month..." simply because his or her experience of that particular month is altogether different from how it is normally perceived in England.

Finally, the way we read any literary work could be conditioned by politics or its worst extension, war. The obstacle that one might see as the worst of all could be the recent history. Could you really enjoy the poetry of your enemies, especially while they were besieging your hometown?

I'd like to draw your attention to one particular poem. The poem that I have in mind is *A Grey Moment* by a twentieth century Serbian poet Momcilo Nastasijevic. There is no point in turning to the original since hardly anyone here present knows any of the languages that would help him to follow the lines. I've translated the poem for this occasion. It's been said that poetry is what still remains untranslated from the original once the translation is done; it is the intangible stuff that is untranslatable. In spite of that truism I've given it a go and the poem reads as follows in my clumsy translation:

223

A Grey Moment

And all of a sudden everything gets grey,
as if everything is burnt out,
but still living

You who share in the secret,
listen, this enduring heart
sails off against all the horrors

And you, who tread in my footsteps,
who even unaware
embark on this strange journey:

It is grey over there,
the core strikes you with greyness,
grey are the eyes of secrets

And when the trees are dying,
neither the sorrow nor the warning, it's only a dry leaf
that by silence strangely strokes the forehead of the sufferer.

I noticed that, while starting on my life in exile, I found it far easier to enjoy lyrical poetry when it came to Croatian or Serbian literature. A lyric is a short poem that expresses personal feelings. It is unconditioned by history and politics and directly addresses the reader's self.

What we notice about this poem is that the poet addresses its reader as a friend who has joined him on a journey. It is not an ordinary journey, no doubt. One wouldn't find it in All Abroad catalogues.

On the visit to that strange land where everything is grey, burnt out but still living, our guide, the poet, talks to us. He tells us that the region is beyond our everyday experience, and that we are on that path even if we are not aware of the journey. It is the journey to the heart of the matter that has retained some of the features of our world

224

as in those lines of enigmatic beauty — *The core strikes you with greyness/grey are the eyes of secrets*. One starts on that journey in spite of everything — *this enduring heart/sails off against all of the horrors*.

It means that we are on a journey to the beyond and that, despite its horrors that we might foreshadow or go through, there is a reward, if I can use the word, for the experience that attempts to summon up in words one's fate or one's ultimate fulfilment. The last stanza talks about the end of the path we were on along with the poet. What awaits the traveller is a moment when *only a dry leaf/that by silence strangely strokes the forehead of the sufferer*. The last word of the poem, the word *sufferer*, as it is the last one in my translation, simply reveals the journey as human suffering itself, referring thus to everyday experience of both the poet and the reader who joined in on the journey.

I may as well be the only one among Bosnians in exile who finds that this Serbian poet brings one peace and solace. But I haven't chosen it for that reason. I just wanted to ask a question. Poetry has never played a role in international affairs nor would we expect it to do so. But do international affairs play a role in the way we look at the poetry of a particular nation? There is no way we could link a lyrical poem from a century ago to what is happening now "on the ground", to use the parlance of the war reporter. But is the answer for readers in exile always so straightforward? What would a Palestinian have to say if I pushed him or her into an absurd position by asking a question that is a far cry from the poem and its poet I've just mentioned: what if Ariel Sharon is in the business of writing love poetry overnight and only making and executing his military plans in the daytime? Would you be able, while in exile, to appreciate his lines regardless of what he does? Would you be able to appreciate the suicide bomber's message as poetry if it passes the literary test?

A Space for the Self:
Kurdish Women Writers in Exile
Nazand Begikhani
(Kurdistan)

Introduction

Writing in exile among the Kurds dates back to the nineteenth century, with the works of Nali and Haji Qadri Koyi. The first Kurdish newspaper called *Kurdistan* was published in exile, in Cairo in 1898. However, Kurdish exile literature became established only in the late twentieth century. As with other exile literatures, it is the result of political upheaval and the dispersion of intellectuals and writers.

The Kurds are divided between Turkey, Iran, Iraq and Syria. There is also a Kurdish community in the ex-Soviet Union — Armenia, Azerbaijan and Georgia. Because of their claims for recognition of their separate national and cultural identity, and because of the totalitarian politics in the region, Kurds in all parts of Kurdistan are faced with upheaval and dislocation. Kurdish intellectuals constitute a considerable part of the Kurdish migrant population.

The division of Kurdistan is reproduced in the division of Kurdish culture and language. Kurds at home but also in exile use three different scripts: Arabic, Latin and Cyrillic. What is more, because the Kurdish language has been, and still is, forbidden in some countries, many Kurdish writers are alienated from their own language and adopt the language of the state. The theme of exile, in all its dimensions, constitutes the main characteristic of Kurdish literature.

Kurdish Community in Europe

The Kurdish community is dispersed throughout Western Europe. The earliest group started arriving after the Second World War. They were members of prominent

226

families and political refugees. Subsequently, from around 1970, a wave of immigrants from the middle and poorer sections of society followed them. The majority of Kurdish migrants and refugees come from Turkey; the others are Kurds from Iraq, Iran and Syria.

By the 1980s, with the establishment of the fundament-alist regime of Khomeini, the start of the Iran–Iraq war and the intensification of the genocide politics of Saddam Hussein, a wave of intellectuals fled Kurdistan and settled in different parts of Europe. It was in the eighties that Kurdish intellectuals in exile started to set up journals and magazines. Later in the nineties and with the develop-ment of communication technology, they established TV and radio stations, along with extensive use of the internet. Women intellectuals have not been absent from this experience.

I wish to focus on the experience of Kurdish women writers in exile. By writers I mean poets, novelists, journ-alists and academics. My study is based on several in-depth interviews with women settled in the UK, Sweden and Holland. Here I am less concerned with a particular genre or style. Instead, I focus upon their identity as women and as exiles and how these themes are translated into their art. My aim is to offer the readers a fairly comp-rehensive introduction to Kurdish women writing in exile.

Experience: Fleeing and Settlement

In studying these women writers, I found that, apart from Dilsoz Hama, a poetess and activist living in Holland, all had fled their homeland accompanying their partner or family. Although women in Kurdistan are faced with all kinds of political, social and economic oppression, the decision to leave rarely belongs to them. Three of these women had to leave the area under the Iraqi and Iranian regime to settle only with their family in the mountains or in another part of Kurdistan. Later, they moved with their family to Europe. Those who left with their partner were encouraged and took the decision themselves. Two of these women were politically active and working in the opposition camp while the others left Kurdistan not because their life was in danger, but because their family or partner was not safe. However, beside political oppression these women were very aware of gender discrimination in their family and in the wider community.

In a society where women are given very little space to be and to express themselves, these women were alienated and silenced. Although leaving and settling in a new place is a painful experience, almost all the women I talked to felt they had greater freedom, as women and as writers, in exile. However, the oppression of exile is omnipresent in their new life.

These women settled in Europe towards the end of the 80s and the beginning of the 90s. Their age is between twenty-five and thirty-eight. Starting from zero, today they all speak the language of the country they live in. All have finished or are in the process of finishing their studies and some of them have obtained professional status. At the time of the interviews, none of these women were single, they are committed to their family life and two of them have children (one child each).

Although they do not face direct political oppression and they feel less subjected to patriarchal restrictions, these women are faced with the burden of "exile." They feel they are exiled geographically, psychologically and linguistically. Unpublished in their adopted languages, they feel isolated and unrecognised. Although they live in a different country from their own, they all write and publish in Kurdish. Mahabad Qeradaghi and Dilsoz Hama publish in their mother tongue in Kurdistan. As for Choman Hardi,[1] Tishka and Zohra, they started their writing activity and publication in exile. I started writing before exile, but began publishing in the *diaspora*.

Translation is one of the great dilemmas. Alienation is experienced intensely by these women. They feel they belong to two different worlds, totally separate from each other. For the majority of these women, writing in

Kurdish becomes a private project not even mentioned in their CV when it comes to applying for jobs. This experience is lived with lots of pain, for writing represents their only real refuge.

This experience brings with itself existentialist ideas reflected in their life and writing. Mahabad Qeradaghi captures this with eloquence: "exile is a permanent feeling for me... I belong to no place. No time is my time... I take refuge in words in order to find a real sanctuary for myself... living with no identity is exile in itself."

Which Identity?

The question of identity is overwhelming in the discourse of these women. Kurdish women writers are in exile on many counts; while the notion of identity, puts us face to face with the "self", I found these women, including myself, negotiating constantly with the conflicting sense of their "selves". Being a writer or poet, an exiled poet, a woman, Kurdish and a refugee, these are a series of classified identities putting the "self" into an unstable position. Here again when they cannot find any place in the external world, words become salvation and a real space for the management of these conflicting identities. The non-recognition of this space by the external world is a source of pain. We have all grown up in Kurdistan. We have absorbed the Kurdish language and culture that has been forged in that particular space. We carry this way of thinking at our core, we are always having to engage in translation, that great leap from one geographical, psychological and historical space to another place with very different reference points.

Speaking personally, I have a strong feeling of alienation and linguistic isolation. While I struggle to write and publish my research in English or French, I find it difficult to get my poems translated. Translation mutilates my poems. With a lost sound or rhyme or an altered metaphor, there are times when I don't even recognise my own poems. I feel detached from them and everything else around me.

This existential feeling is very much linked to the notion of time and the idea of death. However, the dominance of existential themes in the work of these women does not take the direction of absurdity and indifference. Kurdish women writers in exile are involved in political activities and speak out against totalitarian regimes in the homeland. Most of them are also active as feminists and carry out campaigns against patriarchal hegemony and the injustice it generates. Feminist themes are also present in their work.

Love is another overwhelming theme in the work of these women. Love as ultimate power, as an absolute joy and happiness, as reconciliation with the broken "self" and a real space for being yourself.

Conclusion

In this short presentation, I have focused on the experience of Kurdish women writers in exile. Exile as a geographical space but also as an existential feeling is intensely lived and represented by these women. Torn between different identities and the deep sense of non-belonging, these women suffer from linguistic alienation and non recognition, both in their community for being women and in the host society for being "outsiders". However, they are active on many counts and struggle for change and transformation. Writing for these women is the real form of resistance and the strongest way to "be".

[1]Subsequent to this article, however, Choman Hardi's first English-language collection, *Life for Us*, has been published (Bloodaxe, 2004).

Instead of a CV
Predrag Finci
(Bosnia)

Dear Sir/Madam

I was born somewhere sometime and am still alive and kicking. I was only twenty I was when I left my parents' home, found a small room in the *mahala* and dreamed of never leaving my home town. Than, it all happened...

I am partly dyslectic and my glasses don't help me a lot, probably because they were made in my communist homeland and with them I can see only the bright future. Yes, I was born under the red, red star. And I wandered a lot.

Compared to my mother-in-law I was lucky. She hardly ever travelled, but her house was in Austro-Hungary, in the Kingdom of Yugoslavia, in the Independent State of Croatia, in the Socialistic Republic of Yugoslavia, in the Serb Republic and now it is settled in Bosnia.

After the war had broken out I received an invitation from London University — more a sign of solidarity than academic honour — to be their guest (fellow) for one semester, but I had the feeling that I was going to stay in the UK for much, much longer. I used to travel to many countries; I did not buy much so I had no reason to fear customs. But then I felt a bit uneasy: a smuggler who is smuggling himself.

After a while I started looking for a job. In a local Job Centre they didn't need philosophers, except those of pizza-delivery orientation. I was also thinking — because of Voltaire and Wittgenstein for different reasons — of turning to gardening or to become a night porter, but that definately wasn't my vocation.

So, I ended up at a University once again. *C'est la vie*. I didn't like school, especially languages. I spent all my life in different schools as a pupil, student, assistant, lecturer, professor. I was never eager to travel but I travelled a lot and learned several languages (I speak my Bonglish fluently now). I never liked a so-called "warm current" in philosophy and I became one of a kind. I was temporary in different countries, a temporary refugee, a temporary visiting fellow at Universities. Temporary, temporary, temporary... Luckily enough, life is temporary too. Or so I hope.

References: two people whom I talk about more often than anyone else, although I'm permanently in dispute with them, are Plato and Nietzsche, but they can't provide me with any letter of recommendation. At least, not for the time being. Monsieur Descartes is not of relevance in this matter, for my dictum is: "I am not, therefore I think".

As you certainly know, philosophising is a lonely job. My loneliness is a combination of my individualism and the influence of cheap westerns. As an essayist of successfully unpublished books in English, a foot soldier in a philosophical army with an inclination to desertion, the poet of a long, unwritten poem which is hidden in my essays, a writer who sometimes believes that he would end his days in one of his texts (although aware of the fact that the last text wouldn't be written by me but by my doctor), all my adult life I have been interested in only three questions (of Being, Aesthetics and God), questions I think of not only on my *Philosophishe Weg* from my flat to Tescos but which came to me even in my dreams, and now, after thirty years of reflection I have finally understood those questions. And I hope against hope to find an answer, risking not getting any, but why stop now when I am losing in the game in which there is no winner or loser...

Sincerely yours

Finci from Finchley

PS: As I already mentioned in so many words, of all my other interests, film is possibly the greatest. Some of my favourites, like *The Third Man*, I have seen more then a hundred times and watched it even during turbulent times, when I dreamed of being woken up by a cuckoo-clock, rather than by the cannonades of an ever-promised-and-never-to-materialise Renaissance.

Or, how about Spielberg. Which of his film quotes do I prefer now? One from the Ukrainian Jewish émigré mouse who sings on his way to the US "No cats in America" or the other one, "E T phone Home"? My home? I clearly remember my first lesson in English. I still see it (present simple) or am seeing it (continuous). And it is only Monday today.

Linguistic Exile:
The Case of Beur Writers

Farid Aitsiselmi
(Algeria)

The works of French writers of Algerian immigrant descent focus mainly on their life in France. None of them explicitly describes the migration process which really concerns their parents rather the writers themselves. The generation who were directly involved in the migratory process have written virtually nothing about it because the great majority was brought up in the poverty of colonial North Africa. They did not receive any formal education and often could not read or write in French or Arabic.

For instance, the literary representation of Algerian immigration in France is the work of young authors who in most cases are not, strictly speaking, immigrants. They are Algerian by birth and upbringing and some of them were very young children when their families moved to France, but they have all acquired French citizenship. They are, at least in the literal sense of the word, at home in France.

These descendants of primary migrants from North Africa are also known as "Beur". The use of this term is widespread: the main community radio station which started broadcasting in the eighties is called "Beur FM". However, this term is rejected by some such as Azouz Begag because it has been used with political and ideological aims to refer to them as a separate ethnic group impervious to integration and even more to assimilation into French identity.

> *'Cette standardisation a notamment pu servir des desseins politico-idéologiques visant à les désigner comme réfractaires à l'intégration, voire à l'assimilation à l'identité nationale.'*
> (Begag 1994:75)

The Beur community are very active in the cinema, music and literary field, amongst others. A Beur novel can be defined as a novel which was written by a young person of North African origin who was born or who spent his or her youth in France, and which features Beur characters.

In this essay, I will refer to a number of Beur writers but I will focus on three novels to illustrate three main stages in their quest for a place which they can call home. The first novel, *Le Gone du Chaâba* by Azouz Begag (1986), deals with childhood and the conflicts caused by the transition from home to school. The second stage is the transition from school age to adulthood and exclusion in *Le Thé au Harem d 'Archi Ahmed* by Mehdi Charef (1983). Finally, there is the shock of realising that their home does not lie in their parents' country and the acceptance of their hybrid identity within France, their new home. This requires an earthquake, both physical and cultural, in *Zenzela* by Azouz Begag (1997).

Arabic: Home for the Parents

A linguistic analysis of these novels enables us to see how each generation has used language as the expression of their culture and identity.

In *Le Gone du Chaâba*, the author describes his childhood in a shantytown (called the Chaâba) in a suburb of Lyons in the sixties.

For the main character, little Azouz, home is the Chaâba, a piece of Algeria in the heart of France. Not in terms of its physical geography but certainly in terms of the mental world of its inhabitants who were moulded in the tradition of an Islamic country whose culture they carried with them when settling in France. *Le Gone* is precisely about the battle between these rival cultures fought in the mind of the a little boy, Azouz, in his daily migration between home and school. By going to the French school the child migrates daily between two contiguous but culturally different universes within France.

In the three novels, Arabic is clearly the parents' language. But in *The Chaâba* it is also the language that all the family including the children use to communicate with each other. So for example when the post arrives the father calls Azouz, the little boy to translate the mail into Arabic. When his teacher asks Azouz whether he can understand Arabic, Azouz answers that he always speaks Arabic with his parents.

> *Oui, je parle toujours arabe avec mes parents.*

The language that he speaks at home with his parents is mixed with French words assimilated into his mother tongue, Arabic. Azouz gives us some examples of this language. For example the Arabic word for *allumettes* (matches) is *li zalamite* and for *automobile* (car) the word is *la taumobile* and for *chiffon* (cloth) the word is *le chiffoun*. It's easy and everyone can understand.

> *Savez-vous comment on dit les allumettes chez nous, par exemple? Li zalamite. C'est simple et tout le monde comprend. Et une automobile? la taumobile. Et un chiffon? le chiffoun.*
>
> Le Gone du Chaâba

Although Azouz is proud of his parents' language, he becomes — with his father's encouragement — quickly aware of the importance of French, the language of education, if he is to build his home in France and get anywhere in French society.

He decides that at some point that he will no longer be the Arab of the class and that he must be treated as an equal by the French.

> *A partir d'aujourd'hui, terminé l'Arabe de la classe. Il faut que je traite d'égal à égal avec les Français.*
> Le Gone du Chaâba

He works hard and gets excellent results   but is then immediately rejected by his friends from the Chaâba. He no longer belongs with them because Arabs never get good marks in school and they certainly do not sit in the front row with the French boys.

French: Home for the Second Generation

With time passing, French begins to displace the linguistic heritage of the parents. This is illustrated in Charef's novel.

In *le Thé Mehdi* Charef describes the dead-end existence of a young Beur in his late teens in a working class suburb of Paris. His mother, Malika, is concerned with her son's social situation — he is unemployed and has no qualifications — but more importantly she is worried because he is losing her language and he no longer understands her when she speaks to him in Arabic. She wants him to do his military service in Algeria where he will learn about his country, he will learn his parents' language and he will become a man. Otherwise he will no longer have a country, no roots. He will be lost.

> *Je vais aller au consulat d'Algérie, dit-elle maintenant à son fils, la Malika, en arabe, qu'il viennent te chercher pour t'emmener au service militaire là-bas! Tu apprendras ton pays, la langue de tes parents et tu deviendras un homme... sinon t'auras plus de pays, t'auras plus de racines. Perdu, tu seras perdu.*
> Le Thé

In order to be able to live in their new country and to communicate with their own children, the parents have had to learn French. In *le Thé au Harem*, Mehdi Charef describing the mother says that she speaks French with a funny accent and the gestures of a Neapolitan.

> *Elle parle un mauvais français avec un drôle d'accent et les gestes napolitains en plus.*
> Le Thé

He gives us several examples, for instance when she tries to convince her French neighbour, Josette, who is about to commit suicide not to jump off the balcony:

> *Ya! Chousette, fi pas ça, Chousette et li Stiphane y va pleurer, y va chercher la maman partout ... Je ti li trouve du travail, moi, Chousette, je ti li trouve ... à la cantine de l'école ... serveuse, ti seras! ... Ya Chousette ya Allah a Rabbi ...*
> *Ci une bien place ... Chousette ... ti tranquille à la cantine pour toujours ... et ti seras content, ya Chousette ... si ti pli ... Demain Chousette ... je dimande l'embauche pour toi ... ci une place propre, i bien piyi ... demain!*
> Le Thé

Similarly Begag tells us that his mother spoke French a little with the milkman who used to deliver dairy products to the Chaâba. Everyone would laugh when she spoke French even the milkman to whom he had to translate his mothers' order.

> *Ma mère n'a jamais parlé le français. Si, un peu. Avec le laitier qui venait apporter deux fois par semaine au Chaâba le lait et le beurre. Elle faisait rire tout le monde, même le laitier à qui je devais traduire la commande.*
> Le gone

La Tchatche: Home for the Teenagers
Some Beur teenagers and young adults have created their home in the *banlieue* housing estates. They are no longer able to understand or speak their parents' language and with basic education and little hope for employment they

do not feel at home in mainstream French society. They have created their own language known as la *Langue des cités* or *la Tchatche*.

In Rachid Djaïdani's *Boumkoeur* (1999) the main character, himself a young adult finds it difficult to understand his friend, Grézi, who is only a couple of years younger. "Grézi's generation have invented such a complex dialect that it is impossible to understand."

> *La génération de Grézi a inventé un dialecte si complexe qu'il m'est impossible de le comprendre.*
> Boumkoeur

He describes the language as *an incomprehensible mixture of Gypsy language, Arabic backslang and a bit of French*:

> *Toute sa tchatche n'a dans mes oreilles aucun sens, il y a du gitan, de l'arabe, du verlan et un peu de français.*
> Boumkoeur

In *Le Thé au Harem*, Charef gives us some examples of Verlan, or backslang as used by his main character:

> *"Renoi"* for *Noir* (black) or *"Keubla"* for *Black*, *némo* for *monnaie* (money) *"keufri"* for *fric* (money).

This language started as an identity marker for a group of young people living at the margin of mainstream French society and who were no longer at home in their parents language but did not feel at home either in standard French. It is now used extensively by French youths of all backgrounds in and out of the *banlieues* and is so widespread that a number of books and dictionaries have been written to describe it, among others, *Goudailler*, (1997) Pierre-Adolphe, *et al.*, (1998).

Going back "Home"?
In France, the Beurs feel rejected by Frenchmen because they are *Arabs*. In Boumkoeur, Djaidani tells us that in France "he has always felt humiliated and yet he is French".

La société à ce jour m'a toujours giflé, m'a toujours humilié, pourtant je suis français.
Boumkeur

Some Beurs have tried going back to Algeria which is seen as the place where their roots lay. Algeria is often perceived by the children of primary migrants through the descriptions passed on by their parents who have transmitted to them an idealised land across the Mediterranean Sea.

In *Zenzela* by Begag we follow the protagonist, Farid, in his journeys between the two countries, torn between the two sides of the Mediterranean Sea.

In Algeria, his father is no longer a stranger. He has his place in the community to which he belongs. He becomes "a man" again "someone with friends and a history of his own".

Ici, il était quelqu'un, (in italics in the novel) *avec des amis, une histoire*
Zenzela

His son, Farid, who was brought up in France belongs to the group of *zimmigris* (immigrants) who visit the country during the holidays but who do not really belong there. So within what they presumed was their home country the Beur are also seen as outsiders. While Farid was at the balcony a neighbour calls him the *passer-by.*

Et toi, le passager, descends nous rejoindre…
Zenzela

The shock of feeling foreign in a place which was regarded as home triggers a mental earthquake and reappraisal of his life in France. Farid realises that France is his home. His best friends are called Patrick and Jésus, and he is deeply in love with a French girl, Anna. He has made his choice but he realises that he would have to "erase the hard-disk and open a new life folder".

240

effacer le disque dur...et ouvrir un nouveau fichier de vie.
Zenzela

This sense of exile felt by the Beur is expressed in *Les ANI du Tassili* by Tadjer in which after an unsuccessful attempt to settle in Algeria, the protagonist is thoroughly homesick for France. He remarks: *I'm glad to be leaving "home" so that I can get back "home"*.

Nina Bouraoui deals with what can be considered another stage on the way to integration into French society. In her novel, In *Garçon Manqué,* the tension between the two cultures in her social life are also replicated within the family home because she is the daughter of an Algerian father and a French mother.

In her novel, we can see the evolution in language use from Arabic, clearly the mother tongue of the first generation, to standard French which is Nina's mother tongue since her mother is French. This linguistic sign of integration does not however alleviate the conflict between her father and her mother's culture. At the other extreme to Begag's parents who speak French mixed with Arabic words and have a heavy Algerian accent, Nina's protagonist speaks French mixed with a few Arabic words. This mixed language expresses clearly what she refers to as a fractured identity.

> *Je parle avec des mots d'arabe intégrés à ma langue maternelle. ... J'ai deux passeports. Je n'ai qu'un seul visage apparent. Les Algériens ne me voient pas. Les Français ne me comprennent pas. ...*
>
> *Etre séparée toujours de l'un et de l'autre. Porter une identité de fracture. Se penser en deux parties. A qui je ressemble le plus? Qui a gagné sur moi? Sur ma voix? Sur mon visage? Sur mon corps qui avance? La France ou l'Algérie?*
> Garçon Manqué

Where's Home for the Beurs?
These novels illustrate how the Beur writers express their hybrid identity by the language, but where do they belong?

Nowhere, if we believe Nina Bouraoui. For her the term Beur and Beurette (feminine of Beur) are used to replace terrifying words such as Algerians, Maghrebians, North Africans.

Her generation is neither French nor Algerian. They are a wandering people, nomads, ghost children.

> *On ne pourra plus dire Arabe en France. On dira beur et même beurette. Ça sera politique. Ça évitera de dire des mots terrifiants, Algériens, Maghrébins, Africains du Nord. Tous ces mots que certains Français ne pourront plus prononcer. Beur, C'est ludique. Ça rabaisse bien, aussi. Cette génération, ni vraiment française, ni vraiment algérienne. Ce peuple errant. Ces nomades. Ces enfants fantômes.*
> Garçon Manqué

Nina claims to be indeterminate, unclassifiable.

> *Je suis indéfinie. C'est une guerre contre le monde. Je deviens inclassable. Je ne suis pas assez typée. "tu n'es pas une Arabe comme les autres." Je suis trop typée. "Tu n'es pas française."*
> Garçon Manqué

One cannot speak of physical exile in the case of the Beur writers in the sense that they have not left one country for another but what is striking in their writing is the strong feeling of linguistic exile that they express in the act of writing in a language other than what is considered to be the mother tongue.

In *Garçon Manqué*, Nina Bouraoui cannot resort herself to choose one camp or the other. She eventually makes the decision to remain in the inter-space between her two cultures and to write in French bearing an Arab name.

> *J'écrirai en français en portant un nom arabe. Ce sera une désertion. Mais quel camp devrais-je choisir? Quelle partie de moi brûler?*
> *Ne pas choisir c'est être dans l'errance. Mon visage algérien. Ma voix française.*
> Garçon Manqué

In all their books Beur writers play with language to reinforce this feeling of hybrid identity — French and Algerian and this is immediately apparent from the titles of their novels. Although they all write in French and they are at home in France, the Arabic references in the titles are emblematic of their foreignness and the ambiguity of their status as French writers. For example Begag mixes regional dialect with standard French and Arabic. In his title, *Le Gone du Chaâba,* the word *gone* means a young boy or "a lad" which the dictionary labels as a regional word used in the Lyons area. In fact a lot of French people outside this region would not know this word. In this title Begag signals what he sees as his identity and his home: he is a *gone*, i.e. a lad from Lyons but he is also from the Chaâba which is a piece of Algeria in France. Chaâba is the Arabic name given to the shantytown where Begag's family lived in a suburb of Lyons. Similarly the title of another novel by Begag is *Zenzela* which is an Arabic word meaning earthquake.

Conclusion

As the writers or their protagonists cannot find their place in society, so their books are unclassifiable and cannot find a place on the shelves in French bookshops. These writings can be found under the French literature section, emphasising the citizenship of the writers but in some bookshops they will be stocked under the Maghrebian literature section, emphasising the origin of the writers. Others class them under the Francophone section and other still under a migration section emphasising the transitional characteristics of this literature. Hargreaves (1996) provides arguments for and against each of these labels and suggests that Beur might be the most appropriate classification for the moment but this term is bound to disappear as the writers integrate into French society to find their place in French literature.

...the corpus which has so far been produced, like the word Beur itself, seems more likely to prove a transitional step along the road of incorporation into the mainstream of French cultural production...

Hargreaves

Bibliography

1. Begag, A. (1986) *Le Gone du Chaâba*. Paris: Seuil.
2. Begag, A. (1997) *Zenzela*. Paris: Seuil.
3. Bouraoui, N. (2000) *Garçon Manqué*. Paris: Stock.
4. Charef, M. (1983) *Le Thé au harem d'Archi Ahmed*. Paris: Mercure de France.
5. (1997) Three generations of Francophone North African writers in Exile: Driss Chraïbi, Tahar Ben Jelloun and Mehdi Charef. Houssaine Afoullous. in Coulson, A. (ed) *Exiles and Migrants: Crossing Thresholds in European Culture and Society.* Brighton: Sussex Academic Press pp.144 — 153
6. Djaïdani R. (1999) *Boumkoeur*. Paris, Seuil.
7. Goudailler, J.P. (1997) *Comment tu tchatches! Dictionnaire du français contemporain des cités*. Paris, Maisonneuve.
8. Hargreaves, A.G. (1996) Writers of Maghrebian origin in France: French, Francophone, Maghrebian or Beur? In, Ibnlfassi, L. and N. Hitchcott (eds) *African francophone writing*, Oxford: Berg pp. 33-43.
9. Pierre-Adolphe, P., M. Mamoud, G.Tzanos, (1998) *Tchatche de banlieue* Paris, Mille et une nuits.
10. Tadjer Akli 1984 Les ANI du Tassili *Introduction*

Writing in Africa:
a Costly Undertaking
Sulaiman Addonia
(Eritrea/Ethiopia))

The experience of Steve Biko, the famous South African writer, outlines the difficulties facing contemporary African writers. In defiantly announcing, "I write what I like" in the face of the oppressive apartheid regime, he set the challenge for African writers: prepare to give the ultimate sacrifice of all — yourself.

Biko declared his motto in 1969. His reason was that black South Africans' path to liberation lies in the consciousness of their situation — a goal he vowed to achieve through writing. Having realised the power of his words, the then South African government was determined to thwart his mission. His imprisonment on August 1977 led to his murder inside Pretoria prison cell in September of that same year.

For African writers of the postcolonial period, Biko has been a metaphor for determination towards a cause regardless of what happens next. The challenges facing his 'followers', though, were to become multiple: there is the poverty, widespread across the continent; the African governments themselves; and exile — itself a source of agony for many writers.

Living in a continent where poverty has continued to rise over the past century; witnessing the endless death tolls caused by civil wars, and AIDS, has left many writers wondering whether it is worth pursuing their art. They often question why they should write for people dying, people struggling to feed themselves, and people busy trying to survive the cruelty of life? Under these circumstances, many writers perceive the arts as a luxury rather than a necessity — a point of view which leaves many writers uninspired.

However, there are those who, having witnessed the severity of African daily life, chose to let their work depict the reality of their world. It is this group of writers that attracts the attention of African governments — often tyrannical and oppressive.

But why do these writers endure such grievances for the sake of pursuing their writing? The answer lies in how they define art itself. While most artists seem to think politics is inimical to art in that art is a personal expression, most African writers seem to think otherwise. Aware of the injustices, violence, and victimisation their fellow human being are going through, African writers have made the plight of their people the paramount topic of their work.

Simon Mol, an exiled Cameroonian writer, says: "A writer who finds himself in an environment which is strongly under political influence, to the extent that this impacts on the economy and lives of the people, has a moral obligation to react because writing is a humanistic and dramatic art.

"Being a writer has endowed me with courage and engraved in me a principle to defend the minority and oppressed wherever I find myself."

It is this philosophy that has led him to a life in exile and far away from loved ones and his country Cameroon.

"My work as a reporter for *The Sketch* — an independent weekly newspaper branded as radical — has attracted anger from the authorities. The authorities would be so hostile to us that at certain points the main office would be closed for an entire week following a particular publication. They have driven us away."

Simon Mol is not alone. There are other writers who have suffered the wrath of African governments and were either murdered or exiled. Among them are some of the greatest African writing such as Chinua Achebe, Ngugi Wa Thiong'o, Niyi Osundare and Ken Saro-Wiwa.

Dr Kwadwo Osei-Nyame, a literary critic and lecturer of African Literature at the School of Oriental and African

Studies (SOAS), London, has no doubt that the environment under which African writers operate has left its toll on their writing.

"Writing, being part of the current state of the writer's mind, is bound to be affected by the circumstances under which African writers carry out their work." Dr Osei-Nyame explains.

"Certainly, African writers are dissatisfied with their society, and their writing reflects this. At home, as a consequence of poverty, they see the collapse of publishing houses, which means fewer publications. They also face political repression."

Exile has been an alternative home for many African writers. But to many it is questionable whether it stimulates their writing. According to Dr Osei-Nyame, exile may emotionally drain African writers. "Exile itself is paved with difficulties for writers, they face tremendous disadvantages such as racism, marginalisation, and isolation from their own society and audiences. Exile then, although it provides a safe place for writers, does not necessarily positively affect, say, their productivity."

AE (not his real name), a writer from Eritrea now living in the UK, agrees and says that at times he is close to giving up writing altogether. "What makes me feel in such a way is the fact that having escaped all these obstacles at home, I have to face new obstacles here in exile.

"Everything is different here. At times I miss my family and at times I struggle to feed my stomach with bread or my mind with ideas. I chose to be a writer, but yet I am in pain every time I take my pen to write. I wonder why I must endure the same s*** over and over again."

Simon Mol takes the opposite view and explains that, being in exile has enriched his potential and has benefited him in terms of experience. He remarks: "I know it is difficult to be an African writer. At home, you are in an environment where you are made accountable for every single word that falls from your lip and pen. When forced into exile, you suffer its many unpleasant experiences."

"Yes, I face these difficulties as many African writers do, but I don't feel anger."

He adds that his writing has improved. He attributes his progress to the multiple experiences and the effect these have had on him. Whether negative or positive, they have meant he could learn from them and enrich his creativity with ideas. "A writer develops in the course of his life both as a result of his experience and writing".

One question remains: "what if"? What if African writers were free from political constraints, free from economic poverty, their continent and their people free from all these murderous diseases — would we have seen a different African Literature to that which exists today?

When Steve Biko started to write articles under the title "I write what I like", he knew he was leading the movement for a free South Africa, but what he did not know was that he was also to become the symbol for those who chose to write in the continent. He paid with his life to convey what he knew best and many African writers were to follow suit. They too were to endure many sacrifices just to write what they wanted. Some were executed, some imprisoned, some exiled, but above all they continued to write.

Living in Exile

Mahdad Majdian

(Iran)

It is difficult but rewarding to open yourself up to
understanding and receiving what lies there for you: bite
the apple of truth! It is extremely hard to live in a different
place where you lose access to your points of reference,
your values, and your codes and to whatever makes you
feel real and stable. However, it is rewarding to break
down your prejudices to come to terms with the reality of
the present, to stop judging and to start listening, seeing,
touching, for then you can compare your new perspectives
with your past and understand your real self and values
with no need for disguise.

Poetry is a way of achieving three things. The first is to
capture the sense of the present which automatically
brings you into the realm of the present. Living in the
present means living with reality, which means having
concentration and direction: to touch life. It is through
creating poetry that you come to terms with your past in a
controlled manner, it is a way of exploring your past,
acknowledging your failures, your sufferings, your break-
downs, in a way that will not cause further trauma. In
confronting the pain, you will instantly discover the cure.
This is about discovering yourself. Lastly, writing poetry is
a way of exploring life, planning the future, learning about
how to categorise elements of life and overcoming the
feeling of being lost. We human beings live in a wave and
so we cannot help the overwhelming fall every now and
again. But we can equip ourselves with tools and
procedures that facilitate our climbing back, to enable us
to rise up and enjoy once more the excitement of being.
This can be viewed as a need for constant rebirth and is
the essence of the development of human beings. This is
another interpretation of the famous saying "Process

counts and not the end result" so process is what changes us, what gives us an opportunity to develop, to distance ourself from prejudice and from being judgmental.

People that come to this cosmopolitan society from so many countries, cultures and faiths, have a Utopia in mind and they are sure to be disappointed by what they come across, what they see. But that is the point: it is these concepts of Utopia that will finally get us to the real Utopia. So keep up your Utopias, write them, express them and spread them. What medium is stronger than poetry?

Breaking the Silence of the Soul: Issues Raised by an Anthology of Turkish Speaking Women's Writing in London

Aydin Mehmet Ali
(Cyprus)

Introduction

The anthology of Turkish Speaking (TS) women's writing is the culmination of shared experiences of Turkish Speaking women living in London. It gained momentum with the Short Story and Poetry Competition for TS women organised under the auspices of FATAL (For the Advancement of Turkish-speakers Art and Literature). The anthology reflects and embraces many of the issues of claiming, reclaiming, recreating and being part of a communal memory for TS women. It is also part of our resistance to the status quo. The background to the anthology, the context within which women are writing as well as the social and literary issues it raises will be explored.

Background

TS occupy a special position within a language community which is made invisible in British society. I have dealt with these issues of invisibility and the impact of racism on the communities for the last twenty-three years as a community activist in a number of publications and conferences (*Mehmet Ali*, 2001a; 1985; 1986/1987; 1989). The invisibility of the communities is a direct consequent of the British assimilationist and integrationist policies on race and culture and their impact on the lives of the Black and Bilingual communities.

The TS communities have a presence in Britain of over fifty years which began in the 1950s. Migration on a smaller scale still continues. Although accurate statistics are not available an estimated one hundred and fifty thousand to one hundred and eighty thousand Turkish speakers may be living in London. The major population movements for the different TS communities were as follows: Cypriots arrived primarily in the mid-1950s and early 1960s, Turkish people in the late 1970s and early 1980s and the Kurdish communities in the mid-1990s although some came in the late 1980s (Mehmet Ali, 2001b; Kucukcan, 1997). Despite the high visibility of the communities in certain parts of London and in certain areas of employment such as the kebab shops, restaurants, supermarkets or association with certain criminal activities such as the trade in drugs and in women from the ex-Eastern European countries, the communities are made invisible within British society. And within that invisibility women occupy a special place. In political and community organisations women are not visible, are marginalised and not present on management committees. Very few women are known in their own right, mostly being referred to as someone's mother, wife or daughter. The low educational achievement levels in the TS communities (Mehmet Ali, 2001c) and other factors impact on the needs and aspirations of women. Service delivery authorities rarely are able to work directly with women.

TS women are also central to absorbing the pain and trauma of living in racist societies. Racist attacks on the husband at work or on her children at school or in hospitals are absorbed by her compounded by the isolation she may feel of living in Britain (Mehmet Ali, 2001c). She is also controlled through "honour" codes, as the "honour" of TS society is channelled through women. Although the individual positions of women vary and may be determined by their class and educational background or whether they belong to the Cypriot, Turkish or Kurdish communities or whether they are first or third generation women, certain issues such as domestic violence and racism are common concerns. No matter how articulate you may be in English or how well you may have adapted to British society or your level of professionalism, as a TS woman you will have to deal with racism and its impact on your everyday life.

Turkish Speaking Women and Writing

I became interested in TS women writing in 1985 when a group of us organised a conference for women. We asked them to bring something they had created to be exhibited on the walls of the conference. While some women brought handicrafts a seventy year-old Cypriot woman brought her poetry and performed it for the one hundred and fifty participants. She was followed by her grand-daughter of twelve who had won a prize for her poem at school. However, one of the most moving moments at the conference emerged when an eighteen year old young woman was talking about her experience as a victim of domestic violence. She described how she had left her husband's house and had gone to the hospital, where one of our members (TS women's group) was working, to seek refuge. She held a ten-day-old baby in her arms and a plastic bag containing all her belongings. She had run away. We found her a refuge. The mechanism of gossip, very prevalent in the TS communities, went into overdrive focusing on the *namus* (honour) not only of the family concerned but also of the communities. Messages went back to her village, in a remote part of Turkey, that she had become a prostitute and was now in a brothel. And as women who had placed her in the "brothel", we were also prostitutes and a danger to the TS communities in London. Although threats were made against us and the mosque tried to mobilise people against us, fortunately for us, it failed because we were well known in the communities as community activists with a long record of responding to the needs of people and helping to defend and claim their rights.

Her mother came to Britain and discovered the truth. She was at the conference listening to her daughter telling her story. The young woman was the first TS woman we persuaded to tell her story of domestic violence publicly and to demonstrate that she was able take action to change it. She had the whole conference in tears as she touched the lives of many women there. When her daughter finished, the mother told us she was poor and could not offer us money or a present to express her gratitude for taking care of her daughter and being there when she needed someone in this strange land, London. She wanted us to accept her gift which turned out to be an epic poem, a "lament", about the story of her daughter. She "sang" about how she had raised her daughter after the death of her husband, how she loved and cherished her and married her to the young man and entrusted her to his family, how she longed for her and missed her when she left for London. She cursed "fate" for what it had brought her and her daughter and how heart broken she was when she learnt that she was tortured and beaten up. She could not read or write but had created a poem for us.

These early experiences were the first signals that all sorts of women were creating poetry in London whether in a written form or not and irrespective of the cultural settings within which they were operating. Despite the fragmentation of lives, social networks, structures and cultures women were able to maintain, transfer and recreate in new settings mechanisms of personal survival.

In 1987, I became more involved in poetry when I organised a number of bilingual and trilingual poetry readings including some for TS women and Cypriot-Turkish and Cypriot-Greek women.

For many of the women I have since met, I discovered that writing is about survival. When asked, they tell you they write to keep sane. This has an impact on the way that the work can be performed or made public and selected for inclusion in publications. They write to remember, to re-shape, to redefine, to make sense of their past as some came as refugees and escapees of wars. Some write to make sense of their present situation to come to terms with their changed and destroyed social positions. Some may have been teachers, trade unionists, writers, intellectuals or in other professional fields but in London, having to work in sweat-shops, factories, restaurants or supermarkets and suffering humiliation. Through their writing they try to look at a different future; they try to imagine one. Some are seeking or creating new identities. They fictionalise life, making sense of it and accepting it. Just as the writing of African-Caribbean women and that of other Black women, history and culture are central pre-occupations for women living and writing in London. These reasons for writing echo the definitions of the role of feminist criticism by providing,

> "... a clue to how we live, how we have been living, how we have been led to imagine ourselves, how our language has trapped as well as liberated us, how the very act of naming has been till now a male prerogative, and how we can begin to see and name — and therefore live — afresh."
> Rich

Some of the women included in the anthology are well-educated, possessing degrees or doing post graduate research while others are primary school graduates. Some are professionals, others are workers in factories, restaurants, shops and supermarkets. They are first, second and third generation. Some are refugees, others lesbians sharing their work with other women. Some women write in Turkish, others in English; some experiment with both languages.

The other misconception in our communities is that women's writing is dismissed as only being concerned with "love" and therefore not "serious". So not only does white British society dismiss and make us invisible but in our own societies our writing is marginalised. Women write about love and about racism, longing for "home" and belonging, people and lives left behind or lost forever, desire for a different life, gay and lesbian relationships, sexuality, religion, *namus*. We write about politics and how it impacts on our lives both in Britain and "back home". We write about social issues about violence and just as in other communities, domestic violence.

255

Just to illustrate how one woman writer challenges and sabotages some of the taboo subjects ruling her life such as the Muslim religion and sex, can be demonstrated in the following unedited excerpt written in the form of a diary:

2 February

9 stone and feeling groggy and fat.

After the festivities my father came up to me and pulled a long face. "It is time you were married."

I hackled somewhat, then went into the bath and vomited. Then I went an pressed my top and tried to gauge what century it was. "I don't want to marry." Although nearly twenty-one.

Been invited to a party but can't go because I would get a reputation. Bad for a girl to get a certain notoriety. A Muslim girl does not drink, does not smoke, in fact she does not do much. I smoke secretly. If I get cancer I'll be found out. I drink as well, I don't indulge much but then I do occasionally. I don't have sex.

February 3

Time is 9 o'clock. 10 cigarettes (good) 0 sex (good) alcohol 2 glasses (fine).

Been invited to this party and I can't go. I think the reason being is that it's an all night party and of course I might get laid ... I tie my headscarf closer and go out. I hate everyone and everything and there is nothing I can do to change it.

I could fall in love and marry that would be nice. I look a cross between a bird and a sensible man's pain. So who would marry me?

I have been trying to write a novel but can't get beyond the first few pages. Being a painter is what I want to be. I was always good at Art. Some outlet but parents won't allow it.

256

The image is very important and it is blasphemy to paint nudes and see nudes and give them an image. My friend Jenny says Muslims are so original and pure and she wishes that she was as pure as us!

She does not know what she is talking about. I know: why don't we swap places, she could pretend for a night that she is me. ...
Fatma Durmush

In an understated the piece sabotages way a number of taboos in the TS communities such as an unmarried woman of twenty-one stating that she wants to be laid, wanting to go to a party without her family; both unacceptable and contrary to the behaviour of a *namuslu* (respectable) young woman.

My work has also been described as breaking taboos and, not only in the TSCs, by dealing with subjects such as gay relationships, suicide and domestic violence. One of my stories dealing with a gay relationship in the Cypriot communities has been recently published having been selected as one of the winners of the New London Writers Competition organised by London Arts (Arcadia, 2003). Others have appeared in another anthology of refugee and exiled women's writing (Langer, 2002).

The Place of Poetry
Poetry is the preferred genre of literature in the TS communities. Its popularity may be linked to the oral traditions in the "home" communities. Both men and women write poetry. The "machoest" of men can write poetry without losing credibility and may be considered desirable, possibly as a measure of "sensitivity". This is in contrast to men who may be labelled "sissies" for writing poetry in Britain. However, a gender difference seems to exist amongst published and those regarded as leading poets. While in Turkey the world of poetry is dominated by men, in Cyprus, the most original voices and leading poets are women. Anthologies in Turkey barely include five or

six women while approximately half of those included in Cypriot anthologies are women (Kurdakul, 1986; Behramoglu, (1987); Yasin, (1994); Northern Cyprus National Ministry of Education and Culture (1989); Karaalioglu, (1983); Fuat, (1986). What is quite clear is that women are more challenging in poetry alongside some gay poets, in tackling taboos around the Muslim religion, spirituality, eroticism and questioning social relations.

Poetry has high visibility in the lives of the TS communities. Daily newspapers and many magazines publish poetry alongside magazines devoted to it. Many events are inaugurated, celebrated through poetry. Competitions throughout the years of schooling and beyond also ensure poetry a special place in the lives of the TS communities. While poetry may be used to bolster existing power relations and maintain the status quo, it is also the most common form of questioning, resisting and undermining it.

In Britain there is very little awareness and appreciation of the special position of poetry in the lives of the TSCs. Some recent attempts such as the inclusion of UK based TS poets in *Mother Tongues*, the journal of Modern Poetry in Translation and the special edition of *Agenda* poetry magazine dedicated to Turkish poetry have been welcomed. I played a significant role in both of these ventures by translating and ensuring the inclusion of women poets.

Another characteristic of women who write is that they hide their work. When I ask to see it, having heard from others that they write, they rummage through cupboards, draws, books, purses, pockets to unearth and bring out samples of their work. The "famous" TS poets in Britain are male. Much more able to promote themselves and thus make a statement that it is their right to be writing poetry more than women. Poetry and being a poet is serious business and needs dedication and single mindedness and thus assumed to be men's business. These assumptions which undervalue and marginalise women's creativity are but reflections of societal views. It may be absurd to make such a comparison but, while women may cook, men are the chefs. Just as women may write poetry but men are the poets. Thus poetry becomes masculinised.

FATAL: Short Story and Poetry Competition for Women

In 1996 I organised the first short story and poetry competition for TS women in London under the auspices of FATAL, a group I set up in 1987 to advance the arts and literature amongst Turkish speakers in Britain. Our aim was to encourage more writing by women and flush out those who were writing. We ran the competition for three years. We had a good response which was evidence that women were writing and producing good quality and varied work. The competition gave us the opportunity to give women's writing high visibility in the TS communities by establishing links with book-shops (both Turkish and English), the local Turkish language radio and newspapers and even local restaurants who supported the venture by giving prizes. We encouraged the winners to read and talk about their work on the radio while we arranged for it to be published in the local press. We wanted to encourage other women to write but also to share their work.

In 1998 we added a section for fourteen to seventeen year-olds as there was a demand to participate; previously the competition was limited to women aged eighteen and above. In addition, creative writing workshops were set up to help women improve their writing skills, confidence building through the sharing of work, empowerment and to highlight the value of creative writing. A number of issues emerged which needed to be negotiated with the women including what was the "correct" language, "Cypriot or Istanbul Turkish", were there "correct/ proper" ways of expression, what needed to be "corrected" and why?

Issues Raised by the Anthology

I could have chosen to do the anthology on my own but decided to involve a group of women in the process. My starting point as an adult educator committed to the approaches of empowerment inspired by amongst others, Paulo Freire, were central to that decision. The group of women includes award winners and judges of the competitions. Some of the issues we are dealing with are as follows:

- ❖ should the work be bilingual and be published in the language it was produced
- ❖ should the work originally written in Turkish be translated into English as the book will be published in Britain
- ❖ should it include work from across generations and different age groups
- ❖ should the book include controversial work from refugees and political asylum seekers, some of whom may be Kurdish, which may fall foul of the official circles in Turkey
- ❖ should the work include writing from lesbian women or on gay and lesbian relations which are taboo subjects in our communities
- ❖ how do we create cross-cultural access to the work
- ❖ how do we prevent the ghettoisation of TS women's writing
- ❖ should we restrict the genre of work to be included
- ❖ how do we decide on quality
- ❖ how do we select the work of women

Most of the time we are aware of the need to be inclusive and not to impose definitions. Rukhsana Ahmad's paper on Feminists or Traditionalists: *Women Writers and the Urdu Literary Canon* (1999) is a good reminder not to force definitions of feminism on women who seem to be doing extra-ordinary things. In the group there are those who define themselves as feminists while others do not.

We feel that the work of the women will reflect the definitions of themselves and their life philosophies. We are also aware that the reconstruction of women's history has been a central concern for contemporary feminism and that studies of women's writing have played a vital role in that process (Frith, 1997).

In putting the anthology together one of the major issues we face is lack of funding. Within our own communities our individual efforts are not taken seriously and when we approach British funding bodies we face marginalisation. We are treated as though we are "Turkish delights" until we assert our vision of what we want and how we want it. Our wish to produce a bilingual anthology has caused problems as British society has never accepted bilingualism as the norm and repeated policies have denied the cultures and languages of the communities. These find their way into the processes of the funding bodies who insist that the work is in English. When we submitted an application for funding two years ago and asked assistance in ensuring that it was appropriate, it was denied. Funding authorities seem to have pet projects which they support over a number of years. Cuts in local authority funding and other agencies have diminished further the chances of publishing from local bilingual communities.

Conclusion
Inevitably the anthology will challenge the domination of men in literature in the TS communities in Britain. It will also contribute to the establishment of other languages as representatives of British literary life. Another question is how will the literature created in London impact on the literatures of Turkey and Cyprus, the literatures we have come from. And how do we contribute to the literatures of Britain?

Technical issues such as marketing, distribution and editing are also of concern. It would also be useful to experiment with other bilingual communities and with other arts, theatre, mime, music in that cross-cultural presentation. We also realise that we are the first in working on such an anthology in our communities. We hope that we help to break the silences of the soul of so many of our women by breaking our own silence.

Bibliography

1. Behramoglu, A. (1987), *Son Yuzyil Buyuk Turk Siiri Antholojisi (The Great Turkish Poetry Anthology of the Last Hundred Years)*. Istanbul, Sosyal Yayinlar.
2. *Diaspora City*, The London New Writing Anthology (2003), London, Arcadia Books.
3. Frith, G. (1997), 'Women, Writing and Language: Making the Silences Speak'. In Robinson, V. and Richardson, D. (eds.)(1997*, Introducing Women's Studies* (second edition). Basingstoke and London, MacMillan Press.
4. Fuat, M. (1986), *Cagdas Turk Siiri Antholojisi (Anthology of Contemporary Turkish Poetry)*. Istanbul, Adam Yayinlari.
5. Karaalioglu, S. K. (1983), *Cagdas Turk Siir Antholojisi (Anthology of Contemporary Turkish Poetry)*. Istanbul, Inkilap ve Aka Basimevi.
6. Kucukcan, T. (1996), *The Politics of Ethnicity, Identity and Religion amongst Turks in London*. Unpublished PhD. University of Warwick.
7. Kurdakul, S. (1986), *Cagdas Turk Edebiyati (Contemporary Turkish Literature)*, Vol. 1 and 2. Istanbul, Broy Yayinlari.
8. Langer, J. (2002), *Crossing the Border*. Nottingham, Five Leaves Publications.
9. Mehmet Ali, A. (1985), 'Why are we Wasted?' *Multi-Ethnic Education Review*. Vol. No.1. London, ILEA. pp.7-12
10. Mehmet Ali, A. (1986/1987), 'Language and Language Education: a critique of the Swann Report'. *Language Issues: Journal of NATESLA*. Vol.1. No.2. pp. 37-40.
11. Mehmet Ali, A. (1989), *The Turkish Community in Britain — some comments and observations on the immigration patterns, and legal and social position*. *Language Issues, Journal of NATESLA*. Vol.3. No.1. pp. 19-23.
12. Mehmet Ali, A. (2001a), *Turkish Speaking Communities & Education — no delight*. London, FATAL publications.
13. Mehmet Ali, A. (2001b), The *Migration of the Turkish Speaking Communities to the UK* in *Turkish Speaking Communities & Education — no delight*. London, FATAL publications.

14. Mehmet Ali, A. (2001c), *More than one Turkish Speaking Woman* in *Turkish Speaking Communities & Education — no delight*. London, FATAL publications.
15. Northern Cyprus National Ministry of Education and Culture (1989), *Turkish Cypriot Literature — from the beginning to today* — Nicosia, National Ministry of Education and Culture Publications
16. Rich, A. (1971), *When We Dead Awaken: writing as revision*. In Rich, A. *On Lies, Secrets and Silence: Selected prose 1966-1978*. London, Virago.
17. Weissbort, D. (ed.) (2001), *Mother Tongues*, Modern Poetry in Translation, No.17. London, King's College.
18. Yasin, M. (1994), *Kibrisliturk Siiri Antholojisi (The Anthology of Cypriotturkish Poetry)*. Istanbul, Yapi Kredi Yayinlari.

Exile, the Third Zone of Literature
Reza Baraheni
(Iran)

A brief introduction

The major characteristic of literary theory in our time is probably its leadership crisis. Although theory had faced many crises in the past, the new crisis is perhaps fundamentally different from the old ones. Not only novel phenomena have appeared in the arena, but also new factors and participation agents have been added to the crucible of theory. Burning debates on theory draw commentary, deconstructionist objection in the form of participation and presence, and evaluation from cultures subjected in the past to exclusion, servility and genesis amnesia. New cultural geographies are being mapped out and foregrounded in language, literature, philosophy and theory; and old hierarchies are tumbling, new ones are rising. The world of literature and theory is expanding to embrace new functions and challenges.

Not only a revamping and reorganizing is in sight, but also the construction of new spaces and horizons of discourse are on the agenda on a universal scale. Exile, the Third Zone of Literature, is one of those spaces, one of those horizons.

One definition for the concept of national literature is that it is a literature with a reference. The reference may be to a tradition or a set of traditions; to a language or a set of languages; to a volume of possessions or a set of obsessions and idiosyncrasies. National literature is a collective. We are not discussing aesthetics, but we know that each national literature has its own aesthetic set of measures that gauges value, authenticity, hierarchy, relevance and methods of delivery and response. This collective may be considered as a national text, with the collective texts of other neighbouring national literatures acting as a context, and the combination presenting itself as the geographic loci of an intertextual discourse. Although Arabic, Persian and Turkish literatures of the Middle East have had different linguistic and historical origins and horizons, their historical development side by side as geographic neighbours has created structural and thematic patterns of influence and confluence, penetration, interpolation and interpretation, bringing each individual culture under the umbrella of a common cultural narration. The discourse of identity and difference could be applied to these literatures on the basis of a mutual understanding. The same could be said of European literatures of the Renaissance and post-Renaissance periods. The individual narration in each culture in Europe lends itself conveniently to a common polylogical process radically different from a similar process belonging to the common narration of the three Middle Eastern literatures. But this is only one of the ways of looking at nations and national literatures.

The rise of colonialism and imperialism has changed the literature and the literary geography of the world during the last three hundred years. The national literatures and cultures of non-European countries, in lieu of a neighbourly participation in the mutual process of action and interaction, have found themselves overwhelmed by concepts and structural frameworks completely alien to both their own roots and those of their neighbours. These alien elements have not evolved as the continuation of indigenous time and geographic contiguity; rather, they have evolved as the consequence of colonialist aggression and imperialist invasion, introducing disintegration, dislocation and alienation as the major characteristics of cultures living under subordination. The colonized (India), as well as the non-colonized (Iran), each with its own specificity, has felt the traumatic effects of this dislocation.

Disrupted histories have created a rift between the society in which the writers of these nations lived and the literature they produced. The stream of representationality has been problematized, as if these writers and poets were told not to look back, otherwise they would turn into dust, or they would find nothing behind them but mounds of dust. Although new genres, forms, themes and literary devices have evolved as a result of this unequal transaction between those alien to these national literatures and the literary representatives of these indigenous societies, there is no doubt that the governing psychological state on these writers has been one of both enchantment and disenchantment. They have been fascinated by the sciences, the social organizations, the revolutions and democracies, the arts and literatures of the West; but they have equally been disgusted with the West's colonialist and imperialist aggressions. The split personality of these writers has resulted in what we might call a "double alienation," a feeling of estrangement from one's own Self, as well as the Self's Other. This space is one of the most formidable spaces of exile. Writers as diverse as Borges, Hedayat, Nabokov, Al-Ahmad, Marquez, Said, Morrison and Rushdie are ghosts haunting this space.

> *If suddenly you walk on grass turned stone*
> *and think its marble handsomer than green,*
> *or see at play a nymph and a faun that seem*
> *happier in bronze than in any dream*
> *let your walking stick fall from your weary hand,*
> *you're in The Empire, my friend.*[1]

For the writer living in exile, the nostalgia for home, some kind of home, is a shot at familiarity and reference. But home as reference keeps withdrawing into the pits of genesis amnesia. The place where the exiled writer lives is not home, because home means the saturation of time, place and space by primary experience, original memory, non-stop imagination and consistent linguistic attribution. For most exiled writers, their second or third homes are not real; but they are not imaginary either. They possess neither presence nor absence. They simply don't exist. The writer has his own imagination and a language producing the poetics of exile. He is caught in a space from which the old gods have departed, and there is no prospect for the arrival of new ones. He has to create a world in language to replace the reference dead in reality and the reference never to be born in reality. He gets into the world of the ultimate signifier holding a mirror before the Promethean imagination of loneliness, pain and suffering, with his language running the whole gamut of desire and pleasure, hope and salvation. These are perhaps the major features of works by Joyce, Beckett, Nabokov, Italo Calvino and the recent Milan Kundera. Texts keep dreaming and desiring other texts in a Foucauldian "Heterotopia," the non-place of language. During the first years of exile, the writer goes through shocks of memorial arrhythmia, tragic-comical bouts of alzhymeric séances, with subsequent unexpected periods of serendipity, absolutely unaccounted for, and almost completely disassociated from the memory of the past and the experience of the present. The old country one remakes in this process is disturbingly different from the one he had, as if he had found a new continent with which he could do whatever he wanted to. Now, if he tells his stories or writes them, he lives under a different code of existence, more or less like Scheherazade, who started telling her stories, not because she knew all those stories by heart, but because she had to create and relate those stories as she went along, and by creating and telling them, she wanted to buy time and stay alive. The fear of death, and exile, the closest phenomenon to the threshold of death, place the project of narrative on the immediate agenda of one's ontology: You tell a story to live; you live to tell a story. And you wonder: which story?

In the heydays of modernism, beginning with Baudelaire and Flaubert in the nineteenth century and coming, via French symbolists to Henry James, and later to Pound, Joyce, Proust and Virginia Woolf, Western concepts of literature were thought to be universal principles for measuring all world literature. Non-Europeans themselves were as much responsible for this universal distortion as the Europeans, because mimicry of the West was at the root of most cultural and social evaluations which were taking place in non-Western regions. This mimicry was at the heart of the exilic blindness of the East. Jalal Al-Ahmad, the Iranian writer whose treatise entitled *Westoxication* played a very important role in raising consciousness against the malady of mimicry, influenced intellectually the course of events which led to the revolt in Iran against the West, even with some effects on Khomeini himself and his concept of an Islamic rvolution. We see the re-emergence of the concept of mimicry in Homi Bhabha's *The Location of Culture* almost thirty years later. You take the measurements of distant and foreign cultures and apply them to your own indigenous culture, thus turning double alienation into a two-layered exilic blindness. When you are suspicious both of the indigenous culture and the one invading it from abroad, what is your position intellectually and spiritually? A two-layered exilic blindness; something which will happen to you later, when you have exchanged your home for a western country, and are experiencing exilic blindness from the other end of the spectrum. This is the ultimate form of exilic schizophrenia. Wherever you turn, Western modernity seems to have become the future destiny of traditions disrupted by that modernity, whether inside your country, or the country of your exile in the West. The combination of internal traditions with external and incongruous modernity has resulted in the creation of an uneven development in the cultures and literatures of non-European nations. On the one hand, there was the caricature of the West, the mimicry to be taken for the real, the exilic banishment and abandonment of the real in one's own country; and on the other hand, the impossibility of a finalized settling down in one's psyche, intellect and language, into the new format of the so-called guest country with its utterly heedless, but equally fascinating thrust into the unknown called the future. Inside one's own country, because of the unevenness dominating the scene, one could see writers producing realistic, modern and postmodern works simultaneously. Almost the same pattern dominated the exilic world outside, only with differing agent percentages. Now home seemed to be far away, and the modern ways of life seemed by necessity real, almost unrealistically real. A new value system was needed to gauge the dimensions of this polysystemic phenomenon.

Al-Ahmad's *Westoxication*, Edward Said's *Orientalism*, books by Franz Fanon, Gayatri Spivak and Homi Bhabha, works by Hélène Cixous on exilic situations in Asia, Africa and the Soviet Siberia, and the recent concentration of Jacques Derrida on non-Western spaces of religion, race and literature, opened a new phase in the literary discourse of different parts of the world in contradistinction with which inadvertently prescribed Western universals. Writing in exile became a strong presence as writers from different countries moved to the West and lived there.

Where does one place the Third Zone theoretically? Here is what Edward Said says in the introduction to his *Culture and Imperialism*:

> The last point I want to make is that this book is an exile's book. For objective reasons that I had no control over, I grew up as an Arab with a Western education. Ever since I can remember, I felt that I belonged to both worlds, without being completely of either one or the other. During my lifetime, however, the parts of the Arab world that I was most attached to either have been utterly changed by civil upheavals and war, or have simply ceased to exist. And for long periods of time I have been an outsider in the United States, particularly when it went to war against, and was deeply opposed to, the (far from perfect) cultures and societies of the Arab world. Yet when I say "Exile" I do not mean something sad or deprived. On the contrary, belonging, as it were, to both sides of the imperial divide enables you to understand

269

them more easily. Moreover, New York, where the whole of this book was written, is in so many ways the exilic city par excellence; it also contains within itself the Manichean structure of the colonial city described by Fanon. Perhaps all this has stimulated the kinds of interests and interpretations ventured here, but these circumstances made it possible for me to feel as if I belonged to more than one history and more than one group.[2]

There is another dimension to exile that problematizes literature to a degree unprecedented in other exilic forms. Gertrude Stein had said early in the century: "I come from America, but my hometown is Paris." Julia Kristeva has said: "Writing is impossible without some kind of exile." Hélène Cixous has denounced patriarchal philosophy and literature of Europe, seeking her identity in strange lands and among diverse writers of exile, the Russian writer in Siberia, the Brazilian writer of unprecedented female voices, and James Joyce in exile. In the writings of these three major female writers, language is the unnameable poetry of the world. Alterity and estrangement in language are just other names for exile. Exile from the governing role and rules of conventionality, from what Kristeva calls "the mire of common sense," into the strange and unknown world in order to see and hear everything afresh, gives the exilic predicament a new zone, a novel space. It is in the works of these three female writers that we see the language of literature itself as pure exile. No wonder that most of the time, the exilic writers find solace in the writings of Western women writers as against men's works.

The dislocation sometimes draws upon the hidden archives of ethnic groups and oppressed nations and nationalities of many countries and continents of the world, because hope for the survival of the contemporary author seems to require the revival of that which is hidden, and of which we become aware as we move away from the sources and the roots. Exile in this sense means the dismantling of historical memory and the revamping of a new space wherein birth memories, hidden archives of memory, maternal memory and hidden memories of the mother are brought into a new space, the space of the new continent of remembrance. The new country is not only the birth of the new language of that country, but the rebirth of language, both the old and the new. This, we may consider as the positive aspect of exile, as we witness in the works of Ezra Pound, James Joyce, Gertrude Stein, Joseph Conrad, Virginia Woolf and Vladimir Nabokov, in which we see continents rather than countries, languages, rather than a single language.

We cannot simplify things into ready-made categories such as the confrontation between the East and the West, the traditional and democratic societies, the Islamic and Christian beliefs, just as we no longer can classify people now into the conventional male and female. Such categorisations may be convenient, but they may also be prejudicial; they are superficial politics and cheap journalism, unless we enter the mind and writing of those who have chosen complexity as against superficial clarity. The contemporary writer, exilic in the core of his being-because in our age, the exilic and the contemporary are beginning to become synonymous — is coming under pressure from all sides, and his mind seems to be an open space for all kinds of transgressions, genuine and artificial insemination of memories, histories and phantasmagorias of all brands. Theoretical simplifications are not able to account for the rise of the new subjectivity which has hitherto been unknown in culture and literature. It is not only Nietzsche, Heidegger, Adorno, Lyotard, Foucault and Derrida who attack the concept of the Enlightenment as the new metaphysics of the Western world. Writers and intellectuals of the non-Western world find themselves in the more precarious position of yearning for the basic concepts of Enlightenment on the one hand, and detesting, on the other hand, those who pose themselves as the sole representatives of the enlightenment, but rule

271

the world with the iron fist of the dark ages of human history. It is under such conditions that imbalances, contradictions, controversial positions, spontaneous and marginalized concepts and forms, forgotten cemeteries of memories, and archaic archives rise to the surface and declare themselves. We become conscious of this when we consider the fate of the contemporary writer in the non-Western world. Detesting his own stale traditions, hating the onrush of Western hegemony, and attracted to concepts of discovery, progress and modernity, the non-Western writer withdraws into the reservoir of roots which his own traditions tried to destroy on the way to their own historical development and establishment. The hidden archives of humanity rise like huge waves from the past of the cultures of these writers, creating gulfs of interstitiality between archaic worlds and traditional heritages, between the roots of oriental and occidental civilizations, and subsequently, transforming the meaning of the clash of tradition and modernity between the two polarities of East and West, by giving rise first to the literature of post-colonialism, and simultaneously or immediately afterwards, to the rise of a new brand of postmodernism. Here the hidden archives of these writers play a vital role in the literatures of the world, because they are the exiles par excellence of the contemporary world.

When Western traditions of modernity are introduced to countries of non-Western origins as a result of colonialism or semi-colonial oppression, the consequences are unforeseen and unprecedented. Iran is a typical example. Infested by contradictions, the case of Iran may elucidate complexities for many similar cases. One typical example may throw light on a typical instance. Although the concept of the nation-state was introduced to the country with the Constitutional Revolution (1906-8), in the aftermath of the revolution, with the advent of public education in the country, only the language of one nationality, Persian, was recognized as the official language of the whole country, depriving more than 67% of the whole population of the country of the right to read and write in their own languages. The convenience was adopted with the cooperation of the West, whose scholars and orientalists sought to play up the significance of Persian language and culture as the sole identity of a whole nation with diverse nationalities. A perfectly recognizable pattern of conspiracy between the Iranian regime and foreign powers, mainly the British and Americans, with intellectual and political assistance given to them by orientalists in the West and their counterparts in the Iran, deprived almost 70% of Iran's population of their mother languages, literatures, arts and other cultural identities. While the social and national culture of the country was based on the very concrete hybridity of several nationalities living together, the imposition of one language for the education and administration of the affairs of all nationalities, one of the worst patterns of segregation imposed on any nation in world history, created a schizophrenic situation in which Persians were supposed to be masters, and the Turks, the Kurds, the Turcomans, the Arabs and the Baluchies were thought of as second class citizens. The disastrous policy submerged the nation and the relationship among nationalities in a spiritual and intellectual dislocation, as a result of which the mother languages of about 70% of the whole population of the country became a hidden archive. You could speak in the mother tongues of the oppressed nationalities, but you were not allowed to read and write in them. Imagine two thirds of the population of a country turning into translators from their mother tongues into the language of the superior nationality from the day of the inception of public education to the present, about seven decades. More than one third of the whole population of the country spoke Azeri, a language of Uralic-Altaic origin. In 1946, I was forced to lick off the ink from the childish school paper, which I had written every month for a year. In that year, under a democratic

273

regional government, we had learned everything in our mother tongue, but in the aftermath of the fall of that regime, we were forced to write everything in Persian, the mother tongue imposed by the Pahlavi dynasty as the official language of the entire country and maintained in the same capacity even after the Islamic regime took over in Iran. I learned Persian, and English, the reading and understanding of Arabic and French, before I learned the reading and writing of my mother tongue. I never forgot that licking of the mother tongue, the metamorphosis that one's memory had to go through in the process of speaking and writing, and more than anything else, the exilic situation which had become a part and parcel of my entire being. Although Persian became the natural tongue of my decades of writing and intellectual being, and although I benefited from the complexities of my linguistic hybridity, turning it almost to a merit rather than a demerit, I came to realize that there was in me a hidden mother in the form of a hidden language, in the form of such a dynamic space that I could only make up for it by talking about it and by addressing myself and my efforts to the redressing of this lack by birth, by writing about it in any language I knew, and by carrying over the structure of this hidden world towards the hidden voice of a poetry that was almost the equivalent of a kind of disturbed singing; and in my fiction to a labyrinthine underworld in which language is always in the process of a new and genuine birth. A writer giving birth to the mother.

Notes

1. Svetlana Boym, "Estrangement as a Lifestyle: Shklovsky and Brodsky," in *Exile and Creativity*, ed., Susan Rubin Suleiman (Durham and London, Duke University Press, 1998), p. 258.
2 Edward Said, *Culture and Imperialism* (Vintage Books, New York, 1994), pp. xxvi-xxvii

"Exile, the Third Zone of Literature" was first delivered as a keynote address at an international conference entitled 'Building a Writers in Exile Network' held at the National Library of Canada in Ottawa on March 17-18, 2004. The essay will appear in Brick, *a periodical published in Canada and edited by Michael Redhill.*

Poetry and Exile:
Some Thoughts from my Experience
Kamal Mirawdeli
(Kurdistan)

Being in exile puts you in a peculiar position. You feel that
your existential space has turned upside down. Outwardly
you can cope, compromise, accommodate. You read, you
write, you talk, you work, meet people and you are still part
of the 24-hour cycle of time. But the dislocation of space
creates a different internal order: a different play of time,
and stream of sub-consciousness. Gradually you find reality
is overtaken by dreams: daydreams, midnight dreams and
nightmares. The past in the form of its presence there
overturns the equation. It is this powerful presence of the
past and the elsewhere in the reality and overwhelming
nature of dreams, which destabilises your presence here:
you can only be here by being absent there. But the dream
flow of there ensures that for most of your unconscious and
even conscious time you are really somewhere/nowhere. In
your real life daily practices you are absent: you can be
absent-minded, away, thoughtful. There is always this
unavoidable inner odyssey, which makes sure that you have
no real presence anywhere. Given the demands of active
life, work, necessities of survival and pressure to be, this
can result in an unbearable condition. A schizophrenic
experience dualistic existence with each dimension trying to
negate the other. What makes matters worse is lack of a
solution. For there is no solution for exile once it settles in.
It's your life burden, your destiny, full stop. At least that is
how it worked for me.

In the Kurdistan of the mid seventies, the time when I
started to write, the poet had a position between a prophet
and a political leader. He was the voice in a society
controlled by a system of tyranny whose main obsession
was the suppression of voice and the elimination of all

means of expression. Free media, free meetings, free voices were nil. For Kurds, this tyrannical system, even in this twenty-first century, is functioning with a fundamentalist extreme racist effect. In Turkey, for example, even the words Kurd and Kurdistan and the use of Kurdish geographical names are political crimes. They are viewed by the ruling racist establishment as a threat to national security.

However, your experience as a Kurd is not confined to total denial of identity and suppression of natural human impulse for self-realisation and self-determination. In fact the dividing line between political/national repression and physical elimination is very thin. For racism, which is universally practised by the regimes ruling over Kurdistan against the Kurdish people as a matter of course, is a violent creed by its very nature. Racist views and attitudes are easily translated into offensive language, oppressive legislation and physical aggression. Lack of any kind of democratic accountability or international responsibility further facilitates this technical transformation. As Kurdish human and cultural aspirations, both at individual and collective level, are historically interpreted by the ruling regimes as threats to national security and divinity or unitary or chauvinistic states, or as conspiratory devices of foreign powers, then any expression or demonstration of Kurdishness entails a violent repressive response, progressively reaching the level of genocide.

And it was genocide, real cultural and physical genocide, which I experienced in my country South Kurdistan under the Iraqi regime of Saddam Hussain.

I was born and lived my childhood in a Kurdish village which throughout my memory had never been under direct control of any foreign power. I had the good fortune of being immersed in full Kurdishness as an identity and way of life. My father was a known poet writing in Kurdish and fluent in Persian and Arabic. As a child, I saw in my father's library the pictures of Salahuddin, Shaikh Said, Sheikh Mahmud and Qazi Mohammed. These were books

277

on Kurdish history and many collections of poetry of famous classical and modern Kurdish poets. On the other hand, the geography itself, that is the village and its location, embodied voices, colours and characteristics of Kurdishness.

Our home was located in a narrow valley with a small river dividing it into two opposite stretches of land covered with trees, orchards and small farmland plots.

We were self-sufficient in every way. We had more than twenty types of fig and grape. We had every other fruit: peaches, pears, pomegranates, melons and watermelons. We had cattle and a variety of domestic and wild vegetables. The river traversing the valley of Marga was small. But as it streamed down from higher to lower grounds, it was cleverly utilised to operate eighteen water mills providing different kinds of flour to villagers in the area. There were craftsmen for every purpose: carpenters, shoemakers, tailors, barbers, builders, dyers. There was a strong deep-rooted local culture. Ballad singers (*beytewan*) and story tellers (*Hikayetewan*) were abundant. On winter evenings my aunt used to relate to us Kurdish epic tales some of which would last for a whole week or more.

Then there was the ever-lasting omnipresent mountain. The symbol of Kurd and Kurdistan. The only steadfast friend of the Kurds throughout history. Just opposite our home was the mountain known as Barda-qlisht which meant "the split rock". It represented a cave-like opening at the summit of the mountain. There were huge rocks. On one of them a statue of a woman with a baby in her arms. The form was gradually eroded by weather. Perhaps it was the image of the Virgin Miriam. Then there is on the southern side of the mountain a hill called Gewra Qala "Great Castle" which was understood to be a pre-Islamic citadel of Kurdish Kings. At the back of our home, was another hill called Mila-qiran which means "the neck of annihilation". This in the popular memory referred to the slaughters which happened during the Islamic invasion in the seventh century. I want to say Kurdish mountains are full of archaeological sites and signatures that can reveal a lot about the genealogy of power and history and civilisation of the Kurdish people. (But imagine now, only last week, the Turkish prime minister, who does not hide his pride in being a Turkish poet, sent a memorandum to all civil servants instructing them to prevent the use of Kurdish geographical names as this encourages "separatism"! Isn't it shameful for Europe to accept these people as civilised and democratic?)

In Kurdistan, the land experiences four full seasonal lives with each season erupting in a different exhibition of romantic or sublime natural sensuality. Rainfalls, snows and storms in winter, followed by a Nawrozian spring of green grass, blossoming trees, singing birds and playful animals. Then a dry summer of long, hot sunny days doing its best to ripen fruit, regenerate the farming land and offer a generous harvest of variety of wheat, barley and other cereals. Then graciously arrives autumn: a romantic queen with tragic tears of lost love and a pale panoramic view of the world playing a sad nostalgic tune of the absolute eventuality of every living instance.

You never know the value of what you have until you lose it and then miss it. The missing of There is in itself a traumatic experience. But it becomes more complicated and horrid when you know that what constitutes you as an identity, history and psychology has been destroyed. Gone forever. It is at this point that you feel and realise that you have lost some very precious part of yourself which perhaps can only survive in dreams.

I never imagined how much the human brain could store and create. I am still puzzled by the infinity and often metaphysical nature of my dreams. Dreams in themselves were a kind of subconscious configuration in which symbolism is an essential mechanism. For the first ten years in London I never had any dream about my London life. I was always there in my villages and towns.

The powerful persistence of dreams was the result of conscious anxiety and fear due to the genocidal events taking place in Kurdistan between 1981 and 1990. Especially 1998 was the climax. It was in March of that year that the Kurdish town of Halabja was decimated with a chemical attack. In the same month the village of Marga in which I was born and had my primary school education, was obliterated. Then the town Qaladiza, in which I had my secondary school education and then taught as a teacher, was bulldozed and all its population, around one hundred and fifty thousand were deported to the south of Iraq or concentration camps. In the same year, one hundred and eighty-two thousand women, children, old and young people were uprooted from their villages and taken to unknown destinations in the south of Iraq. No one yet knows what has happened to them.

In exile, you lose your audience, your constituency and with it much of your inspiration and motivation. For whom do you write now? How? What do you want to achieve?

I usually wrote and still write poetry primarily for myself. It is totally subjective in the first instance. I write poetry to recognise and reassert my humanity, to give back equilibrium to my relationship with the external world, to remain sane, to give myself a haven in times of loneliness, alienation, anger and anguish. I write also to reassert my national identity and my love for my people and my language. But it is through being subjective, being your true self, that you can express your full existential and human dimension best. Then you will be surprised how universal poetry can be. I like poetry to be lyrical, and be an insurance for such feelings and emotions which are increasingly challenged and submerged in a society becoming more and more technical, more and more materialistic, more and more selfish, more and more driven by values, agendas and superficial attractions set by unaccountable commercial lobbies who direct their attention to the utmost exploitation of basically beastly instincts of mankind: sex, violence and getting richer and richer. In particular, I write poetry to assert that love is the sole value of human life that can still give a meaning to life in spite of all the absurdities, contradictions and hypocrisies we experience.

When you suffer, you understand suffering. You can have a different reading of events and appearances. You have a dream to change the world. You have never given up conquering cruelty with love. You have concern for the environment, human rights and justice. You want peace. You value democracy and civic society. You admire the human capacity for unstoppable progress, creativity and technological revolution. And you think the West, Europe is the place where all these ideas are embodied in institutions, images and expressions.

I was in exile here in the 80s of the last century when genocide was raging in Kurdistan. There was news and images of death and destruction everyday. My village, my town along with four thousand other villages and towns were obliterated. This news and these images were constantly being recreated in hundreds of configurations over and over in dreams and nightmares. There was a political urgency for survival. What could poetry do in these circumstances? Poetry seemed to me too innocent, too feeble and too mythical to respond to the enormity of genocide at least in its immediacy. Can all the poetry of the world stop the killing of a child let alone the destruction of a people and a culture? I became so hopeless about the image and impact of poetry in a world dominated by cruelty that for a long time I was alienated from it, I could not even read poetry. This meant really becoming a zombie. Add to this total disappointment with the Western world, Europe and its claims of democracy and human rights. Genocide was an officially declared policy of the Iraqi regime. And it was happening not only under the eyes and noses of Western democracies but also with their full support and collaboration. Saddam was armed to the teeth. Chemical weapons were used as a routine strategy to eliminate the population. People were being packed in military trucks like cattle and transferred to Arab deserts for Saddam's experiments in biological warfare. There was no news, no voice and no expressions of concern. Only the silence of lambs.

As a writer I was expected to be with people on the streets to demonstrate, to lobby, to shout. To draw the attention of the world to our plight. Instead of poetry I wrote petitions, appeals, political articles. I set up community organisations, Kurdish magazines and newspapers to make people aware of what was happening. Academically, I studied history, literature, philosophy and economics. But none of these could diminish the amount of depression and despair I was suffering from. Is there anything more painful and traumatising than seeing young people slaughtered like sheep, your villages and towns razed to the earth, your culture and civilisation destroyed and you are helpless to do anything about it?

Thus the stream of daily dreams and nightly nightmares continued.

Only after I was able to return to my country in 1992 after ten years of exile, did they begin to diminish. There was some reconciliation between the past and the present, between exile and origins, between poetry and politics. I started to write poetry again both in Kurdish and in English.

I survived. Poetry helped me to survive and it survived with me. I still write for myself, my inner self, when I feel a strong impulse to shed some poetic tears, share some romantic inclinations or show some realistic aspects of a world still ruled by cruelty. Above all, I managed to keep in my soul a safe poetic haven for love. And love will keep me going on living, writing and dreaming beautiful dreams.

The Semantic Gap
(A Problem of Communication)
Esmail Kho'i
(Iran)

The text of the author's speech at a gathering in memory of the late Ali Akbar Saidi Sirjani, organised by CODIR on 12th January 1995 in the Grand Committee Room, House of Commons, London

This is 1995, only five years to the end of the mind-liberating twentieth century.

Not so in Iran, however.

In Iran, history, human history, that is, does not begin with an assumed date for Jesus Christ's coming into the world in order to save the Human Soul from Sin. It begins with an accepted date for the Prophet Mohammed's Departure from Mecca to Medina in order to save himself from his tribal enemies. We are, therefore in the year 1373. That is, of course, according to the Islamic solar calendar, which is more "cleric" in use than the solar one, according to which the year is currently 1415.

Now, I, too, know that the perpetual flow of indifferent moments constituting "physical" time must remain absolutely unaffected by our choosing to single out any part or portion of it as the expanse of human history; and, likewise, that our own society's amount or degree of historical development cannot increase in any way through our deciding to push the beginning of our history back in time, ie by selecting a more ancient event as the marker of our historical time zero. And I shall never stop wondering why it was that the Shah-an-Shah Ariamehr thought that such a thing could be done. A few years before his downfall, however, he did decree the Islamic calendar to be replaced by a Royal (Shah-an-shahi) calendar, according to which we should currently be living in the year 2553, that is, almost five hundred and eighty years ahead of the Western World!

283

But the Shah's nationalistic arrogance, in deciding against the Islamic Calendar, is supposed to have been among the cultural reasons for the revolutionary demise of monarchy in Iran. And the fact is that in the Christian calendar year 1979, the Revolution in Iran began Islamising our lives by taking us from the royal calendar year 2537 back to the Islamic solar calendar year 1357, or its lunar equivalent 1399, that is, much more or a little less than six centuries behind the twentieth century Christian calendar.

Now, historians should certainly feel amused, rather than confused, by such virtually, pointless manipulations of calendar. But the irony, and the symbolism of it all I find both amusing and confusing. True, even the mighty Nero could not wilfully alter the nature and the chronological order of historical facts and the "objective" relations they have with one another. But is there, could there be, a graspable intellectual scheme to embrace the whole miserable, unstoppable bloody flux and to make some sort of sense of it all?

We know our whereabouts in the calendar. It is in history that we are lost. What we need is a time-map, an internal history clock, to let us know the time. But, for God's sake, I ask you, what time is it? What day, month, what year, what century? I mean, not in any chronological time, as an arbitrary marker of the order of events, but in historical time, as the riverbed for the self-creating flow of progress? One thing is beyond Cartesian doubt: This is the present time; we, too, live in the present moment — the Now. But, chronological time aside, is our historical Now the same as that of the Western world? I think not. I cannot help envisaging a yawning gap, wider than over five centuries, between the two.

Europe had the beginning of her Renaissance in the fifteenth century, Christian calendar. With it, Europe was "born anew". Most importantly, "It marked the transition from the medieval to the modern world". And the modern world is politically characterised, first and foremost, by the separation of the Church from the State.

Now, we too, had hoped and dreamed that the Iranian Revolution of 1979 (Christian calendar) would bring us our own national cultural and political Renaissance and that it would mark the turn of the fifteenth century Islamic calendar as the beginning of our transition from the medieval to the modern world.

But it didn't.

Maybe it could have.

But it didn't.

The moment the Revolution succumbed to the back to front ideology of Imam Khomeini, it turned against itself. It did bring us a short-lived "Spring of Freedom". But our "Spring of Freedom" soon turned into a Jurassic Park of theocratic monsters and monstrosities, the first necessary pre-condition for whose existence was to devour anything and everything that looked and smelled and tasted like something civil. And the purification and redemption of the Iranian Society from it came, in the name of God, to be the Revolution's agenda.

Salman Rushdie's insight is astonishing, where, in his *Satanic Verses,* he speaks of "the Commencement of the Imam's Untime" (1988, Viking, p. 215)

Here is his "Imam" thinking, i.e. dreaming aloud:

> We will make a revolution... that is a revolt not only against a tyrant, but against history. For there is an enemy beyond Ayesha, and it is history itself. History is the blood-wine that must no longer be drunk. History the intoxicant, the creation and possession of the Devil. Of the great Shaitan, the greatest of lies — progress, science, rights... History is a deviation from the Path, Knowledge is a delusion, because the sum of knowledge was complete on the day Allah finished his revelation to Mohammed. We will unmake the veil of History... and when it is unravelled, we will see Paradise standing there, in all its glory and light.

Of course, the Imam's dream has not, could not, fully fulfil. His Islamic Republic has not, cannot, take us back in history to the primal innocence of the year zero (ie. his Paradise of blissful ignorance). But his faithful followers have managed to set us on our backward move. And they have, among many other things, done a lot of unravelling of History itself. They have re-written large portions of it, to make it fit the official truth. And the official truth is an ever-growing lie; and the bigger it gets, the more difficult it gets for the Iranian people to relate it to people outside the Islamic republic, especially to the people in the modern democratic world.

You see, we — you and us, have an ever-growing communication problem. There is an ever-widening semantic gap between us. To communicate, we must use words. But the most crucial words do not mean to you the same things they mean to us.

For example, the sentence, "The economy of our country is in ruins", when spoken by anybody in the modern world is (only) an expression of his or her high dissatisfaction with the (present) economic state of affairs in his or her country. But when I say that our national economy is in ruins, I mean just that: That is, the very base of our national economy has been literally destroyed.

The next example, must naturally, be the word "poverty". The phrase "living below the poverty line" must have a miserable ring to your ears. But the majority of those living below the poverty line in your country would be among the happiest people in Iran, should they go to live there, provided of course, that they take their legal rights and privileges along with them. There are centuries of difference between living in poverty and dying because of it.

Or, again, when you are angry enough to find it adequate to speak of "the slavery of women in our society," you are apt to be speaking of things like women's lack of equal opportunities in finding or having jobs, or their lack of equal pay for doing the same job, or the uneven distribution of top social positions among men and women, or an unmarried girl's having to travel to a foreign country in order to have an abortion, and/or other things equally backwardish, unjust and even inhuman: but not, not at all, unquestionably anachronistic, insufferable, unjust and heartlessly inhuman like any single one of the things I have in mind when I speak of the slavery of women in Iran. When I speak of the "Slavery of Women in Iran", my use of the word "slavery" is much nearer to its usage in the literal sense.

You won't believe me, I know.

But that is alright.

I come from another time, another world. Remember?

I come from a world in which one and one woman equals two women, but only one man. In legal matters like inheritance and acting as witnesses, that is. Or when a woman is murdered and the murderer or his family or tribe would want to pay her life-price.

Life-price?

Oh yes. I come from a time when the life of a man too, has a price. The only difference is that it is twice the life-price of a woman. Both of them are cashable in the Islamic republic's currency. Or in terms of live camels, if you happen not to trust the Islamic Republic's banknotes.

And would you believe me if I told you that a widow can have no say in the upbringing of her own children, if, and until when, her father-in-law is around? And, that after he is gone — dead, her oldest brother-in-law is supposed to assume that responsibility?

And what about marriage?

Oh my God! It must be the end of the world, if a shameless girl wants to have some say in her own marriage!

And who is that wretched woman, buried up to her waist in the ground, with her skull smashed and her left eyeball hanging out?

Oh, nobody really. She was stoned to death this morning. She had a lover. The lady was in love!

Or again when you use the word "University", you naturally find it natural to mean to be speaking of "a place of higher learning, in which there are professors and students". That "the professors should be teaching and the students should be learning", you would find an obvious tautological statement unworthy even of making.

Not, however, in my use of the very same word.

When I speak of "University", I am speaking of a place of learning in which there are still some professors and some students. But, and that is the point, in our "Islamically cleansed and rebuilt" universities, there has been a revolutionary role reversal. Between the professors and the students, that is. The Hezbollahi students ie those among our university students who take great pride in being among the self-sacrificing members of the Party of God, have kindly taken upon themselves each morning to teach our professors what to say and what to do, as well as what not to say and what not to do, in their classes if (and of course, only if) they do not wish to be given the revolutionary sack and suffer all the things that will come after it.

Or again, for example, take the word "prisoner".

When you grumble, rightly no doubt, about the prison conditions in this country, you must be talking about things like lack of hygiene or rehabilitation opportunities and the like.

But, would you, could you, find it possible to believe me when I say that I come from an age in your own actual time in which fellow prisoners have to stand up in overcrowded cells, in order to make room for their tortured comrades to lay down?

Granted.

Not all prisoners are political prisoners; and it is fundamental ie moral for governments to decide which is which. But when, for example, a British government official declares "We do not hold political prisoners", he or she is saying something that not only the British Government says. He or she is saying something with which some, at least, of the British people agree. They are terrorists, they would say. They have broken the law.

They have killed people. That is why they are in prison.

My reference, when I speak of "political prisoners", is, however, specifically to those of your mass media who have recently become conscientious enough to use the term "prisoners of conscience". And now you go ask the Islamic Republic if they hold any "prisoners of conscience".

"Prisoners of Conscience?!" What's that?!

"Political Prisoners!"

Oh that ! Yes. We did have them up until a week ago. But then we gave them a choice: Repent or die...

And what happened?

Some of them repented. Here is one. You can ask him. We do not hold political prisoners. Islam does not permit us to do so. Ask him. Here. He has learnt his lesson.

I know you would not, how could you, believe me. But there is, has been, an easier way of constantly keeping the Islamic Republic political–prisoner free: you have to be against Islam, in order for you to become a political prisoner in the Islamic Republic. But to be against Islam is to be against human nature. For Islam is the natural religion of human beings. It follows, logically, that those who are against Islam ie Islamic Republic, are not, cannot, be human beings. Those we hold in prison are, therefore, animals, not human beings. And it can only be the enemies of Islam who call such animals "political prisoners".

And you have certainly not grasped my meaning if you still ask:

Is it true that in the Islamic Republic's prisons, they make political prisoner share cells with rapists, maniacs and murderers?

Yes of course. What is wrong with caging animals like animals?

Or again, take the word censorship. It is almost exclusively in relation to the cinema and the video industries that you find occasion to use the word. And your censors do not have to work under assumed names, lest some director or actor demented with anger should seek and find the opportunity to skin one or two of them alive. They use their scissors wrongly, I think, in order to protect the public or the young from violence, criminal teachings or dangerous sex exercises. And what is more, they have a definite code of practice, a set of rules and regulations, reflecting some shade of public opinion.

But when I speak of censorship, I am speaking of what is happening to the whole of Iranian poetry, to the whole of Iranian literature, to the whole of Iranian art, to the whole of Iranian culture, indeed to the whole of Iranian life. Life, yes, life itself is under censorship in Iran today. Women have to strictly observe the Islamic Hijab. Even the innocent beauty of little girls has to be "well" covered up, lest some depraved sex maniac in the street should glance at them and entertain and, God forbid, enjoy sinful thoughts.

It should be obvious, however, that the Islamic Republic's distrust of human beauty comes from an attitude towards life that is far gloomier than any of those leading to the "familiar forms of censorship". Censorship in its familiar sense has, I think, always been the official outcome of the religious, social and political authorities fear of the individual's freedom of thought and creativity. And as such, it has of course, been no revolutionary innovation of the part of the Islamic republic in Iran. We had it in the reign of the Shah as well. But we have really never had it so bad. There is a great difference, as great indeed as the distance between Heaven and Earth, between censorship done as an official job in the name of a King and censorship performed as a religious duty in the name of God. There is nothing by way of the butchery and destruction of works of science, philosophy, literature and art, the censor would not be prepared to do, when censorship is done with the clear conscience of a self-righteous servant of God. That the self-righteousness might only be feigned is beside the pint. The butchery and the destruction remain real. Of all the powerful tools the Islamic Republic authorities use in their fundamentalist

290

endeavours to force modern Iranian culture and life into their ways of thinking and feeling and being, nothing is indeed more real than censorship.

Whole books and periodical are banned and barred from publication. Whole films are burned. Whole paintings and other works of art are destroyed. And you have no right to question the censors why. Do that and you will be persecuted, imprisoned, tortured or worse. Armies of researchers, writers, poets, publishers, university professors, school teachers, film producers, directors, actors and the like are supposed to be attacking the ideological foundations of the Islamic Republic in a treacherous campaign officially described as "the cultural siege of Islam". Censorship is the Regime's defence. "Forbidden to Write" (ie literally forbidden to use the pen!), "Forbidden to Publish", "Forbidden to Teach", "Forbidden to Make Films" and "Forbidden to Act" are among the labels with which categories of cultural crusaders are primarily warned as belonging to that vast campaign of the Enemy Within. And once you are so warned, you would be well advised to accept and bear the distinction in silence. Or else you could embark on a road which would soon enough reach the signpost: "Forbidden to Beathe!" The case only recently, of Ali Akbar Saidi Sirjani, must show that I am far from speaking metaphorically.

I do sincerely feel sorry for Mr. Salman Rushdie. But as far as our mutual understanding of censorship is concerned, his horrifying experience may serve as a transient bridge over the semantic gap between people like you and people like me.

And here is a last example: Human Rights.

Now, most of these rights, you people take for granted and rightly so. But our Human Rights Lords are there in Tehran, the high authorities of the Islamic Republic. And before I may expect to be bestowed with, of course, the "Islamic" version of these Rights, I must prove to them that I am a "human being" — an impossible task unfortunately, because by going against the Islamic Republic, I have waged war against God; which I could not have done, if I had not been a "human being". Because it is not in the Nature of human beings to wage war against their Creator!

You cannot believe me, can you? But I swear to God, I am not making this up. I am talking about real people and actual mentalities. The end of the twentieth century Christian calendar? Yes it is. But they are there. They are still very much there And the problem for me as a poet, is how to describe them, to people like you.

I see a highly cultured, art-loving, old-fashioned, silvery-haired retired English politician venturing to express an opinion on some hot issue, and I see you impatiently putting him down by calling him a political dinosaur. And I say to myself, "If political dinosaurs are people like that, then what am I to call those in power in Iran today?!"

Rural Imagery in Contemporary Somali Urban Poetry: a Debilitating Carryover in Transitional Verbal Art

Maxamed Daahir Afrax
(Somalia)

The deployment of rural imagery in Somali poetry presents difficulties for Somalis in urban settings, and considerably more for those in exile far removed from pastoral settings.

It may be of interest to students of comparative literature that, contrary to the universally accepted view that literature draws its imagery from the environment that has given rise to it, Somali modern poetry produced in an urban setting draws much of its imagery from the rural environment — an established practice inherited from traditional poetry, but not without problems for a contemporary audience. Several scholars have noticed and touched upon the use of pastoral images in modern Somali verse (Andrzejewski 1974; Johnson 1996).

Describing some of the characteristics of the kind of poetry used as an essential part of dialogue in modern Somali plays, Professor Andrzejewski writes:

> It is interesting to note that even in plays, which are a product of the urban environment, almost all the imagery [in poetic parts] is taken from the life and scenes of the countryside. Even among the educated elite there is a great respect for their traditional way of life and culture, which still thrives in the rural environment [...] The speech of the country folk, especially that of the nomads, is universally regarded as the highest form of Somali, and some educated townsmen involved in public life have felt it necessary to spend a certain time learning the arts of oratory from old men in the interior
> (Andrzejewski 1974: 23).

What has hitherto escaped scholarly observation, however, is the debilitating effect of such a traditional technique in modern poetic discourse created by and meant for the new society of the town dweller in Africa today. This essay highlights this problem, exploring how the utilization of pastoral images was useful in the context of traditional/rural Somali poetry, but is not relevant to modern poetry associated with the contemporary urban environment, in theme or audience.

Pastoral Imagery in Traditional Poetry

In pre-colonial times, pastoralism was the predominant way of life for the majority of the Somali population, and this features prominently in the imagery of all forms of Somali oral literature created over the ages. In proverbs, for instance, most well-known sayings are laden with pastoral images. For example:

> *Geelow daaq, daaq, daaq, laakiin maalintaad 'ciin'*
> *daaqdo ayaa laguu yaabaa!*
> O camels, graze, graze, graze, but one fears for you[r life]
> on the day when you graze on [the plant of] *ciin*!

Ciin is a poisonous plant deadly to camels. The saying suggests that camels can eat many kinds of plants, which are too rough for other livestock, but they have to take care not to be too greedy and lose sight of the dangers that may be involved. The proverb is used to warn those people who indulge in wrongdoing because they are too privileged to consider the deadly consequences of their actions.

In the following proverb, the branches referred to are those used to seal off the entrance to the *kraal* where sheep and goats are kept at night. In the morning, the branches must be removed one by one very carefully in the reverse order to which they were laid, as they are so thorny and heavy. The proverb thus instructs one to tackle matters one at a time according to their importance:

> *Oodo dhacameed siday u kala sarreeyaan baa loo guraa.*

One picks up the branches of the outer gate barrier of a *kraal* in the order in which they lie on top of one another.

The presence of rural imagery in Somali traditional poetry is equally profound and even more conspicuous:

Baadida nin baa kula daydaya
daalna kaa badane
Oon doonahayn inaad heshana
daayin abedkaaye
[Sometimes] a man comes out with you to look for lost
     animals,
and gets [even] more tired than you,
But without wanting you to find them at all.
Andrzejewski and Galaal, 1963

This couplet comes from a poem by a well-known early
twentieth-century pastoral poet, Qamaan Bulxan, in
rejoinder to another poet, Cali Dhuux, in a famous series of
poetic contests between a number of pastoral poets, each of
them acting as the spokesman of his clan.[1] It would not only
have been relevant but very useful for Qamaan Bulxan to
utilize the image of a man looking for lost animals; this
would augment his poetic point in the eyes of his audience
of camel herders and cowboys who are certain to have
enjoyed and appreciated the piece because it vividly
depicted an experience they shared with the poet. That is
presumably why the poem has been widely circulated and
preserved in the oral memory of thousands of Somalis.

It is widely recognized that good literature represents
the experience of its time and society. As Wole Soyinka
puts it, poets act "as the record of the mores and
experiences of society and as the voice of vision in [their]
own time" (Soyinka, 1968).

Similarly, the noted poet and literary scholar, Maxamed
Xaashi Dhamac Gaarriye, asserts that the main reason
why we use imagery is to facilitate the audience's easier
acquaintance with whatever the poet wishes to convey, by
portraying it in a picture closely familiar to the recipient
(Maxamed Gaarriye, 1998).

This is precisely the case in the work of Raage Ugaas,
another Somali pastoral poet of singular stature. Sometime
in the early nineteenth century, Raage composed a famous
lament on the death of his beloved wife. The opening lines
of the moving poem are as follows:

Sida koorta yucub oo la suray, koromo buubaal ah
Ama geel ka-reeb ah oo nirgaha,laga kaxaynaayo
Ama beelo kaynaan ahoo, kor u hayaamaaya
Ama ceel karkaarrada jebshiyo,webi karaar dhaafay
Ama habar kurkeedii wadnaha,lagaga kaw siiyey
Ama kaal danley qaybsatiyo,kur iyo dhaal yaabis
Shinni kaaluf galay ama sidii,koronkorroo oomi
Xalay kololo'aygii ma ladin,kaamil reeruhu e.

Like the *yucub* wood bell tied to gelded camels that are
     running away,
Or like suckling she-camels being separated from their
     calves,
Or like communities setting off for a desert trek,
Or like a well which has broken its sides or river which has
overflowed its banks,
Or like an old woman whose only son was killed,
Or like the poor, dividing the scraps for their frugal meal,
Or like the bee entering their hive, or food crackling in the fry,
Yesterday my lamenting roar drove sleep from all the
     camps.
Andrzejewski and Lewis, 1964

To make his audience comprehend the magnitude of his
pain caused by the unexpected death of his life-partner,
the poet summons a multitude of well chosen word-
pictures and familiar situations, using highly powerful
poetic diction (largely lost in the attempted translation).
He has depicted a legion of pastoral situations and their
familiar tragic sounds and collected them together in a
single dark frame. They thus amplify his utmost grief
which is expressed in the form of an uncontrollable,
lamenting roar that continues the whole night and keeps
the entire neighbourhood awake. Being closely
acquainted with these well-drawn images, Raage's
audience is certain to have been utterly moved by his
heartrending account.

Commenting on this poem, Maxamed Gaarriye is not
way off the mark to argue that one of the main reasons
why so many Somalis still memorise this poetic piece a
century later is the poet's complete mastery of these

penetrating images (Maxamed Gaarriye, 1998). But if the same piece was recited to a present-day Somali city lad, it would almost certainly sound like an alien language which, rather than gain immediate appreciation, would at best cry for translation.

However, it is not such a city lad that has to be blamed or accused of being ignorant or having bad taste; he simply has no idea about how camels behave. He has never been exposed to the experience of a nomad community trekking in the desert, nor has he seen 'gelded camels [...] running away'. In my view, it is the poet who continues to speak the wrong language to the wrong audience, and is thus responsible for this kind of communication breakdown.

An old shoe on new feet.

Many Somali contemporary poets or composers of modern songs must have suffered such a communication breakdown in their unsuccessful attempt to impress young town dwellers by using the wrong tools. Habitually, they aim to show their poetic competence by using "high standard" language and highly stylised techniques from the past, such as symbolism (*dedan*), allusion (*sarbeeb*) and rural imagery. This may be relatively tolerable in the case of what we call the poetry of public forum (*maanso-goleed*), that is the serious poetic genres used chiefly to address sophisticated issues of a political and social nature.[2] The use of traditional features in the public forum poetry might well be comprehensible, even desirable, to members of the older generation with some rural background who constitute the main audience for this type of poetry. I have argued elsewhere[3] that the skilful and conscious use of certain elements of tradition — legendary characters in this case — could be useful in terms of linking the past and present, especially in the case of a society experiencing the transition from a traditional to a modern way of life.

In the mid-1960s, a Somali poet, Saxardiid Axmed, expressed in the following poem the growing concern of the general public who felt disappointed after several years of unfulfilling independence:

297

Hashaan toban sano u heesaayey
Hruubkiyo heeryadiiba cuntaye
Lixdankaan haybin jiray maxaa helay?
The she-camel I've been singing about for ten years
Has eaten both the milking vessel and the saddle
What happened to the [year of] sixty I so much longed for?
Maxamed Afrax, 1994

Like many others at the time, the poet depicts the independent Somali state as a suckling she-camel by the name of *maandeeq*, a well-known image created to symbolise the country, the state and the sovereignty.

The poet wished to convey the message that independence, which was gained in 1960, was beginning to fail the expectations of the people who struggled for it.

In this particular case, although he uses pastoral imagery for modern urban communication, one can assume that the poet's employment of the image of a "she-camel" eating its "saddle and milking vessel" (which alludes to a popular Somali saying), posed no remarkable problem then, given the nature of both the audience of the time (closer to tradition) and the seriousness of the theme. However, when such techniques from the past are used in today's modern songs, targeted at a younger audience with no rural background at all, we are confronted with an entirely different situation.

The modern song is one form of Somali modern poetry where the use of rural imagery is most irrelevant. Indeed, it is paradoxical that this art form, which still uses pastoral images extensively, is meant for the consumption of the younger generation of town dwellers and that its theme is predominantly romantic love — a modern theme almost exclusively associated with the said segment of Somali society. The question then arises of how the use of images drawn from the pastoral setting, at odds with the central theme, is relevant to the audience in this entirely new environment?

If the main purpose of deploying imagery is "to facilitate the recipient's acquaintance" with the content, using alien images would inevitably have the opposite effect. The following song by an acclaimed contemporary poet and playwright, Xasan Shiikh Muumin, illustrates this point. Xasan is by no means less skilful than Raage Ugaas in his competent use of pastoral imagery in a somewhat similar situation, ie to express a moment of intense grief (this time felt by a fictional character, an inexperienced schoolgirl ruined by a heartless playboy who traps her by false marriage and false promises). Trying to appeal to his non-existent sense of humanity, she depicts her plight:

Nin geel badan lahaayoo
Guluf kala carraabay
Gallad wixii uu haystiyo
Gadhoodhkii uu dhamaayey
Gego madhan ka joogoo
Dhallaan gaajo haysiyo
Nirgihii ku gooheen
Ganuunsaday sidiisii
Adaa garan waxay gubee
Garwaaqso waad igu geftee!

Like a man who once had many camels
But one afternoon they were taken by raiders,
His prosperity, and the sour milk he used to enjoy, all gone,
And who sits in an empty corral, his children hungry
And his camel-calves orphaned — thus am I ill with bitter grief.
You know what seared me — then judge it fairly, for you have
   wronged me!
Hassan, 1974

If "every historical epoch writes its own poetry or rather expresses itself in appropriate idiom in the poetry of its most committed and sensitive minds" (Amatu, 1989), every artistic theme requires an appropriate idiomatic structure through which it can be most effectively expressed — a structure which does not obstruct the development of the new art or debilitate its effect. As Abdulfateh Al-Hakeemi argues, old aspects of form have to either adjust themselves to fit "the measurements of the time" or give way to new aspects (Al-Hakeemi, 1986).

In this light, the main subject matter of the sung verse cited above is closely familiar to its target audience; the theme, the characters and the overall situation all truthfully represent the everyday experience of the young urban Somalis of the time. Shallaayo, the victimized young lady who tearfully sings the poem, represents not only herself but also every girl of her age group and society, and this effectively reinforces the poem's appeal to its recipients.

On the other hand, however, aspects of form — the language, imagery and other traditional techniques — are far from familiar to the main target audience. To them, such lines as *Guluf kala carraabay* (Looted in an afternoon raid) and *Nirgihii ku gooheen* (His starving baby-camels howling in his ears), would be as difficult to appreciate as poetry in a foreign language. In this respect, not only are these difficult for the audience to internalise or even visualise, but the language as a whole is too archaic to cope with. Words such as *guluf*,[4] *carraabay*[5] and *nirgihii gooheen*[6] are not only absent from the present-day vocabulary of the young urban Somali, but have generally faded into lexical archaism.

To an audience of pastoral nomads and probably some older people with a rural background, the poem would appear to be an utterly beautiful piece of verbal art; it unmistakably reflects the great talent of its creator, Xasan Shiikh Muumin. To this kind of audience, the continuity of traditional elements in contemporary literature is desirable. Furthermore, if used selectively with a combination of competence and care, the use of some selected traditional features in treating modern themes can be highly effective, as stated earlier. Yet, to achieve the best of both worlds, the poet needs to strike a delicate balance — he or she has to be aware of "tradition as a double-edged sword" (Wright, 1994).

To members of the younger generations in towns, the targeted segment of society in this case, the beauty of the above piece has, as already delineated, been substantially disabled by the use of the wrong elements of form. While Shallaayo, the protagonist, realistically represents the experience of the audience, the language she speaks to them is not theirs, nor indeed is it hers. It is uncharacteristic of a townsgirl of Shallaayo's age and time to use such language and style, which in fact belongs to the author who has imposed it on the wrong character. The actress/singer (Mariam Mursal), who at the time was as young as Shallaayo, may be learnt the text by heart without fully understanding the meaning of the words she uttered.

This obvious gulf between the form of the poem on the one hand and its content and context (including the audience) on the other, is highly problematic. The obvious communication breakdown could have been avoided had the author taken this problem into consideration and moulded his artistic devices into a form more relevant to the setting of his poem — the city environment which has given the poem (or the play it comes from) its theme and characters. This could have been achieved with a relatively slight adjustment in wording and imagery.

To portray Shallaayo's plight — abandoned, pregnant and disowned by her family — in such a way as to make it appeal to the audience's sense of tragedy, the poet likens it to the agony of the ex-camel-lord described in the extract cited above. However, the imagery would have been more effective in the modern urban context if the ex-camellord had been replaced, for example, by an ex-landlord/merchant, suddenly robbed of his property and thrown out into the city streets. Contemporary Somali poetry, which is a product of urban society, represents the experience of a society in transition from a traditional to modern way of life. The poetry itself is in the process of transformation from 'purely' oral methods of composition and transmission to a new form — a mixture of orality, techno-orality (the use of audio and video recording) and written alternatives.

301

Due to this transitional status, the new form still hovers between having to adjust itself to the pressures of modern times and being unable to venture a break with the established poetic devices carried over from traditional oral poetry. Pastoral imagery is one of the three most pre-eminent devices inherent in this tradition, the other two being alliteration (*xarafraac*) and metrical scansion (*miisaan*). The rigid rules of the latter two features regulate the structural patterns of almost all types of Somali verse thus imposing on the new poem some serious 'restricting, and hence, debilitating effects' (Samatar, 1982). While the restraining effect of these latter two devices, particularly the *miisaan*, have attracted the attention of several students of Somali literature, the limitations posed by pastoral imagery is yet to be observed in scholarly work. In this article I have attempted to highlight this aspect of Somali literature which, perhaps, has parallels in the experiences of other cultures.

Despite the general tendency towards "conservatism" universally found in oral and semi-oral cultural forms (cf. Ong 1982), one can assume that, as time goes by, time-honoured features, including pastoral imagery in Somali urban poetry, will inevitably adhere to the pursuing winds of change.

References

All Somali names are given in the official Somali orthography except where they occur differently on the title page. In the Somali naming tradition, surnames are not normally used. Persons are identified by their given name followed by that of their father and grandfather. Libraries with substantial holdings in the Somali field have adopted a system for Somali entries recommended by the late Professor Andrzejewski (1980). This is based on the official Somali script and the order of Somali customary naming. In accordance with this, names of Somali authors in this references list are not inverted.

1. Abdillahi Deria Guled (1980) 'The Scansion of Somali Poetry', in Hussein M. Adam (ed.), *Somali and the World:*

Proceedings of the International Symposium held in Mogadishu, October 15-21,1979 (2 vols.), Mogadishu: State Printing Press, pp.132-40.

2. Al-Hakeemi, Abdulfateh (1986) 'Albaroudi fi Mahkamat Ashi'r', *Athaqafah Al-Ghadeedah*, 5, pp.84-99.

3. Amatu, Chidi (1989) *The Theory of African Literature: Implications for Practical Criticism*, London and New Jersey: Zed Books and Institute for African Alternatives.

4. Andrzejewski, B.W. (1974) (trans. with introduction), Hassan Sheikh Mumin, *Leopard Among the Women — Shabeelnaagood*, Oxford University Press.

5. (1980) "Recommendations for Somali Entries in Library Cataloguing systems", *African Research and Documentation*, 22, pp. 21-2.

6. (1982) (trans. with introduction), Faarax M.J. Cawl, *Ignorance is the Enemy of Love*, London: Zed Books, 1982.

7. and Musa H.I. Galaal (1963) 'A Somali poetic combat', *Journal of African Languages,* 2:1, pp.15-28; 2:2, pp.93-100; 2:3, pp.190-205.

8. and I.M. Lewis (1964) *Somali Poetry,* Oxford: Clarendon Press.

9. Hassan Sheikh Mumin (1974) *Leopard Among the Women — Shabeelnaagood*, Oxford University Press.

10. Johnson, John William (1996) *Heelloy*: *Modern Poetry and Songs of the Somali* (2nd edn.), London: Haan Publishing.

11. (1996b) 'Musico-Moro-Syllabic Relationships in the Scansion of Somali Oral Poetry', in R.J. Hayward and I.M. Lewis (eds), *Voice and Power. The Culture of Language in North-East Africa: Essays in Honour of B.W. Andrzejewski,* London: School of Oriental and African Studies, pp. 73-82.

12. Maxamed Daahir Afrax (1987) 'Ashakhsiyah Aturathiyah fi Shi'r Hadraawi', *Al-Hikmah*, 135 (Feb.), pp.44-50.

13. (1993/4) ' "A Nation of Poets", or Art-loving People? Some Aspects of the Importance of Literature in Present-day Somali Society', *Hal-Abuur: Journal of Somali Literature and Culture*, 1:2-4 (Autumn/Winter 1993/4), pp. 32-6.

14. (1994) 'The Mirror of Culture: Somali Dissolution Seen Through Oral Literature', in Ahmed I. Samatar (ed.), *The Somali Challenge: from Catastrophe to Renewal,* Boulder, CO and London: Lynne Reinner, pp.233-52.

15. Maxamed Dhamac Xaashi Gaarriye (1998), *Caweys Gabay*, video recorded lecture, Dubai: University of Amoud, 2 July.

16. Ong, Walter, J. (1982) *Orality & Literacy: The Technology of the Word,* London: Routledge.

17. Said S. Samatar (1982) *Oral Poetry and Somali Nationalism:*

The Case of Sayyid Mahammad Abdille Hassan, Cambridge University Press.

18. Soyinka, W. (1968) 'The Writer in a Modern African State' in P. Wastberg (ed.), *The Writer in Modern Africa*, Uppsala: Scandinavian Institute of African Studies, pp. 14-36.

19. Wright, Derek (1994) *The Novels of Nuruddin Farah*, Bayreuth: Eckhard Breitinger.

Notes

1. Poetic contest (*gabay-ku-dood*) is an established Somali poetic tradition which takes place frequently, every couple of years or so. It either takes the form of poetic exchanges which are conducted directly at an assembly, with the contestants present, or consists of a series of polemical poems, recited on different occasions, in different places; in the latter case, they are carried by messengers and travellers who learn them by heart. For further details about this poetic combat and the full text of this poem with English translation, see Andrzejewski and Galaal (1963).

2. For information about the unusually important role of poetry in Somali society and the many functions it performs, see Andrzejewski and Lewis (1964); Samatar, 1982; Johnson (1996); Maxamed Afrax (1994).

3. Maxamed Afrax (1987).

4. Aggressive raiders of tribesmen.

5. Set off in the heat of early afternoon to begin a long desert journey on foot.

6. Baby-camels producing such a painful continuous sound in hunger to attract the herder's attention for milk.

7. For a detailed discussion on these features with ample illustrations see Andrzejewski and Lewis (1964); Andrzejewski (1982); Abdillahi (1980); Samatar (1982); Johnson (1996b).

BIOGRAPHIES

Sulaiman Addonia is a half Eritrean/half Ethiopian writer living in the United Kingdom. After fleeing one of the longest conflicts in Africa, he lived in Sudan and Saudi Arabia. He has a BSc in Economics, and an MSc in Development Studies, both from the University of London. He has written for the *New Statesman, Underground Focus* magazine, *Emel* (a Muslim lifestyle magazine), *KIT Theatre Special* (online magazine); and is a column contributor for the forthcoming *Bulb Magazine* (a political teen magazine). He also writes fiction, mainly short stories.

Maxamed Daahir Afrax is a novelist, critic, playwright, journalist and literary scholar who writes in Somali, English and Arabic. His major published works include three novels in Somali: *Guur-ku-sheeg* (1975), *Maana-faay* (1979) and *Galti-macruuf* (1980), and a historical novel in Arabic, *Nida Al-Horiya* (1976), in addition to many short stories published in different magazines and newspapers in Somalia and abroad. He has written two plays; his first play was entitled *Durbaan Been ah* (A Deceptive Drum) and was staged in 1979 by a then famous theatre group in Somalia called Danan Artists. In the field of criticism and literary studies, Afrax has authored many articles and research papers and has also published a book of theatre criticism and historical analysis of Somali drama entitled *Somali Drama: Historical and Critical Study* (1987). He is also the co-author of *The Somali Challenge: from Catastrophe to Renewal,* (1994). The author's new book in Arabic is entitled: *Nadaraat fi Athaqaafah As-Soomaaliyah* (A Window to Somali Culture). In his creative writing, Afrax denounces such evils as political and moral corruption and social injustice. When in 1980 his novel *Gulti-macruuf* (Pseudo-civilised) began to appear

305

in serialised form in *Xiddigta Oktoobar,* a leading national daily newspaper, the government took offence at its denunciation of the political corruption and moral decadence of the ruling elite, which were set to lead to the current Somalia disaster. The publication of the story was discontinued at its thirty-seventh episode by orders from the authorities and the author was muzzled. Soon after that, Afrax had to leave the country in 1981 and has been in exile ever since. After a period of political activism against the government of Siyad Barre, he settled in Yemen where he completed his BA degree (1988) and joined the Ministry of Information and Culture as head of its Theatre Research Unit and, later, as assistant director of the Publishing and Translation Department before he moved to London in 1991 where he is now based. In London, while doing his PhD in literature at the University of London, he founded and edited a unique literary periodical in English and Somali called *HAL-ABUUR, Journal of Somali Literature and Culture.* He is currently President of the Somali-speaking Centre of International PEN. After several years of full involvement in UN missions and in the international efforts towards peace-building in Somalia in various capacities (UN advisor, Djibouti Government consultant, independent researcher etc), the author finally decided to re-focus on or revitalise his writing vocation. Since early 2002 he has either written or revised and completed the manuscripts of three new books in English, Somali and Arabic. The latter two books were published simultaneously in Kenya and the UAE in 2002 while the third *The Changing Shape of Somali Poetry,* in English, is awaiting publication.

Ibrahim Ahmad was born in Iraq in 1946. He graduated in Law from Baghdad University. He has published five volumes of short stories and one trilogy entitled *The Child of CNN.* He left Iraq in 1979 and now lives in Sweden.

Farid Aitsiselmi was born in Algeria. He graduated in Modern Languages from the University of Algiers where he taught English Language and Linguistics until 1994 when he moved to England to take up a job as a lecturer. He is now a lecturer in French Studies at the University of Bradford where his area of specialism is Language and Linguistics. His interests include language and identity with special reference to the migrant population of Algerian origin in France. In 2000, he edited a book entitled: *Black Blanc Beur: Youth Language and Identity in France.*

Zuhair Al-Jezairy is from Iraq where he worked as a journalist. He has had twelve books published including a novel, short stories and books about politics. For three years he lived with the Kurdish *peshmergas* in remote villages in the mountains. His book *Paper of the Mountains* is based on these experiences and is a mixture of fact and his feelings. His novel *Idealistic Cities* was written as a result of his experiences living in no-man's land. He has worked as a producer for the Arabic television service, APTN, based in London.

Mir Mahfuz Ali was born in Dhaka, Bangladesh, Mahfuz is a performance artist, renowned for his extraordinary voice — a rich throaty whisper brought about by a bullet in the throat fired by a Bangladeshi policeman trying to silence the singing of anthems during a public anti-war demonstration. He studied at the University of Essex. His work has appeared in *Index on Censorship* and various other magazines. He is currently completing a novel on his experiences in Bangladesh and Britain.

Ahmed Omar Askar was born in Hargeisa, Somalia. He studied medicine at the National University of Somalia in Mogadishu and took specialised courses on tuberculosis and lung diseases in Finland. Dr Ahmed worked for the national health services in Somalia as a Regional Medical

Officer of Health and Tuberculosis in northern Somalia. He has written poems and plays about health and education in the Somali language. Dr Ahmed left Hargeisa with his family when the outbreak of civil war destroyed his home town in May 1988. He was granted asylum in Finland in 1989.

Fadhil Assultani was born in a small town near the city of Hilla, south of Baghdad. He studied at the University of Baghdad, worked as a journalist, and taught in Iraq, Morocco and Algeria. He began writing poetry in the 1960s. He has been working on a complete Arabic translation of Whitman. His poetry is characteristically modernist in its imagery and intimate rhythms. In addition to his publications in Iraqi and Arabic journals, he published a collection of poetry entitled *Burning in Water*. He is the editor of the literature section of the Arabic daily *al-Sharq al-Awsat*.

Afshin Babazadeh was born in Tehran, Iran in 1963. He left Iran as a student in 1979. He has published two collections of poetry: *Letters to The Sisters of Stones* in Persian (1991), and *Breakfast In Better Circumstances* in Persian (1996). A selection of his poetry was translated into Swedish (1998). Three further collections await publication; *Bodilies* in Persian, English and German, *Cow* in Persian, and *When I Lie Next To You* in Persian.

Reza Baraheni was born in Tabriz, Iran. He is professor of Comparative Litaerature at the University of Toronto and President of Canadian PEN. He is the author of more than sixty books of poetry, fiction and literary criticism in Persian and English and has been translated into all the major European languages. The French publisher Fayard has published three of his novels since 2000, and two of his works were recently directed by the French director Thierry Bedard in the main section of the Avignon Theatre Festival (July, 2004). His books include the

Crowned Cannibals, a collection of prose and poetry, and *Les Saisons en Enfer du Jeune Ayyaz*, a novel. *His God's Shadow: Prison Poems* is a collection of poems based on a period of 102 days spent in solitary confinement in Iran, during the time of the Shah. He was also imprisoned in the autumn of 1981 and the winter of 1982 by the Islamic Republic of Iran. He has been active for the last thirty-five years in trying to promote democratic liberties in his country.

Nazand Begikhani was born in Iraqi Kurdistan in 1964 and has been living in exile since 1987. Her first degree was in English Language and Literature and she then did an MA and PhD in Comparative Literature at the Sorbonne, Paris. She published her first poetry collection *Yesterday of Tomorrow* in Paris in 1995. Her second poetry collection will be published in the near future. Many of her poems are translated and published in French, Persian and English. Apart from writing poetry, Nazand is an active researcher and advocate for women's human rights. She is the founding member and co-ordinator of the organisation Kurdish Women Action against Honour Killing (KWAHK) and the International Kurdish Women's Studies Network. She has published many articles on gender issues in Kurdish, and in French and English.

Sherko Bekas was born in 1940 in Sulaymania in Southern Kurdistan and was educated in Sulaymania and Baghdad where he published his first collection of poems in 1968. His poetry reflects his close association with the Kurdish liberation movement which he joined in 1965, working with the movement's radio station — the Voice of Kurdistan. During the period 1984-87, he lived with the Kurdish *peshmergas*. Since 1987, Sherko Bekas has lived in Sweden where he continues to write. In 1987, he was awarded the Swedish PEN Club's Tucholsky Prize.

Nafissa Boudalia is from Algeria and now lives in London. She is a poet and painter and occasionally returns to her country to paint at great risk to herself. She has worked as a journalist since 1969, originally working for Algerian newspapers *El Moudjahid* and *Algérie Actualités*. In 1967, she won the Prix St Germain des Prés in Paris for her poetry. Her collection of poems *Réflexions sur l'Algérie* (1989) focused on the political situation in Algeria, especially the position of women.

Sofia Buchuck was born in Cusco, Peru. Her collection of poetry entitled *Al otro lado de America* (On the other side of America), was published in Mexico in 2003 and she has been published in a range of anthologies. In 2004 she was awarded a silver medal by PoetryVoices.com in the USA. Since 1991 she has performed Latin American music at festivals and concerts in the UK and Latin America and in 2000 *Girl of the Rain Forest* was released.

Ahmad Ebrahimi is a founding member of Exiled Writers Ink! He came to Britain in 1974 for post-graduate studies and subsequently worked as an economist. He later moved to the USA. He published his first volume of poetry in 1974. His poetry, in Persian and English, has been published in many journals and anthologies. He is currently working on an anthology of translations of the poetry of Ahmad Shamloo as well as on a collection of his own work. In the UK he was closely involved with the Iranian PEN Centre in Exile.

Mirza Fehimovic comes from Sarajevo, Bosnia and Herzegovina where he was engaged in freelance journalism and translation of literary essays and fiction. He taught Serbo-Croat at the University of Delhi, India for three years. He has published two collections of poetry, one collection of short stories and a novel.

Predrag Finci was a Professor of Aesthetics at the University of Sarajevo and left the city because of the war in Bosnia (1992-1995) and came to the UK in 1993. He has published five books in his native language (*Epistolary Discourse, Art and Experience of Existence, Origin of Question, On Some Secondary Matters in Arts and Sarajevo's Introduction to Aesthetics*) and several texts in English. *Refugee Blues* was written in 1995. He was editor and co-editor of two refugee quarterlies including *SALON (Sarajevo-London)* and is currently working on his new project as an Honorary visiting Fellow at University College, London.

Abol Froushan left Iran in 1975 to disengage from the welter of student unrest in the Shah's Iran, opting to live and study in London. In 1979, he graduated in Engineering from Imperial College, University of London, subsequently gaining a Masters in Social and Economic Studies and a PhD. Abol's career since 1986 has uprooted him many times giving him many opportunities to experience migration, relocation and separations (two marriages, three cultures and two tongues). He writes poetry fused with digital images and sound.

Yasser Ganem was born in Syria in 1971 and is an artist and doctor who has been living in Marseilles, France since 2001. His work has been widely exhibited in Syria and France.

Hadraawi Mohamed Ibrahim "Hadraawi" spent his childhood in a pastoralist environment in Somalia but was educated in Aden, later becoming a student and then a teacher at the College of Education at Lafoole, Somalia. In 1973 he was imprisoned for five years for composing poems interpreted as being critical of the Government. On his release he was appointed Director of the Fine Arts Department of the Academy of Arts and Sciences but left his post to join the Somali National Movement and was a key member of the Ethiopian-based opposition. "Hadraawi" is a revered Somali poet who lived in exile in Britain.

Karim Haidari was born in 1973 in Kabul, Afghanistan where he graduated with a BA in English from Kabul University. He had worked for many years for Radio Afghanistan on a part time basis. He worked for UN Aid agencies in different parts of Afghanistan. He spent fourteen months in prison during the Mujahideen era, escaping prosecution during the Taliban era by fleeing to the UK in June 1999. He currently works for a social care agency providing support to unaccompanied minors particularly asylum seekers. He is currently studying playwriting.

Reesom Haile was a poet and scholar from Eritrea. He returned there after a twenty year exile, which included teaching in Communications at The New School for Research in New York. The first collection of his poems in Tigrinya *Wasa ms Qum NegernTensae Hager*, won the 1998 Raimok Prize, Eritrea's highest award for literature. His second collection in Tigrinya was *Bahlna Bahlbna Our Culture, Our Pleasure*. He died in 2003.

Choman Hardi was born in Sulaimanya, Southern Kurdistan in 1974, grew up there and then lived in Iran and Turkey before coming to England in 1993. She has published three collections of poetry in Kurdish *Return with No Memory* (Denmark, 1996), *Light of the Shadows* (Sweden, 1998), *Selected Poems* (Iraqi Kurdistan, 2003) and one in English *Life for Us* (Bloodaxe, 2004). Her poetry has been read on BBC Radio 1 and 4. She studied Philosophy and Psychology at Queen's College, Oxford, and has an MA and PhD.

Mogib Hassan was born in Yemen in 1974. From the age of fourteen, he was principal singer in a group and also an active member of a students' organisation until he left Yemen for India in 1994. He obtained a degree in Business Management from Mysore University. In 1999 he moved to the Netherlands, where he worked as an Arabic teacher as well as continuing with his writing and taking part in literature activities. Some of his work has been published in Dutch and Arabic. One of the novels he is writing is called *Is it Religion or Tradition?* to be published by De Geus in Amsterdam. The main theme of Mogib's work is politics, women's rights and the empowerment of women in the Arab world. He has also written a number of emotional poems and songs. He has taken part in a project about the empowerment of women organised by Colorado University and in a project involving poets travelling to six different cities in the Netherlands and Belgium. He moved to London in 2004.

Sousa Jamba is an Angolan writer who fled to Zambia at the time of the civil war and later returned to join UNITA against the MPLA government. His first novel: *Patriots* (London: Penguin, 1991) is about UNITA's exile in Zambia. His second novel is *A Lonely Devil*, 1993 and his third *Le Feeling* draws on his experiences as an African exile living and working in London. Jamba has been a correspondent for *The Spectator* and has written for the *New Statesman, Times Literary Supplement*, the *Daily Telegraph* and a number of Portuguese newspapers. After having lived in exile in London for a number of years, he moved to the USA.

Miroslav Jancic is from former Yugoslavia and was in exile in Britain from 1993. He was born in Sarajevo and was a Bosnian writer with three novels, ten plays/film scripts and two books of non-fiction to his credit, all published, staged/filmed in Serbo-Croat. When the war started in 1992, he was the ambassador to Ghana. He returned to besieged Sarajevo to try to help his homeland but was scorned by all three warring nationalistic parties and he had to flee the county. He has had two collections of poetry published in Britain *The Flying Bosnian* 1996 and *Singing Through The Town*, 2001. Miroslav Jancic died in Sarajevo in November 2004. (See www.bosnia.org.uk/bosrep/report_forma for obituary.)

Jorge Jimenez was born in Medellin, Colombia in 1983. For political reasons, his family had to move numerous times and he spent his childhood travelling around the country. In Colombia he was a university student studying computing. He came to the UK in 2002 to join his father, Asdrubal Jimenez, who had been an important lawyer representing the banana plantation workers' trade union. Because he had been forced to leave Colombia when he was seriously injured in an assassination attempt organised by the army, Jorge had grown up without his father and the family in Colombia had to remain silent about human rights issues for fear of being targeted.

One of the rising stars of Iranian poetry, **Ziba Karbassi** was born in 1974 in Tabriz, Iran. She left Iran in 1989 and now lives between London and Paris. She has published five volumes of poetry in Persian, all outside Iran, and continues to write prolifically. Her poetry tackles difficult themes and has received wide critical attention. Her work has been translated into several languages, one volume currently being translated into English by Stephen Watts. She was recently voted as Director of the Association of Iranian Writers in Exile.

Fawzie Karim was born in Baghdad in 1945 and has lived in London since 1979. He has had eight books of poetry published in Arabic as well as fiction and essays. *Dawn is Imminent* is a portion of his eighth book of poetry, the epic *Continents of Pestilence*, published in Beirut. Some of his work has been translated into English by Lily Al-Tai. A collection of his work has been translated into French by Said Farham: *Continent de Douleurs,* 2003, Editions Empreintes, Switzerland.

Abdulkareem Kasid was born and educated in Basra, Iraq. He taught in Iraq and Algeria where he was a university lecturer and now lives in London after having been in exile in Yemen and Syria. He has published five books of poetry, the most recent of which appeared in 1990. His poetry is a blend of modernism, Sufism and references to Islamic and Arabic history. He has lived in France and translated three books of poetry and prose from French. He has worked as a journalist for a range of Arab journals in Baghdad, Damascus and London.

Mohamed Khaki is a Kurdish poet from Iran who writes in both Kurdish and Farsi and has written four volumes of poetry. When he was sixteen, he was imprisoned for three years for possessing an unauthorised poetry book, having originally been sentenced to twelve years. He left for the Kurdish area of Iraq where he worked for a broadcasting station for eight years and, in addition, edited a newspaper. In the UK he works voluntarily for refugees as well as running his own business.

Esmail Kho'i is a leading Iranian poet living in exile. He was educated in Iran and England and began his career in Iran as a lecturer in Philosophy. In the 1960s and 70s, as a founding member of the Writers Association of Iran, he opposed the restrictions placed on intellectual freedom in monarchical Iran, gradually advocating revolutionary change. After the Iranian Revolution of 1978-81, however, he found himself living in an even more oppressive political atmosphere. In the early 1980s, he was forced to spend nearly two years in hiding before fleeing in 1983. Over the last sixteen years, Kho'i has emerged as a most articulate poetic voice of the Iranian diaspora. His anthologies of work in English are *Edges of Poetry: Selected Poems of Esmail Kho'i* (1995), the bilingual anthology *Outlandia*: *Songs of Exile* (1999) and *Voice of Exile* (2002).

Hadi Khorsandi is a veteran Iranian satirist in exile in London. He is the editor of the magazine *Asghar Agha* published in London. By the mid-seventies, Khorsandi was one of Iran's most successful journalists writing for *Ettela'at*

315

and for *Zan-e Rouz* and he also wrote scripts for radio, television and nightclub comedy shows. His work was censored by both the Shah and Ayatollah Khomeini regimes and the publication of some of his critical poems and articles after his return from London to Iran, led to protests by the Hezbollahi mobs who eventually demanded his execution. He fled back to London fearing for his life. An unsuccessful plot to assassinate Khorsandi in London has meant that he must keep a low profile. His work appears in *The Ayatollah and I: New Iranian Satire*, 1987.

Igor Klikovac was born in 1970 in Sarajevo where he lived until 1993, when he came to England. He took a degree in Comparative Literature and Librarianship at Sarajevo University. Parts of his first collection of poetry *Last Days of Peking* have appeared in translation in England, the Czech Republic, France and Slovenia. In 1995, he jointly founded *Stone Soup*, a literary magazine published in London in bilingual format. He now lives in London where he works as a freelance writer.

Fatmire Kocmezi is from Kosova and came to the UK as a refugee. No further information about her is available.

Berang Kohdomani is a poet who was born in Afghanistan and started his career in the Department of Folklore and Culture. He was later appointed a lecturer in the Faculty of Literature at the University of Kabul. From 1989 to 1991, he was based in Tajikistan working for the Academy of Science in matters related to literature. He has lived in London since 1995 with his wife and five children. He has had many collections of poetry published including *Greeting to Corn Poppies*, *Spiritual Meaning of Words* and *The Bitter Chapter of God*. He has also published *The Birth of the Sun*, a collection of contemporary Afghan poetry, *Towards the Sun*, a collection of Latin American poems and *Morning Ballads*, a selection of Latin American short stories.

Jennifer Langer is the founder and director of Exiled Writers Ink! which works to promote the creative expression of refugees and exiles and to encourage cross-cultural dialogue. She edited *The Bend in the Road: Refugees Writing* (Five Leaves, 1999) and *Crossing the Border: Voices of Refugee and Exiled Women Writers* (Five Leaves, 2002) and is editor of the magazine, *Exiled Ink!* She has given and written many papers on issues pertaining to exile. She has a background in Further Education and has co-ordinated several refugee education projects as well as having facilitated creative writing sessions with and for non-native speakers. Her own poetry focuses on her identity as the daughter of refugees and on political and human rights issues. She is currently studying for a Masters in Cultural Memory at London University.

Yang Lian was born in Switzerland and grew up in Beijing, China. He began writing when he was sent to the countryside in the seventies and on his return became one of the first group of young underground poets who published the influential literary magazine *Jin Tian*. Yang Lian's poems became well known inside and outside China in the eighties, especially when his long poem *Norrlong* was criticised widely by the government during the political movement "Cleansing the Spiritual Pollution". Yang Lian became a Chinese poet in exile after the Tiananmen massacre and has published seven selections of poems, two selections of prose and many essays in Chinese, as well as having been translated into more than twenty languages.

Jean-Pierre Faziry Mafutala was born in the Democratic Republic of Congo. Whilst working at the Ministry of Education, he became involved in political activities for the main opposition party but had to flee because his life was under threat. Since 1996 he has lived in exile with his family in the UK. Inspired by the storytelling tradition, he describes his culture, praises the

317

noble deeds of his ancestors and echoes the suffering of refugees worldwide. He is currently reading Politics with Economics at Goldsmiths College, University of London.

Mahdad Majdian was born in Iran. In 2000 his book *Mahomma*, an inner poetic dialogue about the harsh realities of the prevailing situation, was published in Iran by Madavi Publications. Since being in England, in the last three years he has been writing and performing in English in various colleges, pubs, and venues in London. He has a strong academic background and has just completed a new collection of poems in English inspired by his struggles and experiences as a Persian living in England.

Antonio Joaquim Marques (Kiluanji Kush) is an Angolan poet resident in Sweden who speaks seven languages. He has published several collections of poetry — *Journey of Search* (1989), *Mystic Verses and Scarlet Voices* (1990). In 1991 he originated a poetry form called ETU with the publication of a volume entitled *Sun Woman*. In 1993 he published *Flames of New Dreams*. In recent years, he has completed a trilogy of poetry entitled *Turbulent Passages*. Other work includes *Green Shadow*, *Cadences of Rain* and *Wonderful Ways of Poetry* (keynotes on creative writing).

Semezdin Mehmedinovic was born near Tuzla, Former Yugoslavia and took a degree in Comparative Literature at Sarajevo University. He was editor of several journals in the late eighties. With its urban inflection and focus on everyday life, his early worked marked an influential turning point in contemporary Bosnian poetry. He wrote and directed *Mizaldo* or *The End of Theatre*. He edited a remarkable wartime magazine *Fantom Slobode* (Phantom of Liberty). He left Sarajevo in 1995 and now lives in America where he works for Voice of America. His main publications are *Modrac* (1984), *Emigrants* (1990), *Sarajevo Blues* (1995) and *Devet Alexandrija* (2002).

Aydin Mehmet Ali was born in Cyprus and lives in London. She is an international education consultant specialising in multiculturalism and bilingualism and has been involved in anti-racist work across Europe. Her book, *Turkish Speaking Communities & Education — no delight* (2001) has been highly praised. She set up FATAL (For the Advancement of Turkish-speakers Arts and Literature) which includes Cypriot, Turkish and Kurdish artists and writers. She has organised numerous arts and literature festivals, arts exhibitions, writing workshops and short story and poetry competitions for Turkish speaking women. She has contributed to *Mother Tongues, Modern Poetry in Translation* (2001) and *Agenda* (2002) magazines and her short stories have appeared in *Crossing the Border*. One of her short stories was selected in the 2002 London New Writing Competition organised by London Arts and published in *Diaspora City* (2003) by Arcadia Books and *Index*. She is well known for her conflict resolution work amongst Cypriot-Greek and Cypriot-Turkish communities. She has contributed to *Weeping Island*, a recent collection of Cypriot writers living in Cyprus and the Diaspora. She translates contemporary Cypriot and Turkish poetry and has organised bilingual poetry readings and workshops. She is the editor of *Turkish Cypriot Identity in Literature* (1990). She is working on an anthology of Turkish Speaking Women writing in Britain. Her writing has been characterised as "breaking taboos".

Hilton Mendelsohn was born in Bulawayo, Zimbabwe (then Rhodesia), studied Marketing and in 1993 began writing for *The Chronicle*, Zimbabwe's second largest daily newspaper. He moved to the UK in 1997 and began work with the Movement for Democratic Change in 2000. Because of this work he has not been able to return to Zimbabwe and has been threatened with arrest if he does so. He works with various Zimbabwean organisations in the UK and is a founder of Writing Wrongs, an exiled Zimbabwean writers' group.

Kamal Mirawdeli is a Kurdish poet and writer who left south Kurdistan to live in exile in Britain in 1982 after arrests, intimidation and threats to his life by the Iraqi regime. His native village and town were obliterated in Saddam's chemical Anfals in 1988. He returned to his country for short periods between 1993-4. He studied for an MA in Philosophy of History at Essex University in 1983 and gained a PhD in Literature from the same university in 1987. He has written widely on politics, philosophy and literature in Kurdish, Arabic and English. He has published three collections of poetry in Kurdish. His first collection in English is entitled *Passage to Dawn* and was published in 2002.

Abdirahman Mirreh was born in Hargeisa, Somali and died in Norway. He attended school in Aden, South Yemen before obtaining degrees at the University of Leipzig in 1969 (Tropical Agriculture) and 1976 (Anthropology). He then studied and worked in Norway before being involved in farming in Hargeisa in 1982, where he was when war broke out. He was twice imprisoned and fled to Norway. Anthologies of his work are *A Gob Tree Beside the Hargeisa Wadi* (1995), *Songs of a Nomad Son* (1990) and *From an Acacia Landscape* (1996).

Simon Mol from Cameroon, was forced to flee political persecution and has been living in Poland since 1999 after being granted asylum. He fled Cameroon in 1995 after the publication of articles in which he denounced a corruption. Upon arrival in Poland he applied for refugee status. Currently Mol continues to write poems and prose, which are regularly published in the Indian monthly anthology *Poet International* and other Indian, British and American reviews. He also works as a staff writer for the *Warsaw Voice*. He has been published in several anthologies and *Africa My Africa* (2002), is his first published collection, with the poems in English and Polish.

Mabiala Molu was born in Kinshasa, Democratic Republic of Congo and has a degree in English. He was co-founder of the club "The Fantastic Band" and editor of *Zairean Student* was well as having written many articles in both French and English. He currently lives in Paris. His collection of poems *Aujourd'hui Le Soleil* contains work in French, English and Lingala.

Agim Morina is from Kosova where he studied Albanian Language and Literature and Graphics at the University of Prishtina. He worked as a journalist and designer and came to Britain in 1998. He currently teaches Albanian to adults.

Muepu Muamba was born in the Democratic Republic of Congo in 1946 and is currently in enforced exile between France and Germany. His poetry, stories and essays have been published in Africa and Europe. Much of his work has been translated into German from French.

Shereen Pandit from South Africa, was a law lecturer and political activist and edited a community newspaper in South Africa before coming to Britain in 1986. She started writing fiction in 1996 and has won short story competitions, had her stories published in magazines and is a freelance journalist for publications which include the *Times Educational Supplement*. She has done many readings of her work, most notably at the Celebrate South Africa and Spit Lit Festival 2001 and 2002. She is currently teaching journalism for the Round House, London.

Nasrin Parvaz first came to the UK from Iran in 1978, at the age of twenty, to study. When the revolution broke out the following year, she returned for a brief visit to her family little realising that it would be fifteen years before she would come to Britain again as an exile. She was arrested in 1982 and was released in 1990. In 1993 she fled to the UK and claimed asylum. In London, she studied for a Psychology degree, after which she did a Masters degree in International Relations. She published a book *Beneath the Narcissus,* 2002 in Farsi which has been translated into English.

Ghazi Rabihavi is from Iran and published his first book in 1980. Since then he has written seven books. *From This Place* was published in Iran in 1991 and consists of eight short stories. *Daisies* was made into a successful film. Rabihavi's second book *Geesu,* is a novel published in 1994. After migrating to the UK, he published the books that were banned in Iran: *The Iranian Four Seasons* and *Merriam's Smile*. In 1997, Harold Pinter introduced Ghazi to the British public by producing his play *Look Europe!* which was performed in London, Amsterdam and New York. Subsequently, Ghazi wrote the play *Stoning*. In July 2000 *Fourplay* was performed in London while *Voices* was performed in San Francisco. In 2001 he wrote and directed *Prey* a short film in London. His latest work is *Captured by Camera* based on the true story of Ahmad Batebi, a film student serving fifteen years in prison in Iran for being photographed by a journalist during student demonstrations.

Nazaneen Rakhshandeh was born in Tehran and has been living in England since 1976. She studied Comparative Literature, Sociology and Garden Design and currently lives and works in London as an English teacher. She has had a series of readings in London as well as overseas. Her collection of poetry *Runway of Words* was published in London in 2003.

Refiq Sabir was born in Qaladiza in south Kurdistan in 1950. He gained his first degree in the Kurdish language from the University of Baghdad in 1974. He joined the Kurdish movement in 1978 and his life as a *peshmerga* became the source of many of his poems. He obtained a PhD in the cultural history of the Kurds from the University of Sofia in 1988. He is presently living in exile in Sweden where he has published a complete volume of his poetry. He was one of the new post-Goran generation of modernisers of Kurdish poetry.

Dursaliye Sahan was born in Turkey in 1958 and has lived in London for about twelve years. She has written since childhood and usually writes true life stories. In 1988 the national newspaper *Gunes* awarded her second prize in Turkey and in 1999 she won second prize in Turkey awarded by *Halkevleri* for her book *Londrada Bir Kadin, Dondu* and in addition won first prize in Northern Cyprus for her short stories. She currently writes for several Turkish women's magazines.

Hastie Salih is originally from the Kurdish region in Northern Iraq and spent her childhood in Wales and Germany. She has published short stories, poems and articles in Germany and currently works as a GP in London. Hastie is a member of Amnesty International and Oxfam.

Himzo Skorupan came to Britain as a Bosnian refugee from former Yugoslavia in 1992. He had worked as a journalist and had had six novels published in Bosnian. He wrote two unpublished books whilst living in Britain. In 2000 he published *O'CAJ* (Despair) and *O Tea*, a collection of short stories which was written and published in Bosnian, in Sarajevo.

Darija Stojnic is from Sarajevo, Bosnia, Former Yugoslavia where she lived until the outbreak of war in Sarajevo in 1992. She came to England as a refugee in 1993. She now works as a counsellor having completed a Diploma in Integrative Counselling with specialisation for refugees. Darija writes short stories some of them having been published in *Salon*, *The Big Issue* and in the anthology *Crossing the Border*. She also works as a journalist writing a column for *Bosniak Post* which is published in Norway.

Sokol Syla was born in Kosova where he was an English and PE Teacher. He was a member of the LDK, a prominent political party and was imprisoned by Milosevic from 1998 to 2000. In 2002 he fled to Britain for political reasons and now lives in Ipswich having had to leave his wife and four children in Kosova.

Dubravka Ugresic is from Croatia and currently lives in exile in Berlin. She is the author of children's books and collections of short stories and has translated from and written extensively about Russian literature. Her books include *Museum of Unconditional Surrender* (1996), *My American Fictionary* (1994) and *Thank You for Not Reading* (2003). Before she left Croatia, she was among five prominent Croatian writers who prized independence above the new "National State Culture" and were subsequently attacked by the press as traitors.

Shadab Vajdi is a poet and linguist from Iran. Her poetic works in Persian are *A Bend in the Alley, A Song for Little Hands* and *To the Memory of the Thirst of the Southern Mountain Slopes*. The anthology of her poetry in English is entitled *Closed Circuit*. Shadab Vajdi studied Persian Literature and Social Science in Iran and acquired her PhD in Linguistics at SOAS, University of London where she is currently lecturing. She has also translated into Persian Paul Harrison's *Inside the Third World* and Liang Heng's *Return to China*.

Saadi Youssef is one of the leading poets of the Arab world. Born in 1934 near Basra, Iraq, he has published thirty collections of poetry and has also composed numerous essays, journals, short stories and two novels as well as translations of international poets and novelists from English into Arabic. He taught Arab Literature in the high schools of his country, then in Algeria, before occupying a post in the Ministry of Culture, Baghdad. He left Iraq in 1979, and after living in Yemen, Beirut,

Damascus, Aden, Nicosia, Belgrade, Paris, Tunis and Amman, settled in London. His latest major anthology, the first in English is entitled *Without an Alphabet, Without a Face*, Graywolf Press, 2002.

Gulay Yurdal Michaels was born in Arcadiopolis on the European side of Turkey, raised in Adana in the south, educated in Istanbul and lives in London. In 1998, Gulay returned to Turkey to teach English but was dismissed for having mentioned the Kurdish language in class so had to return to London. With Richard McKane, she translated the poetry of Ergin Gunce, *A Flower Much as Turkey*, 1995.

Haifa Zangana was born in Baghdad and graduated from the School of Pharmacy, Baghdad University in1974. A year later, she left Iraq to work with the Palestinian Red Crescent in Damascus, Syria. She edited and published Halabja in 1989. *Through the Vast Halls of Memory*, her first novel, was published in English in 1990 and in Arabic in 1995. Three collections of short stories followed: *The Ant's Nest* (1996), *Beyond What the Eye Sees*. She is a founder of 'Act Together', a women's group opposing the war on Iraq.

Crossing the Border:
Voices of Refugee and Exiled Women

Women and children make up 80% of the world's refugee population, yet their voices are seldom heard. In *Crossing the Border*, thirty women from Somalia, Afghanistan, Algeria, Iran, Iraq, Kurdistan, Turkey, Northern Cyprus, Bosnia, Kosovo and the Congo tell their stories. All the women are refugees or are living in exile. This is the first anthology of refugee and exiled women's writing.

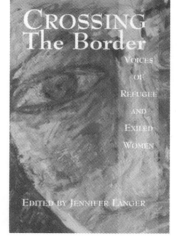

The book is divided into sections on women in conflict; women incarcerated; departures; voices in a strange land; living memories and thoughts and cries of pain. As well as the women's stories, told in fiction, non-fiction and poetry, there are articles on women's lives and women's writing in each of their countries of origin.

The editor, Jennifer Langer, is herself the daughter of refugees and her own family's story is included. Jennifer works with refugee communities in London where she set up Exiled Writers Ink.

327 pages,   0 907123 63 5,   £9.99